Model Dioramas Handbook

PARK
SOMEWHAT SAFE
SELF STORAGE

Model Dioramas Handbook

Mat Irvine

Crécy
www.crecy.co.uk

CRÉCY PUBLISHING LTD

First published in 2024 by Crécy Publishing.

A CIP record for this book is available from the British Library

Printed in Turkey by Imak Ofset

ISBN 9781800352780

Crécy Publishing Limited
1a Ringway Trading Estate,
Shadowmoss Road,
Manchester
M22 5LH

www.crecy.co.uk

MIX
Paper | Supporting responsible forestry
FSC www.fsc.org FSC® C111584

FRONT COVER MAIN Modelling with a water-based theme usually has to rely on other accessories and scratch-building, as seen here with a SupermarineWalrus amphibian and vehicles including an RAF Austin Tilly. *Model and photo by Patrick Pycke*

FRONT COVER TOP AFVs still seem to still dominate model dioramas, and this example incorporates a photographic background. *Model and photo by Spencer Pollard.*

FRONT COVER MIDDLE TOP A Tamiya Honda S600 sports cars being serviced in a scale garage. Besides the more obvious garage tools and equipment, note also the details such as the posters on the wall and the scale model glider! *Model and photo by Spencer Pollard.*

FRONT COVER MIDDLE BOTTOM The completed Back to The Future Part III diorama. The smoke is made from teased-out cotton-wool.

FRONT COVER BOTTOM Close-up detail of the area behind the Catalina fuselage. The crests of the waves have been added using a broad (10mm) brush, blended in 'backwards', in the direction of the wind. *Model and photo by Kevin Khoo.*

BACK COVER MAIN Space and science-fiction is beginning to be catered for as far as accessories and dioramas are concerned. Here, the Monogram Battlestar Galactica Viper diorama has accessories provided as 3D-printed parts from Cozmic Scale Models.

BACK COVER TOP Another war-time scenario. An anti-aircraft gun, figures and a wrecked City Hall building. *Model and photo by Spencer Pollard.*

BACK COVER BOTTOM A production Natter (not that they really went into production), which has the wider tail-plane. This is on the production launch pad. The vehicles come from Tamiya's 1:48-scale range.

Dedication

To Andrew P. Yanchus

Andy Yanchus first worked for Aurora, then as a colorist for Marvel Comics. In the recent years he had been the advisor to the newly-formed Atlantis Model Company. He was an avid collector of model memorabilia, and an excellent builder and painter, especially of figures. He was a good friend for approaching 50 years. Always there with help and advice, though not slow to point out if he thought you were in error!

Unfortunately he died on 11th September 2021, but I'm pleased that I have been able to include a few of his builds within these pages.

He was a highly knowledgeable historian on all matters to do with model-making, and I still often think, when tackling a particular problem: 'Ah, Andy would have known.'

Contents

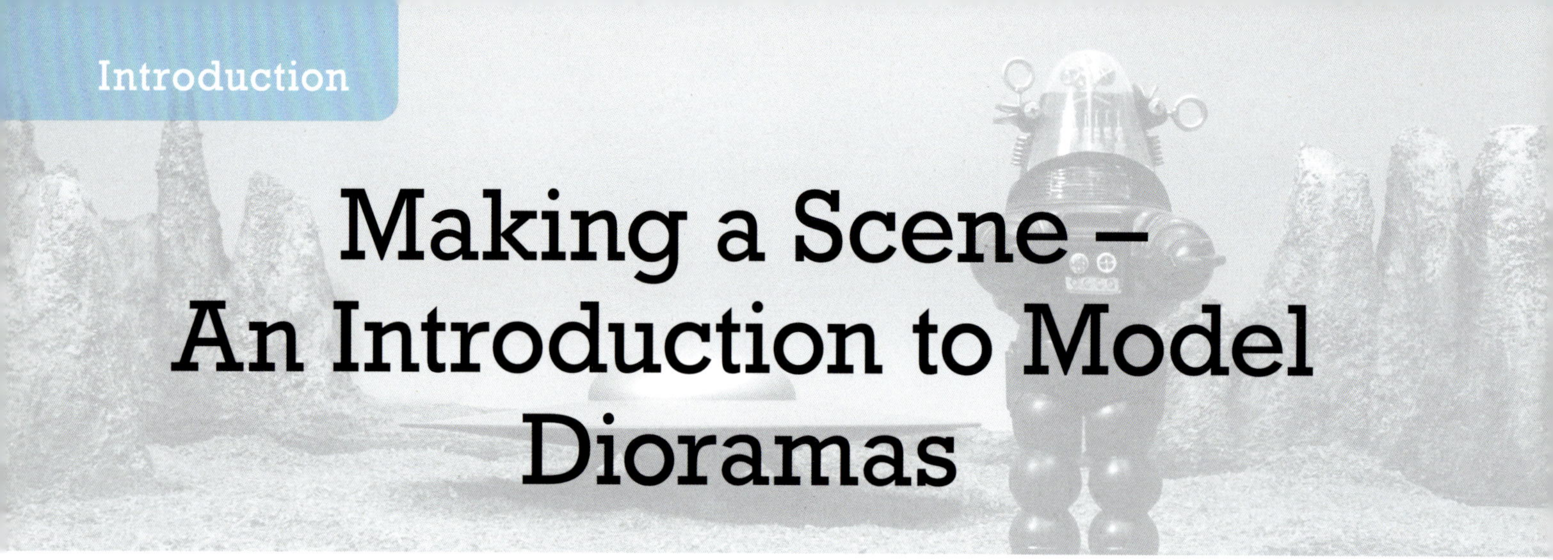

Making a Scene – An Introduction to Model Dioramas

Dioramas are not a new idea, they have been around for years. These days though, the term is invariably associated with scale models, usually built by amateur modellers using commercial plastic kits as the starting point. These models are then incorporated into some sort of appropriate setting on a base to create a scene.

Consequently, this is the area that the majority of this book will concentrate on – though how it all came about is not ignored, and the first chapter examines how, when, where, why and by whom the first 'dioramas' were created.

There are of course many other books about building dioramas, but virtually all deal with specific – some very specific – subjects in intricate step-by-step detail. This book is in no way intended to replicate what these previous books have already covered, but instead it aims to provide an overview of the subject, showing general techniques and materials, rather than very detailed builds focusing on specific subjects (though there is one chapter covering that area).

This is not a book about building the actual models themselves, or the specific tools and equipment used to build them. It is assumed that if you are interested in incorporating models into dioramas, then you will almost certainly have some experience of building the models themselves. Of course, many 'modelling tools' are used in various aspects of building dioramas, so Chapter 3 does cover the basics as far as general tools and equipment are concerned.

The primary aim of this book is therefore to provide an overall view of model dioramas, examining how the traditional model companies – the 'mainstream' companies – started to include 'diorama accessories' with their kits, which was happening even from the very beginnings of the industry – now well over half a century ago.

Next, this book looks at how these companies started to manufacture separate kits of diorama parts and accessories, and at the arrival of the specialist names (the 'garage'- or 'cottage'-industry manufacturers), that came about specifically to make various alternative and accessory parts for existing kits; only then to branch out to make complete kits of individual vehicles and subjects that the mainstream companies would never contemplate – even with the wide remit of many of them these days.

The book looks as the materials required for building dioramas, from simple bases that contain only a few items, to larger structures that need far more work and effort in

An example of small diorama, here using a catering version of the Citroën H van, from Ebbro, set up in the corner of what appears to be a southern European town.

ABOVE An example of a diorama depicting a building interior, showing a Sherman tank undergoing repair. *Model and photo by Spencer Pollard*

LEFT An example of a relatively simple, but effective small diorama showing the Adams (now Glencoe Models) covered wagon crossing the 'Wild West'.

their creation. It covers the materials that can be used to create features such as earth, vegetation and water – from seas and oceans, to what you may find in a bucket.

Oddly, one of the earliest subject areas for 'hobby dioramas' is not really thought of as fitting into the diorama mould – railway layouts. Never really termed 'dioramas', they are usually just called 'layouts', but they fulfil all the requirements of a diorama, and would likely be the largest such projects built by the average amateur model maker at home. However, techniques are much the same: whether for a landscape based around the railway tracks of the classic English branch-line with a small diesel shunter; the American Wild West and wood-burning locos; a smaller base displaying a Hawker Hurricane readied for take-off; a Panther tank stuck in the mud of a battlefield; or a Monte Carlo Mini in the snow.

The largest 'diorama' subject likely to be built by the amateur model-maker – a railway layout.

A Monte Carlo Mini by itself is not a diorama,...

... but adding a base starts the process,

... and the addition of a figure is another step forwards. Maybe it needs a road sign?

The idea of dioramas also extends to the professional world of modelling, whether it be architectural models for display to clients, model displays in museums, or the special-effects industries of films and television with miniature sets. All these categories actually tend to use very similar materials and techniques to those used by the modeller at home, albeit in the professional world they do tend to be on a much larger scale.

Of course, there is then the decision as to what would make a good diorama? A new model kit may give some indication with its box-art, or maybe an old photograph shows a scene that could be recreated in miniature, or maybe it is just down to your imagination.

The book also looks into some of the terms used. When does 'a base' become 'a diorama', and how does the term 'vignette' fit into things – assuming that it does.

Overall, the book aims to show the wide range of techniques and materials that can be applied, and even if you are a car modeller and have never put an aircraft kit together, let alone placed it in a diorama setting, you may get some ideas from the other side of the airfield fence. Maybe it's even worth a try mixing and matching subjects from different disciplines – there are many aircraft kits in 1:32 scale – but then this is also one of the conventional car scales, so an aircraft could be displayed with the pilot's other mode of transport. Taking the most popular aircraft scale, that of 1:72, this is close to the UK's model railway 00 gauge – otherwise known as 1:76 scale – and with the small military scales of 1:72 and 1:76, this gives many more possibilities.

Dioramas tend not to follow strict rules or regulations, unless you are entering a competition, where you may have

ABOVE The idea for a diorama can start with the image on the box, here the Airfix SRN-4 hovercraft.

RIGHT The SRN-4 box art recreated in '3D' for the Classic British Kit SIG (Special Interest Group). *Model by Alan 'Beanie' Bean*

American petroleum company Sinclair uses a fibreglass brontosaurus as its 'trademark' – found at gas stations throughout many southern US states (Shawnee, in Oklahoma shown here). Perhaps in inspiration for a diorama?

Atlantis Models reissued the original Revell gas tanker with Sinclair markings, so the addition of an old Pyro Models brontosaurus – painted bright green – completed the Sinclair gas-station look.

Combining two interests in a single dioramas. Here an aircraft, the Revell 1:32-scale Bell X-1, meets a car – a Gowland and Gowland (later Revell), MG-TC sports car. The standing figure of Chuck Yeager was produced by ReHeat Models.

ABOVE Adding a building and figures to an aircraft scene is natural for wartime subjects. Here, a Spitfire is seen with relaxing pilots outside a Nissen hut, complete with washing and 'scramble' bell, while the ground crew service the aircraft. *Model and photo by Ian Peacock*

RIGHT Dioramas are often thought of as being the sole preserve of 'the outdoors', but of course dioramas set 'indoors' are equally applicable, as in this highly-detailed garage scene. *Model and photo by Spencer Pollard*

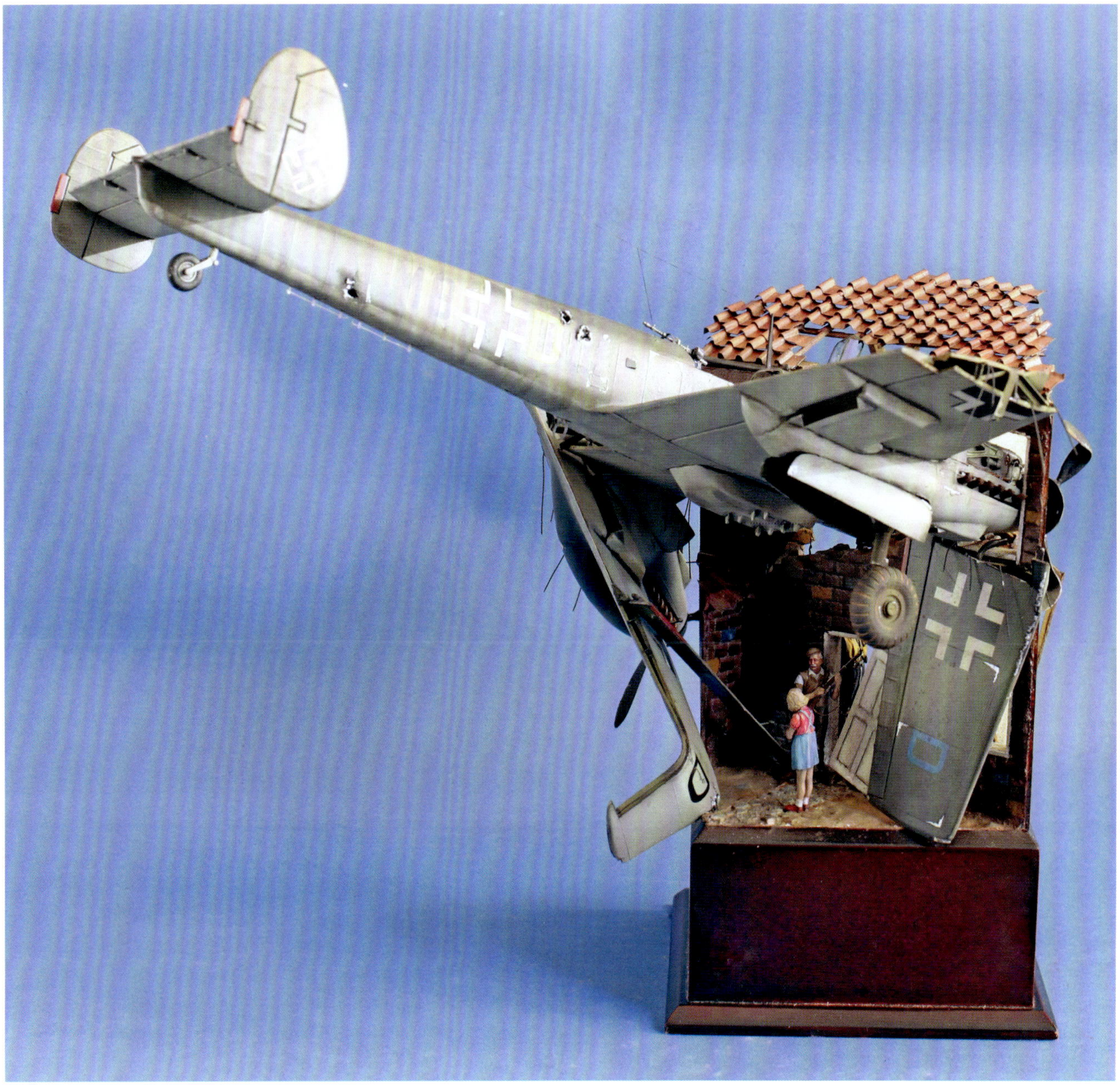

An old newspaper photograph of a Messerschmitt Me-110 that crashed into a house in southern England became a starting point for this intriguing diorama. *Model and photo by Suresh Nathan*

The fall of the Berlin Wall, seen here as a 'full-size diorama' at the USAF Museum, Dayton, Ohio. This could be reproduced fairly easily as a small-scale diorama, as Revell makes a kit of a Trabant.

to trawl through the 'small print' to discover what is allowed or not. As far as the hobbyists themselves are concerned, they will generally ascertain whether a model is 'a model on a base' or 'a diorama', but there are no real hard and fast rules. Dioramas don't actually have to be large, or actually include any figures, hardware, or structures. A landscape, with little in it, can still be a diorama. Although they are invariably assumed to be set in the great outdoors, there's no rule that says they have to be. Dioramas can be made to show interior scenes, such as an aircraft in a hangar, or a car in a garage. Maybe a diorama doesn't even need a solid base – you can

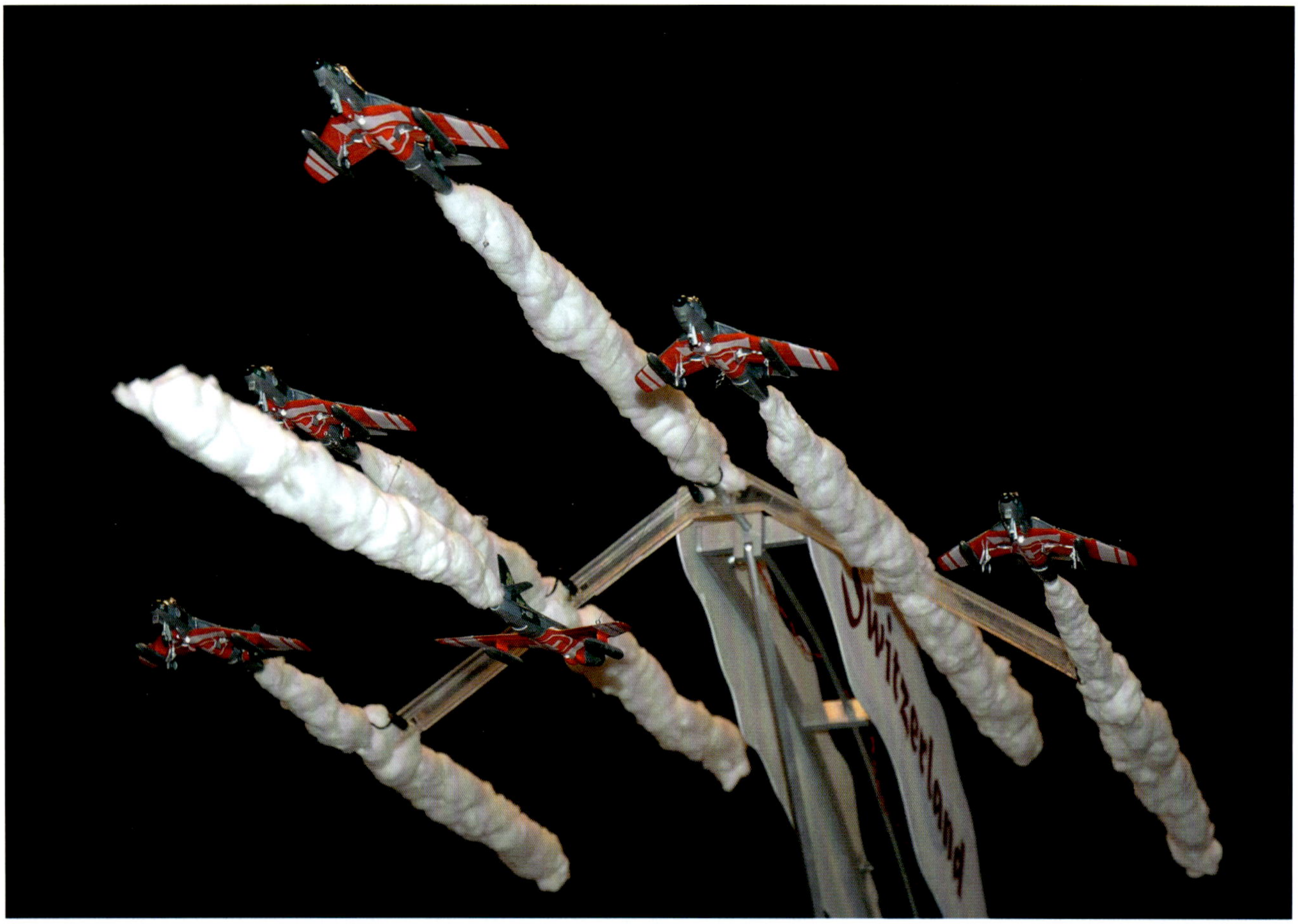

ABOVE Maybe not thought of as such, but flying aircraft can also make a diorama – here the subject is a display by the Swiss aerobatic team, the Patrouille Suisse, using Hawker Hunters.

RIGHT Ideas can also be taken from books. Lee Child's creation, Jack Reacher, ironically doesn't like driving, but the books provide great details of all of the cars he gets involved with in the novels. Here, the subject is a 2005 Mustang, as driven by a local TV anchor, Ann Yanni, in the book *One Shot*. Note the book cover illustration features a floor of a multi-story car park, reproduced in the diorama.

Items included in dioramas don't necessarily have to be to the same scale. Here a Moebius 1:11-scale Robby the Robot stands in front of a 1:144-scale Polar Lights C-57D spaceship, both from the *Forbidden Planet* film.

Adding details of a build to go with a model can be effective. Here, the Italeri model of the Cessna piloted by Mattius Rust that landed in Moscow's Red Square in 1987, is detailed in the news report displayed alongside.

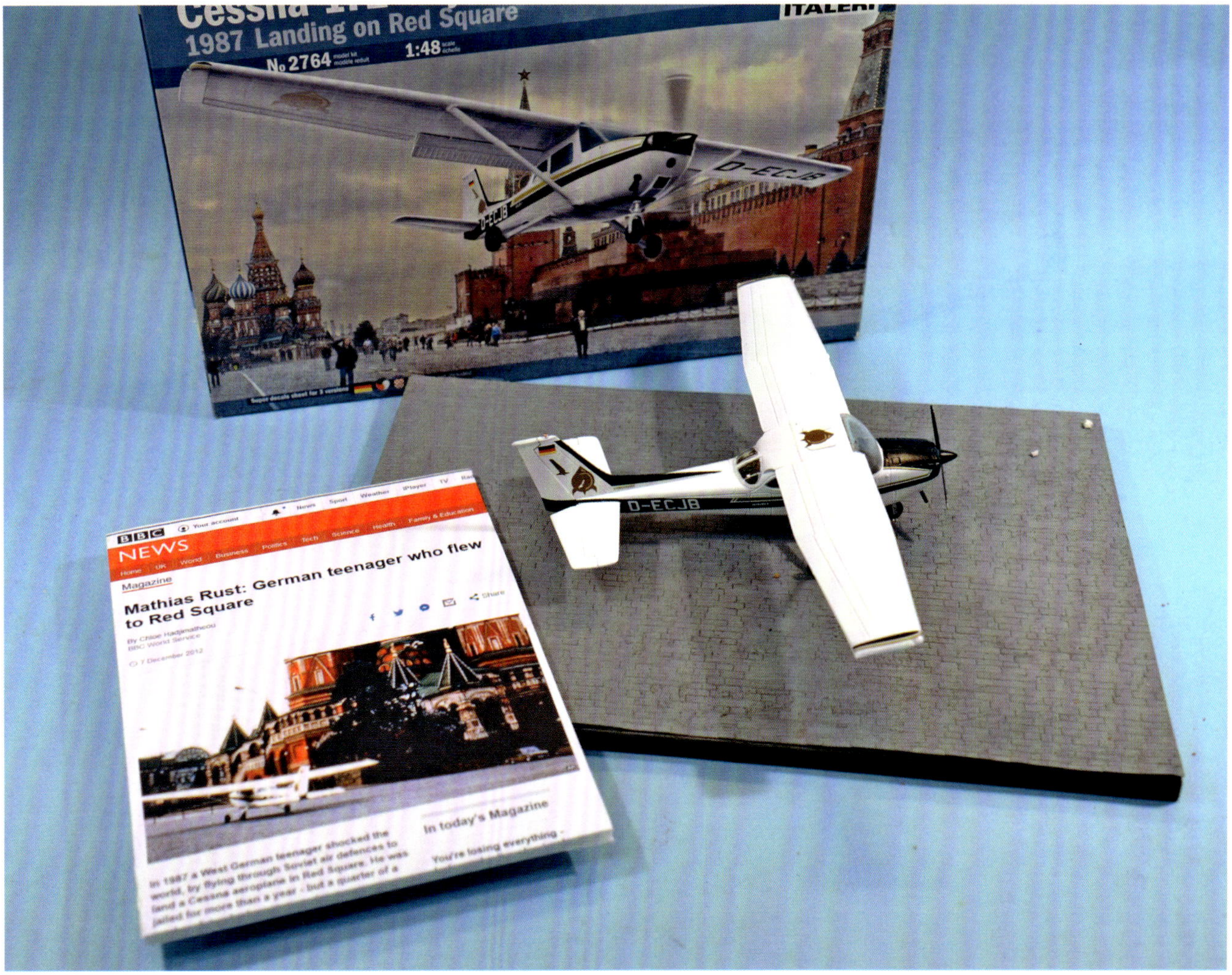

Spaceships 'in space' are generally even more difficult to interpret in a diorama than aircraft. However, here Mark Blackwood and Simon Goodall have achieved the desired effect with the *Millennium Falcon* being pursued through an asteroid field, with a '3D' asteroid, and '2D' Star Destroyer painted on the backdrop.

have dioramas of flying aircraft, or spaceships for that matter, though then methods of support have to be devised.

There is also a matter of scale. The majority of the elements that make up the parts of a diorama will be at the same scale, but you can have forced-perspective dioramas, where the far distance is not necessarily the same scale as the foreground. In addition, elements of a diorama can include items that are not in scale at all – they could, for example, include a copy of the book from which the diorama illustrates an extract, or the photograph on which the diorama is based.

There is really only one rule when it comes to building model dioramas – use your imagination.

Mat Irvine
April 2024
www.matirvine.com

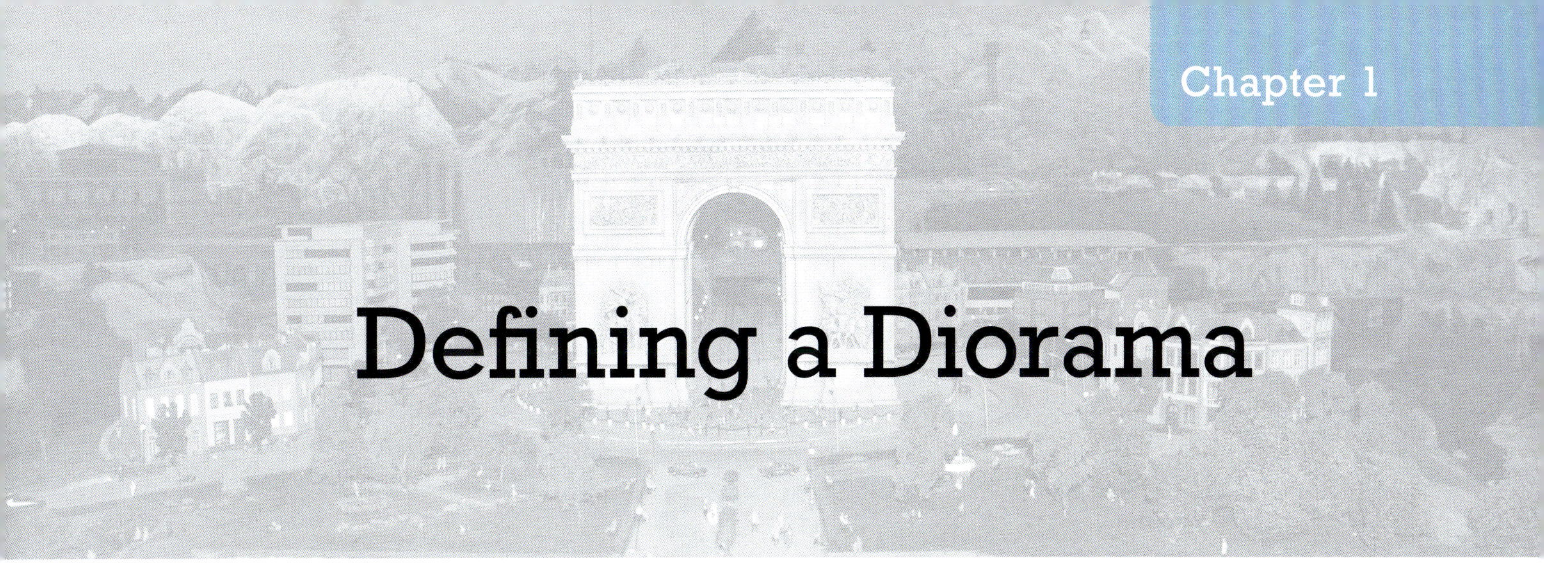

Chapter 1

Defining a Diorama

As this is a book on model dioramas, it is probably good idea to establish exactly what a 'model diorama' actually is?

You will almost certainly know what it is when you see it, but when it comes to trying to precisely describe it, that is far more of a problem.

WHAT EXACTLY IS A DIORAMA?

These days the term 'diorama' seems to be almost exclusively reserved to describe model makers extending the use of an existing model (invariably plastic) kits, adding to these to create a scene – or diorama. Perhaps a typical battlefield scene on a base around 2ft^2 (600mm^2), with a variety of tanks, figures and lots of mud… However, it all began long before there were scale-model plastic kits.

Mention of dioramas invariably brings thoughts of tanks and wartime scenarios – here a Sherman tank on patrol. *Model and photo by Spencer Pollard*

Another war-time scenario. An anti-aircraft gun, figures and a wrecked City Hall building. *Model and photo by Spencer Pollard*

Air museums can provide diorama ideas. Pima Air Museum in Tucson, Arizona has seven 'Century Fighters' – F100 through to F106 (no F-103 that only reached prototype stage) parked outside. Pima also has an F-107, but that is inside – and the kits for all the aircraft can be obtained.

THE DIORAMA

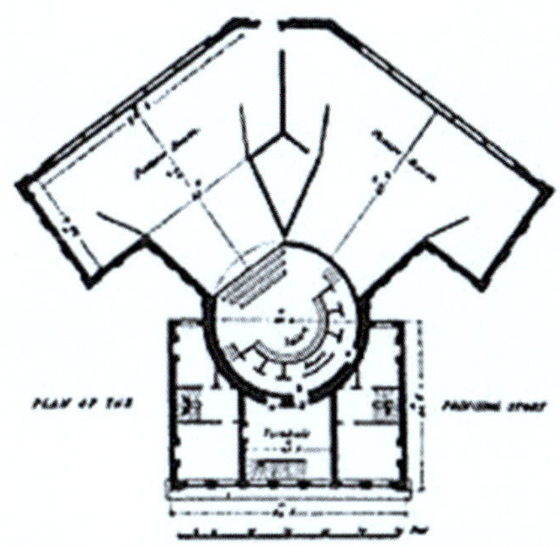

(a) Ground plan of the Diorama building, London, by A. Pugin and J. Morgan, 1823

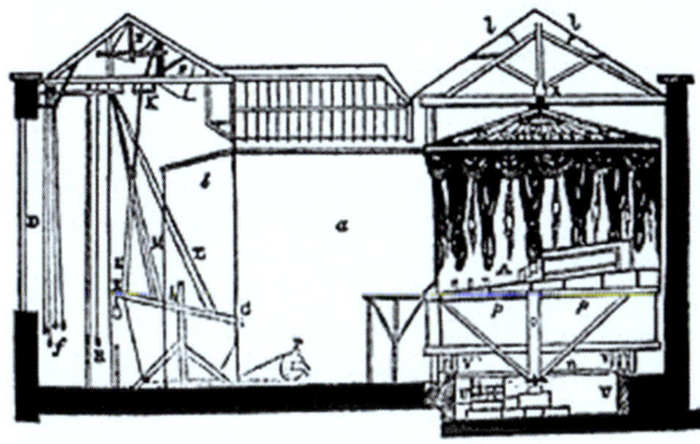

THE DIORAMA.

Most dictionary definitions still tend to take the slightly old-fashioned view, describing a diorama as: 'Of a miniature scene, viewed through an opening.' This definition is very much based on the original creation of what became 'dioramas', which were used in a theatrical setting. To this end these dioramas could be accompanied by lighting effects, to 'change the scene'. An example is the use of translucent backdrops, which can be altered with lighting changes – with the lighting on the front you see one scene, but with the same backdrop lit from behind you get a completely different view. This is termed a 'Pepper's Ghost'.

This dictionary definition comes from the inventors of the very first dioramas – at that point called 'theatrical dioramas' – introduced in France around the beginning of nineteenth century.

It was also of course at a time before the advent of photography, cinema or television, though intriguingly, elements of the first would soon be introduced by one of the instigators of the very first, original diorama display, in Paris 1822. The creators of this display were Louis Daguerre and Charles Marie Bouton, and it was Daguerre who went on to develop, later that same decade, elements of the very first efforts at photography – the Daguerreotype.

Daguerre (1787–1851) was also an accomplished painter, architect and theatre designer, all of which talents were used to produce these dioramas. Bouton (1781–1853) was primarily a painter, specialising in the perspective of buildings. The two men developed what was basically a 'theatrical event' – or 'theatrical illusion'. The first example of this occurred in a specially constructed building next to Daguerre's studios in Paris, between 1822 and 1823.

TOP LEFT One of the inventors of the 'diorama', Louis Daguerre. *Image – public domain*

TOP RIGHT An engraving depicting what the Daguerre and Bouton 'theatrical diorama' was like for the audience. *Image – public domain*

ABOVE A diagram showing how the Daguerre and Bouton theatrical diorama was set up in London, with a movable screen. *Image – public domain*

The taxidermy possums in a museum in Vermont can arguably be classed as a diorama.

These events consisted of painted scenes, usually of notable buildings, but incorporating elements of movement. This could be in the form of the previously mentioned translucent backdrops, so that different aspects of the scene could be shown. One of the earliest examples was a painting of Chartres Cathedral, where lighting effects were used to light windows, put waving tree patterns on the walls, and to change the sunlight throughout the day. They could also depict a specific event – for example a train travelling along a track, but – with the appropriate scene and lighting changes – it could be involved in a train crash. Theatrical events are, after all, invariably dramatic!

However, these 'theatrical dioramas' were large, as the backdrops could be up to 25m wide, by 15m tall. This meant they had to be fixed in place, and the whole event could consist of up to 20 such displays. Consequently, the 'dioramas' could not be moved, and the audience had to be moved instead. So, the audience crowded into a central cylindrical auditorium, facing one diorama, and after that diorama had been viewed, and had its sequences had been operated, the auditorium was revolved to the next diorama.

TAKING LIBERTIES

Interestingly, the idea of moving the audience, not the stage, has a modern counterpart. In 1983, American magician David Copperfield wanted to make the Statue of Liberty, in New York Harbor, disappear, in one of his most famous illusions. To this end, he had an auditorium built on a platform, with two scaffolding towers supporting a screen that could be raised and lowered, hiding and revealing the statue.

During this live TV event, initially the statue is dead centre between the two towers. The screen is then raised, Copperfield intones the usual conjuring mumbo-jumbo, and the screen is lowered – Liberty has disappeared!

What actually happened was that while the screen was raised, the whole auditorium was revolved by a few degrees. Obviously, this was done very slowly and extremely smoothly. When the screen was lowered, the audience saw what they assumed was the same position of the New York skyline, but no Statue of Liberty – she was now hiding behind one of the towers! This was all helped by disorientating loud music being played, a lot of blinding spot-lamps shining in the audience's eyes, and the whole performance taking place at night. Mis-direction is the key to most conjuring tricks, and helped in this instance, as the New York skyline tends to look much the same from across the river!

To bring Lady Liberty back, the whole magic trick was reversed.

Incidentally, this itself could make an interesting model diorama – commercial kits of the Statue of Liberty having been produced.

DIORAMA – THE TERM

It is this method of viewing 'a scene through an opening' from which the word 'diorama' was devised. The word itself comes from two Greek words – a combination of 'di' (actually 'dia'), meaning 'through', with 'orama', meaning 'that which is seen; a sight'. So, we get 'diorama', which translates literally as 'through that which is seen', which follows through to the way Daguerre and Bouton set up their shows.

By the beginning of the twentieth century however, the meaning of diorama was changing somewhat. It was now being applied to a smaller-scale displays that showed a scene and 'told a story', which is more or less the definition that is used today, and which relates to the majority of this book.

However, this is not the end of the story, as 'diorama', especially in the museum sense, can be applied to any staged scene – regardless of scale.

'Diorama' itself doesn't actually indicate a scale, and many early dioramas were life-size, or near life size, and for that matter, still are. A museum of natural history showing animals in the undergrowth is just as much of a diorama as a smaller-scale model of the animals with suitably scaled-down vegetation. It comes back to 'setting a scene' and 'telling a story', regardless of the scale.

All the early diorama scenes would have been made from the ground up, using whatever materials were available, or to use the usual modern terminology, scratch-built. All the materials would have been of the time – primarily wood, maybe with some metal elements, and variations such as plaster and papier-mâché.

FROZEN IN TIME

With modern model-making, plastics have come to fore, not only with the construction kits themselves, but as materials for scratch-building. Invariably, much of the overall time is spent actually creating the main model in the first place when

On its own, an Airfix Mk IX Spitfire is not a diorama...

... but now on a grassy base with ICM figures and Tamiya vehicles, we are definitely in diorama territory.

using a commercial model kit, making modifications and additions, or maybe building an entire model from the ground up. This is not to say that the older, more traditional materials and techniques are not still in use – they are, and are featured throughout this book. However, once created, the model can be placed in surroundings, thus creating the diorama.

It really is the 'telling a story', albeit one frozen in time, that can sum up a diorama in the very general sense. A model of a Supermarine Spitfire simply sitting on its wheels, however well built, is still a model of a Supermarine Spitfire sitting on its wheels. However, put that same Spitfire model on a grassy base, with its pilot readying for flight, maybe with crew and equipment, and even his pet dog gazing up at his master, and immediately it is going to invoke visions of an RAF crewman about to take to the skies, maybe to participate in the Battle of Britain? By placing the model in this environment, it is setting the scene and telling a story. It is these additions that turn a model, albeit a very nice model, just sitting on a base, into something more – a diorama – and that transformation process forms the basis of this book.

Overall, a diorama can be said to capture a moment in time – in effect a three-dimensional photograph (or, in more modern times, a hologram!). The animals in the undergrowth; the Spitfire pilot clambering into the cockpit, rather than some extended narrative. There could be some lighting effects, even the odd moving feature, but the overall scene usually stays the same throughout a viewing.

Of course, things are never as straightforward as that, as later in the book we look at the way dioramas – or as they are generally termed in the cinematic world, 'miniature sets' – are produced for movie and TV filming of miniatures, and where of course 'movement' can very much play its part. The vast majority of techniques used for special-effects miniatures in film and television use precisely the same techniques as the amateur model-maker – though in many cases, at a somewhat larger size.

Ships on the water can also be dioramas – especially if there are other elements involved. Here the author points to the culprit in a *Titanic* diorama at the amazing 'The House on the Rock' in Wisconsin.

ABOVE LEFT Ideas going round in circles? The 'worst movie ever', *Plan 9 from Outer Space*, used the actual model kits of a Flying Saucer made by Lindberg (as an aside, this is the first ever 'all-plastic' space kit). Now reissued by Round 2 (owners of Lindberg) as the model from the movie. Previously, Skyhook Models had produced a small diorama of a scene from the movie, using the same kit.

ABOVE RIGHT Dioramas don't have to be large, and with most hobby builds, aren't, but a lot can be packed into a small base – this wartime scene has 20 figures. *Model by Roger Penny*

DIORAMA – THE DEFINITION

So, we are coming to a reasonably modern definition for a diorama. We end up with: a miniature scene that depicts a certain point in time, or a specific event, (usually) built to a specific scale and containing all relevant elements such as figures, vehicles, buildings, structures, natural scenery, all mounted on a base. Additionally, a backdrop may be part of this, as may certain lighting effects, and even movement. Of course, this definition is very general, and most elements can vary, or may even be absent, with the set-up still being classed as a diorama.

All this really boils down to two options for model makers – a model simply mounted on a base, or a full diorama. The former will take the form of a model of, say, a figure, vehicle or craft, that sits just as it is, the only addition being possibly a flat base, primarily so that the model doesn't fall over, or is easier to move. The latter is a scene that is populated with elements placed on a base that is sculptured to make it a real (or, in the science-fiction or fantasy sense, 'real' in some universe, somewhere'), forming a diorama.

The 'telling of the story', may actually incorporate elements that are not to the same scale as the main object. These may include paperwork, say a book or record cover, or a photograph of the original event that inspired the diorama in the first place, which is displayed as part of the whole scene.

Once those parameters have been established, we are still in the position that things are never quite as neat and straightforward as it would seem. One question is: 'How detailed should the base be?' Put another way, can a model on a base without accoutrements still be a diorama? (This is a

DICTIONARY DEFINITION

This is the definition of 'diorama' in Blackie's Modern Cyclopedia, dated 1898:

Diora'ma, a mode of painting and of scenic exhibition invented by Messrs. Daguerre and Bouton, and first exhibited in 1823. It secures a higher degree of illusion than the ordinary panorama, by a mode of uniting transparent painting to the usual opaque methods, and causing the light to fall upon the picture both from before and behind. At the same time, by means of coloured transparent blinds, suspended both above and *behind* the *picture*, the rays of light can be intercepted and made to fall in pleasure in graduated tints upon every part of the picture in succession.

BASE QUESTIONS

The question 'when does a base that is primarily there for support, become a diorama?' particularly applies if you have decided to enter your creation for a model competition. In this case, you are totally in the hands of whoever has set the competition rules and regulations. This has taxed the minds of many model-competition organisers, who could decree that: 'This model isn't a diorama, as it doesn't have enough diorama elements on its base.' Conversely, they may decide: 'This model is not a free-standing model, as it has too many elements on its base, so is a diorama.'

Consequently, potential entrants to model competitions beware – it can be a minefield, so read the fine-print carefully (though often that isn't clear, and it will be down to the decision of individual judges!).

situation with many a model entered into a competition – see the accompanying 'Base questions' box.) Much is going to be down to what could be expected to be on the base in the first place. Back to our Spitfire on a grassy airfield. One could argue that the plane just sitting on the grass is not a diorama – it needs the people and equipment. But what about a ship, flying boat or sea plane, on the water? In this case, normally there wouldn't be a lot around, apart from the water, but this could still be considered a diorama.

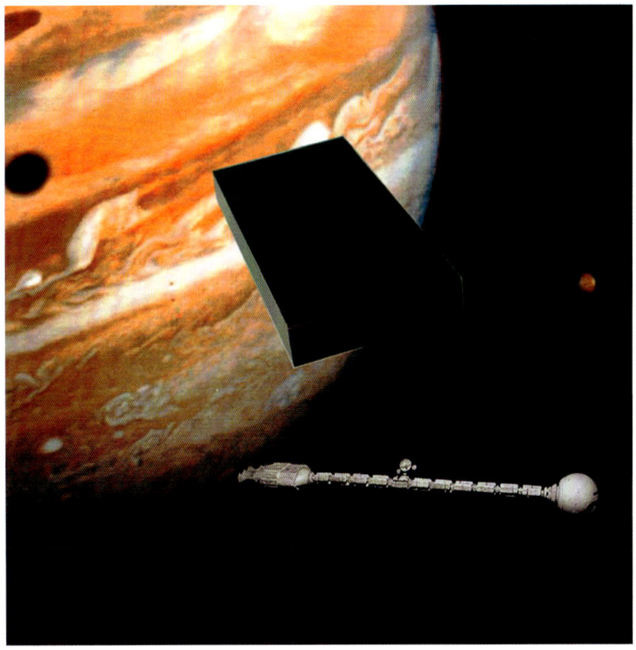

The movie 2001: A Space Odyssey was full of 'vignettes' in the usually accepted sense of the word. The image here is, strictly speaking, not a 'model diorama' as it has been digitally created in Photoshop – but it does feature a small 6in model of Discovery, as made by ReShape. *Jupiter photo courtesy of NASA.*

ENTER THE VIGNETTE!

There is a slightly odd in-between point between a 'model on a base' and a 'vast diorama', which is where another term needs introducing – 'vignette'. If the definition of a diorama is slightly vague, and has been modified somewhat over the years, that is nothing when compared the definition of 'vignette'! Some encyclopaedia listings include a dozen different meanings for 'vignette' – unfortunately none of which includes a mention of models.

The primary definition these days of a vignette comes down to a short descriptive passage in a book, play or film, usually relating to one person. This is something that stands on its own – and if removed does not affect the overall story.

Using a well-known movie as an example (a movie full of models and many diorama miniature sets), there are many sequences in *2001: A Space Odyssey*, especially on board the Jupiter-bound *Discovery*, where astronauts Poole and Bowman are whiling away the time. It could be playing chess with HAL, talking with the 'BBC-12' interviewer via a video link (on what has to be the first impression of an iPad or tablet), making drawings of the hibernating crew members, or jogging round the inner circumference of the craft. These could all be classed as vignettes. Each sequence stands on its own, but take them out of the movie and you don't actually loose anything from the overall story – *Discovery* is still on its way to Jupiter.

As an extension, 'vignette' can also mean a frozen scene that's glimpsed almost as it were 'in a frame', so as an extension to that we come to photographs, but here it specifically refers to a photo – or any graphic image – where the edges have been blurred out, so making the subject stand out. (Many photo-manipulating computer programmes have a 'vignette setting', which adds a 'fuzzy frame' round the main subject.) However, with all these definitions and meanings, there is still no actual mention of 'models' in the traditional three-dimensional sense.

RIGHT One of the Airfix 1:12-scale figures, in this case Anne Boleyn, supplied with a base that includes a small amount of extra detail. These could fall under the banner of vignettes.

FAR RIGHT One the of the specialist manufacturers, ReHeat Models, made resin kits that could also be classed as vignettes. US astronaut John Glenn stands by a bench with a model of his Mercury spacecraft.

TOP LEFT The first mention of vignettes in relation to hobby models seems to have been in the American magazine *Amazing Figure Modeler* in 1980. More recent magazines covering similar subjects, such as the UK *Fantasy Figures International*, also uses the term (noted on the left of the cover, second from the bottom).

TOP RIGHT Intriguingly, another Airfix kit, this time the Vostok launcher, has several elements on a base – two of the three payloads and the rocket – but likely would not be called a vignette or even a diorama, just 'a model on a base'.

ABOVE An example of kit historian Andy Yanchus's large collection of figures on bases, all designed by himself. Named 'Better Mousetrap', the droid, small creature (the mouse?) and the trap made from antlers, could be classed as a vignette. *Model by Andy Yanchus, photo by Pat Yanchus*

RIGHT The wild car customizer, Ed 'Big Daddy' Roth, with several trophies. All the components come from different existing kits, Roth himself in the Revell Mysterion. Once collected on the base, this display could be termed a vignette. *Model by Andy Yanchus, photo by Pat Yanchus*

LEFT Creating a vignette from elements all found in one kit. Here 'Hot Curl' came with the original MPC '29 Ford Woody, along with his surfboard, bike, bedroll and skateboard. Only the base was added.

BELOW At the other end of the scale are literally large-scale dioramas. This has been built for the Gulliver's Gate display in New York City, with the scene centring around the Arc de Triomphe in Paris.

All this isn't exactly helped as the word itself – vignette – derives from something completely different, and actually originates from even earlier times than dioramas. It comes from the small images that invariably appeared at the beginning and end of a chapter in old books. These motifs themselves could vary considerably, but were often a small black and white image of a twisted vine, from which we get 'vignette' – French for 'little vine'.

We still get back to the fact that none of the dictionary definitions for 'vignette' list models or model-making as such. The nearest we get is probably the photograph or illustration description mentioned previously, where the edges have been engineered to fade away, hence making the subject of the image stand out. This is about the nearest we get to a model 'vignette', in that these could be considered as a 'photograph in three dimensions'. So, taking it to the extreme, a photograph, with suitably blurred edges, of a small model with diorama elements, could even be called 'a vignette of a vignette'!

It is actually somewhat unclear exactly when and how the term 'vignette' was first applied to model-making. However, it is certainly far more recent than the term 'diorama' and it may even be as late as the 1980s. It seems to have started

ABOVE Any model on a small base with minimum amounts of equipment, could be termed a vignette (the Airfix Lunar Module shown here)...

ABOVE RIGHT ...however the same scenario, with the same equipment, on a large background cannot be classified as a vignette, even though all the elements are exactly the same (the Monogram Lunar Module shown here).

BELOW Interestingly this appears to be the first commercial model kit one of the Porco Russo kits from Fine Molds, which actually uses the term 'vignette' in the advertising.

with models of figures, and is still mainly applied to that subject matter. The first use of the term can probably be traced to the American magazine *Amazing Figure Modeler*. It was used to describe the classic type of model found in that magazine, where a single figure, which could be in a real or fantasy setting, is surrounded by a few of what could be classed as 'diorama pieces'. This was described as a 'vignette', the term stuck, and the terminology has been adopted by more-recent similar magazines that also specialise in figure modelling.

Consequently it is still is primarily used for a small (in overall dimensions) model where a figure is involved. We are back to the term's literal meaning of 'little vine', so here interpreted as 'little scene'. So, a figure with appropriate diorama accoutrements, on a base around 130mm (5in) wide, could likely be called a 'vignette', but that same figure in the middle of a base that is 1m (3ft) wide almost certainly would not – it would be a 'diorama'. So it really comes down to the overall size and 'feel' of the model's presentation, not the actual model itself.

So it ends up that all vignettes are (primarily small) dioramas, but the vast majority of dioramas cannot be termed vignettes.

WHATEVER YOU CALL IT

Regardless of whether you want to call your creation a vignette, a diorama, or just a model on a base, the techniques and materials used to build the scene are basically the same. While on the subject of definitions, it is a good idea to go through at least the basics of what is required when model-making, not just with commercial model kits, but also when it comes to scratch-building – literally 'building something from scratch' – which is where much of the effort is involved when it comes to building dioramas. We will only take an overall look in this book – there are other books, (some by this author) providing a more in-depth guide.

ABOVE A small selection of kits from 'specialist' model companies. These tend to us various materials – primarily resin, but also white-metal and photo etch – but not injection-moulded styrene.

LEFT A small selection of model kits from 'mainstream' companies, from older names such as Airfix, AMT, Monogram, Revell and Tamiya, to newer brands such as Takom, MiniArt and Glencoe Models.

BELOW Examples of paper kits for all sorts of subjects.

ABOVE The differences between 'mainstream' and 'specialist' companies can be illustrated by kits of the same subject, in the same scale. This is the 1:144-scale kit of Space Ship Two, issued by 'mainstream' manufacturer Revell and injection-moulded in styrene.

RIGHT This is Space Ship Two, as issued by 'specialist' manufacturer Fantastic Plastic – this time moulded in resin.

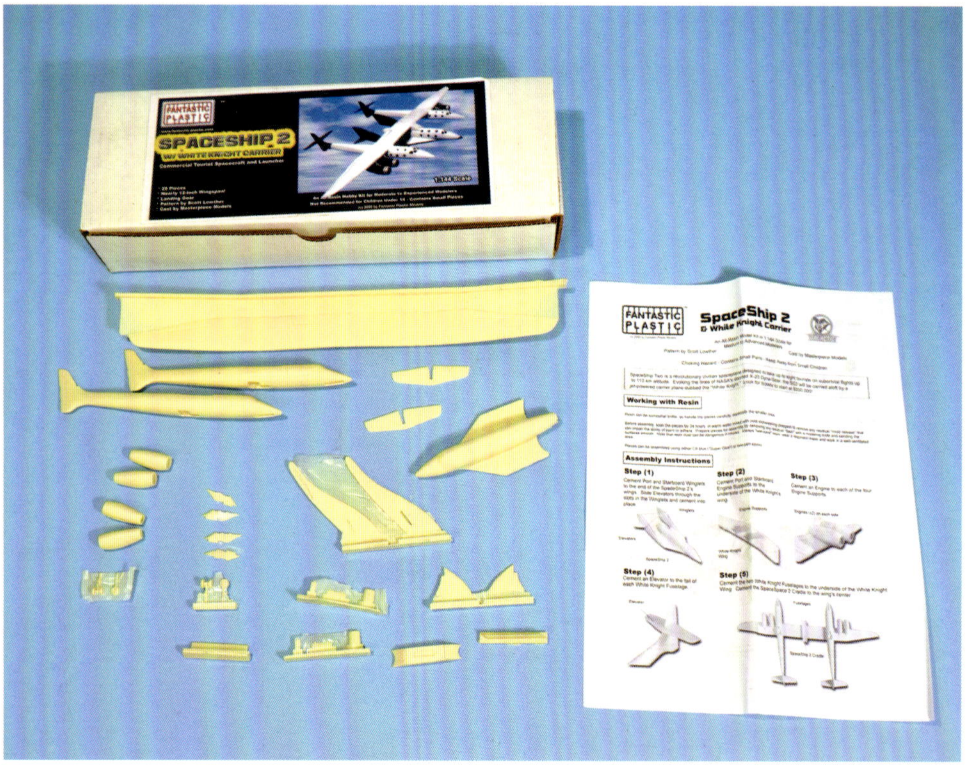

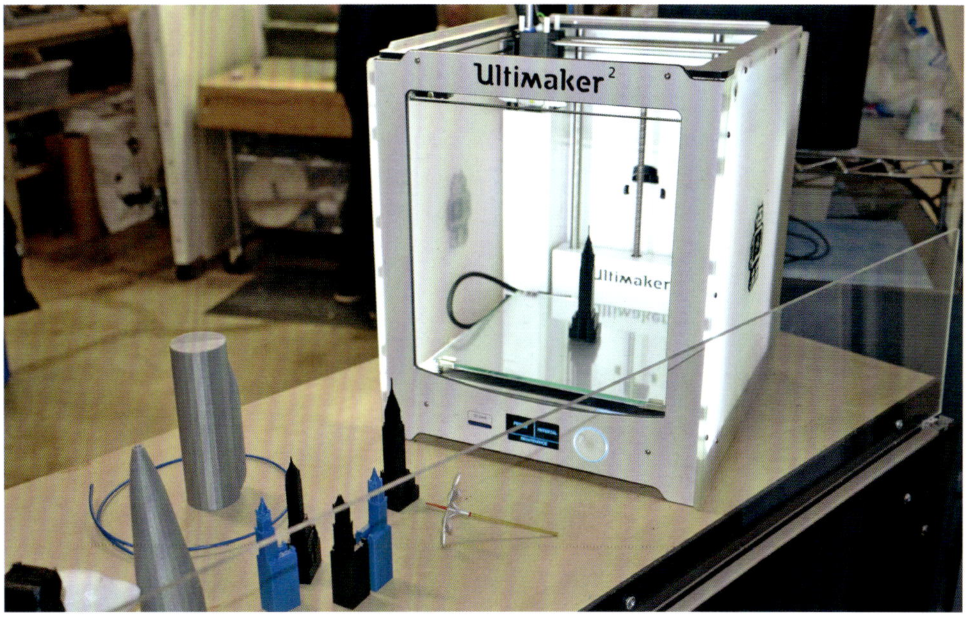

And the future… A 3D printer that can be used by the home hobbyist or small companies to produce small parts.

Almost certainly these days, most model dioramas will start with a model kit, so first let's sort out exactly what a model kit is.

These days, if you say 'model kit', you are almost certainly referring to a plastic model kit. In most cases, with a plastic kit, that fact that it will be injection-moulded polystyrene ('styrene') can be taken for granted. However, there are model kits produced from of all types of materials – there are wooden kits; there are metal kits; there are paper and card kits, and there are kits that involve a mix of these materials, invariably called 'multi-material' kits.

MAINSTREAM vs SPECIALIST

You can – very roughly – split the kit you buy as your starting point into two distinct categories. There are the standard commercial kits from established model manufacturers, such as Airfix, Revell and Tamiya – these are generally referred to as 'mainstream' manufacturers. There are then a vast number of kit producers that come under the umbrella of 'specialist' manufacturers.

These are otherwise known as the 'garage' or 'cottage' industries, because they usually involve one person working, presumably, out of a garage or cottage. These often one-person operations may have begun life by making accessories for existing kits – a weapons load for an aircraft, new wheels for a car, different plating for a tank, extra rigging for a ship, etc – but then expanded to produce complete kits. Invariably, these would be 'niche' models that the mainstream companies would not touch with the proverbial barge-pole.

These specialist companies use a wide range of materials, including resins, photo-etched metal sheets, white-metal parts, even wire, string and card, and vacuum-formed styrene sheet, which is the nearest they get to the polystyrene of a conventional model kit. Of course, even this is not clear cut, and there are specialist companies that now use low-volume production methods where enable them to injection-mould styrene into short-run tooling, so mimicking what the mainstream companies are doing. Conversely, mainstream companies are now increasingly using these specialist materials, and you can often open up what appears to be a conventional plastic model kit box, and you will find, along with the styrene, white-metal, resin and photo-etched parts.

3D PRINTING – TAKING OVER THE WORLD?

Now of course, there is the rapidly growing use of 3D printing, using a wide range of materials – not just plastics, but metal and even food! Is it going to change model making? In the long run the answer is likely yes, but currently, although its use by home hobbyists to produce one-off parts is growing, the situation with the commercial model companies is far less clear. For the commercial manufactures, whereas an injection-moulding machine can turn out a full kit in thirty seconds, the same kit parts would take far longer even with the most sophisticated 3D printer. Currently, the main use of 3D printing by commercial companies, is for kit prototyping. However, specialists companies can afford to wait hours for one kit to be produced, so where very small production numbers are involved, there is a growing range of full kits, accessory parts and items for dioramas made via 3D printing. There are now also many kits and parts that are not available 'ready-made', and instead rely on the fact that many amateur modellers have 3D printers in their homes, so a digital file is produced, which you then buy and download from a website to enable you to print components yourself.

Here the only problem could be the transient nature of the companies that make these files. On-line companies come and go in the blink of an eye, so are these files always going to be available? In the long run, they are almost certainly not going to be the Airfix, Revell or Tamiya of the modelling world.

Consequently many of the original distinctions between commercially available kit types are becoming increasingly blurred, and this means you will have to get involved with tools, glues, paints and processes that will have to deal with more than one type of material.

This area is discussed in more detail in the following chapter.

Chapter 2

Tools, Paints and Glues

Anyone reading this book will, no doubt have some knowledge and experience of building models and working with a variety of tools, paint and materials, otherwise you probably would not have picked up the book in the first place!

However, we will take a look at the basic equipment that you will need for building, for 'plastic' and other materials, which fall into three main areas – tools, glues and paints.

OUT OF THE BOX

Opening the box of a standard plastic model kit will reveal the plastic parts themselves. These are attached to what are correctly termed 'runners', which is exactly as they come out of the injection-moulding machine. Unfortunately many – including some kit manufacturers themselves – still refer to these runners as 'sprues'. That term is incorrect in this context, but the word 'sprue' has passed into the modelling lexicon and

A conventional model kit from recent years – a Hasegawa F-15. There are a lot of plastic parts packed in polythene bags, plus decals, instructions, and in this case white-metal (left) and photo-etched (right) parts.

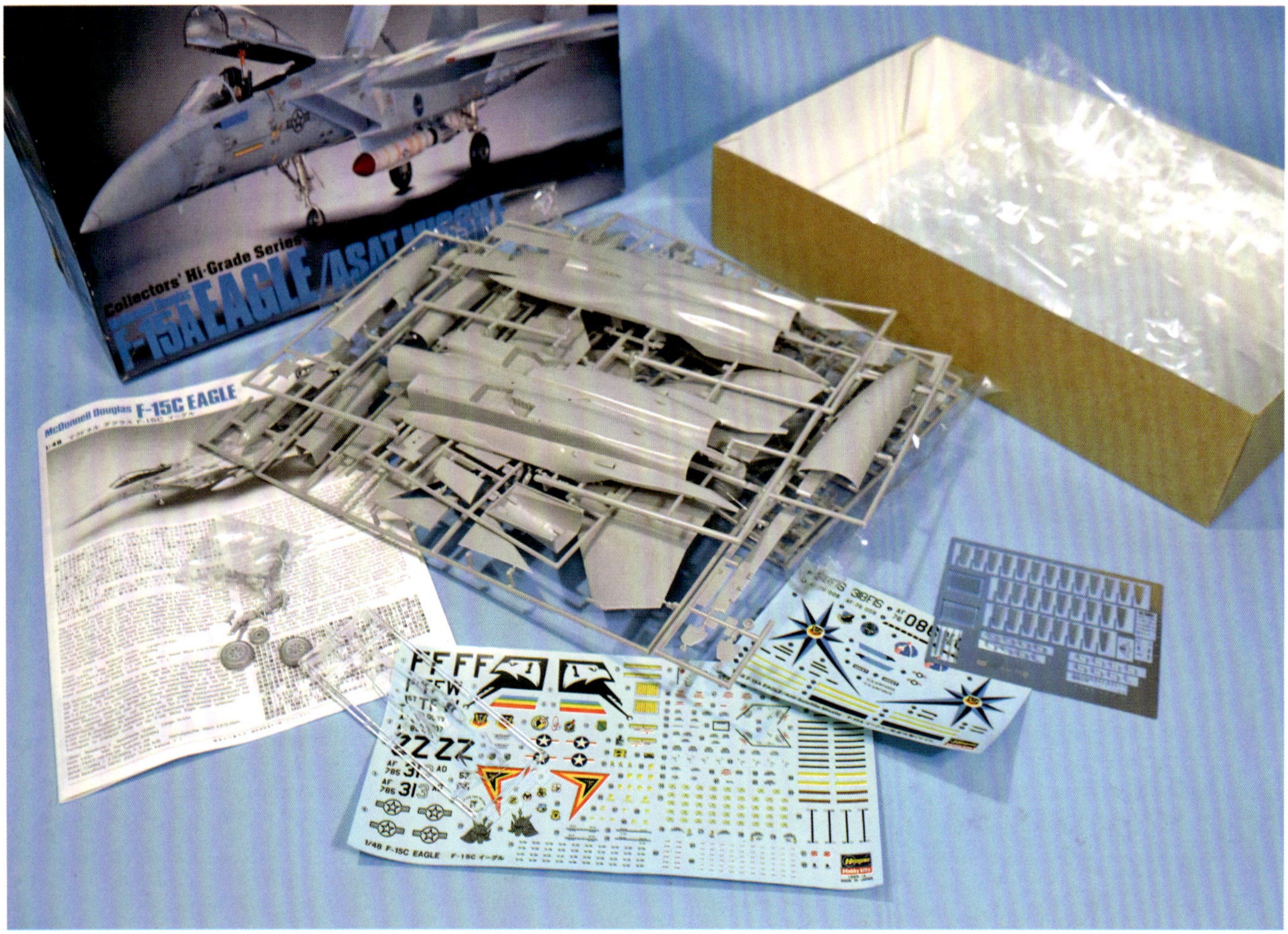

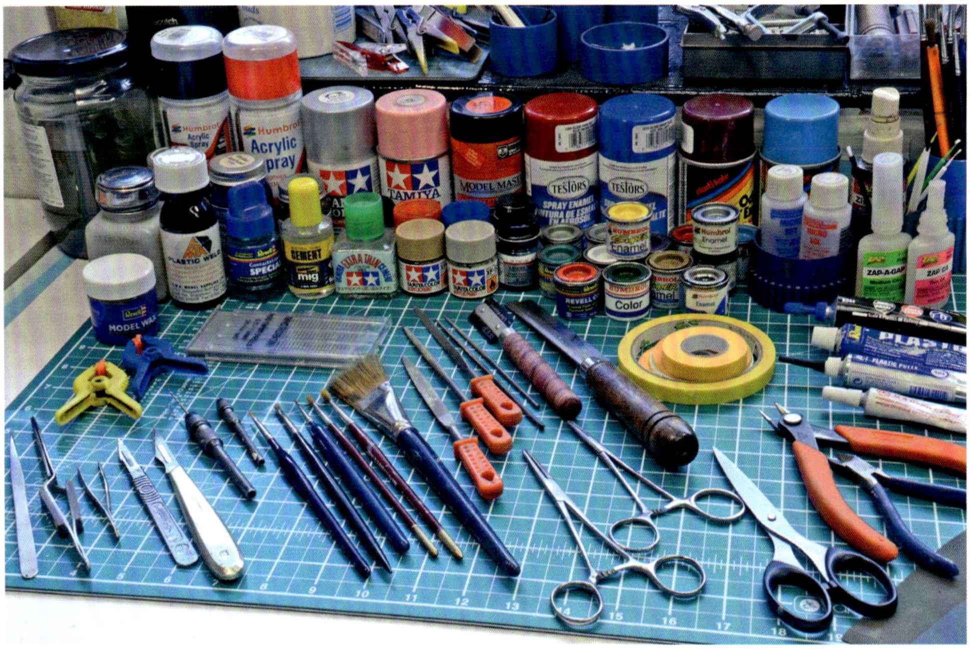

A typical modeller's work bench.

is now extremely difficult to shift. Actually, 'sprues' do exist in the injection-moulding process, but you will not find them in a model kit box. The sprue is the core of molten plastic before it gets injected into the mould, and having performed this task, the excess is recycled. The nearest it ever gets to the kit box is in the form of a small circular plug, usually positioned somewhere near the centre of a runner.

The box will also include a set of instructions, and in the vast majority of cases, a set of waterslide decals. Additionally, these days many kits may include non-plastic parts in the form of photo-etched, white-metal or injection-resin parts. Some even have vacuumed-formed plastic parts, particularly pertinent here as this material is often used for diorama bases.

CUTTING AND TRIMMING

At the very outset, when building any standard plastic model kit you will need some method of cutting and trimming the parts from the runners.

Cutting the parts from the runners can be done in two ways. They can either be cut off using snips, or sawn off. There are specially-manufactured 'modelling snips' for this task, however nail cutters or small electrical wire side-cutters could also work perfectly well.

Razor saws are made for most modelling tasks. These have thin blades with fine teeth, and can be bought in various sizes. Saws can be more suitable than snippers for certain parts, where the 'shock' of the snips 'snipping' can cause very small or very thin parts to snap. Sawing the part from the runner will usually avoid this.

A range of basic tools including razor saws, knives and files.

ABOVE LEFT A range of sanding papers for modellers. In fact the main pieces (right) are ordinary 'household' sanding papers cut down to a convenient size. On the left is a sanding set especially made for modelling, with a range of very fine sanding squares, and also sanding sticks. Top are liquid polishing and modelling wax. All sit on a sanding board, simply made from a sheet of sanding paper glued to a wood base, with another grade of paper fixed to the other side.

ABOVE RIGHT Cutting mats are available in several size, and there is always the option of a piece of thick card as a substitute for a mat.

With the part removed from the runner, you will be left with the slight 'tag'. This is where the plastic was fed into the mould cavity at the point called the 'gate'. Here, careful use of a modelling knife, small needle file or abrasive paper will remove the burr.

For general cutting, a wide range of standard knifes and scalpels is available from modelling suppliers and DIY stores. The scalpels are basically the same as those used for medical purposes, though for these tasks they are listed as 'non-sterile'. Non-sterile they may be, but the blades are equally sharp – extremely sharp – and consequently, although it may be stating the obvious, be careful and handle with respect; though this applies equally to any knife.

Larger knives are also useful, such as those generically referred to by one of the common names – Stanley knives, or box-cutters. They are useful for cutting larger runners, carving parts, and even opening boxes. It's preferable to buy one with a retractable blade. Good-quality scissors will also be required, especially when it comes to cutting up decal sheets.

Cutting tools also include the 'hot-wire' devices and similar used for some foam materials (these are dealt with in more detail in Chapter 8: Buildings).

When talking about cutting, it is also wise to include in the discussion the surface where it is taking place. Working directly on a wooden table or bench top is not ideal, as scars are soon going to appear. A purpose-made cutting mat is a wise investment, and these are available in a variety of sizes. They take general cutting blades in their stride, the surface being 'self-healing' to some extent. Alternatively, a sheet of mounting card could be used, available from art shops.

FILES AND SANDING

Small files – called 'needle files' – are especially made for modelling and similar activities. They come in various shapes, from the conventional flat, to half-round, round, square, and triangular. Larger files can come in useful when dealing with resin kits, where the gates on the runners are far larger than those found on the equivalent injection styrene kits. Files will also of course be very useful for many aspects of building dioramas.

Abrasive paper, still invariable called 'sand paper', is also a must for many tasks. Many grades are available, and for your main supply there's no need to buy special modelling sanding paper, just get the packs from a DIY store, and cut up sheets into convenient sizes.

Sanding papers can be split into two main categories – that which can only be use used dry, and that which can be used wet, but also dry, and is therefore termed 'wet-and-dry'. Wet-and-dry is the most useful, as sanding wet improves the cutting action, and cools the parts so the styrene doesn't tear. Most emery-type 'sandpapers' are fine for this task – these are waterproof and can easily be identified as they usually have a dark grey or black backing. 'Dry' sandpapers – which usually have a yellow or green backing – can also be used for some tasks, particularly sanding expanded polystyrene for landscapes. These papers cannot be used 'wet' as they will disintegrate into a soggy mess!

All sanding papers come in grades – the higher the number, the finer the grade. There are also specific sets of the finest grades made for modellers, and these can be used with polishing powders or liquids for the very smoothest of finishes.

CLAMPING

Parts often have to be clamped together while glue dries, and a wide range of metal or plastic C- or G-type clamps is available from model shops and DIY stores.

Another clamping tool that can be worthwhile is medical forceps. These are extremely useful for not only clamping, but holding small parts for painting. Because they have a slight amount of 'give' to them, and are ratcheted, they can accommodate a fairly wide range of thicknesses.

There is also that old mainstay – the humble clothes peg (clothes pins in the US). Available in both plastic and wood,

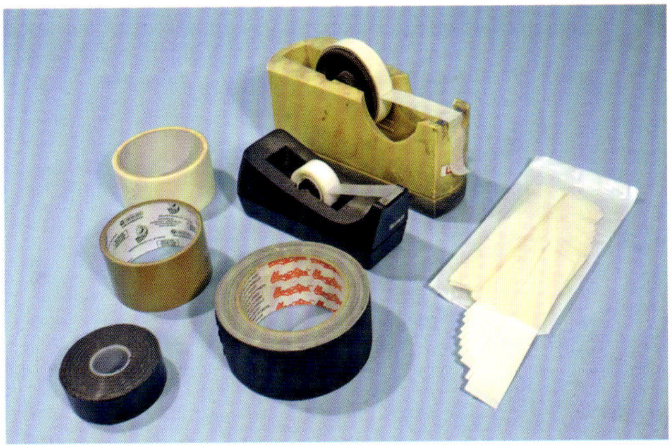

ABOVE Tools for clamping include small clamps, clothes pegs and medical-style forceps.

LEFT A range of tapes of all types – including clear tape in dispenser, general masking tape, electrical tape, gaffer tape (or duct tape) and double-sided sticky tape.

BELOW Specialist model masking tape is available in various widths, and should be used for masking edges. The other areas can be masked with standard tape – upper left and right.

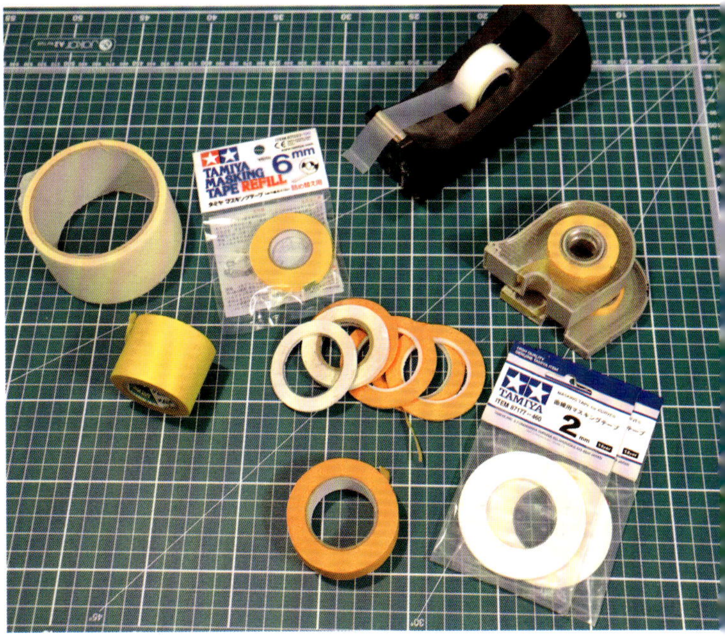

these are very cheap to buy and a selection should be in any modeller's tool box. Another household accessory that can be used for clamping is bulldog clips. Small bench-mounted vices can also be useful – some have a G-clamp to attach to a table edge, while others have a vacuum cup to attach them to a flat surface.

Standard sticky tape will have its uses. Fitted into a standard tape dispenser, the tape can easily be pulled out and cut off with one hand. Double-sided sticky tape is also useful, for example when you may want to permanently hold two flat surfaces together. Foam double-sided tape (which has small amount of 'give' in it) is useful for attaching and holding parts that maybe have a slightly irregular surface, when painting.

Clamps also come into play when devising methods of holding parts for painting.

The classic Humbrol and Revell paint tinlets with enamel paint (centre) and Tamiya acrylics upper centre. The large jar contains enamel paint cleaner (white spirit or turps substitute), while the smaller jar has methylated spirit for acrylics. The large brush (right) isn't used for paint, it is only used for dusting! Next to it are kebab-type sticks, for stirring.

PAINTING

Paints for modellers used to be almost exclusively enamel based. This applied to the original bottled paints from Airfix, similar bottles from Testors and the classic Humbrol tinlet, as well as the aerosol spray cans designed for modellers. However, recently there has been a change to acrylic-based paints for all types of household paint, as well as those especially made for modellers. Acrylic-based paint is deemed (slightly) more environmentally friendly. However, unlike enamel, there are various formulas, and these do not necessarily mix together. Using paints from a single manufacturer is usually safe in that these can normally be mixed together without problem. Cleaning and thinning of acrylics is also different to the process for enamel; some acrylics will clean in water, while other need something like methylated sprit (de-natured alcohol), or the relevant company's own special thinners. Virtually all modelling spray paints are now acrylic, though enamels in tinlets are still made by Humbrol. In addition, and besides the major chemical companies, there are many smaller names producing specialist paints, such as Xtracolor, Alclad, Vallejo, AK Interactive, Mig-Ammo and ZeroPaints. Many of these have to be airbrushed, and a wide variety of airbrushes are available.

The usual process is to first assemble all the parts that will be the same colour, then paint. Other parts will need individual application of paint. With the vast majority of kit parts supplied still on their runners, this is the most convenient 'hand-hold' for painting. Most parts have more than one gate (where they attach to the runner), so remove all you can, but ensure the part still remains held securely. Alternatively, the parts may have to be completely removed from the runners, in which case see if there is locating hole, where you can push a cocktail stick as a hand-hold. You may even need to drill a specific hole for this task, in some out-of-the-way place.

If there are many parts on a single runner that will be the same colour, remove all the gate positions you can, then spray the whole runner. Maybe hold an edge of the runner with a large clothes peg.

Larger parts with an 'inner surface' (such as a car body or hull of a ship) can be held by bending a suitable length of wire rod – a metal coat hanger is the usual source – bent so that it 'snaps' up inside the part. Maybe hold in position with doubled-sided sticky tape. Besides providing a convenient hand-hold, the wire handle also provides a convenient method of hanging the part up to dry.

This now brings us on to where to put the parts to dry. Drying paint is just as susceptible to dust contamination, as it is when being painted – in fact more-so as drying takes a longer time.

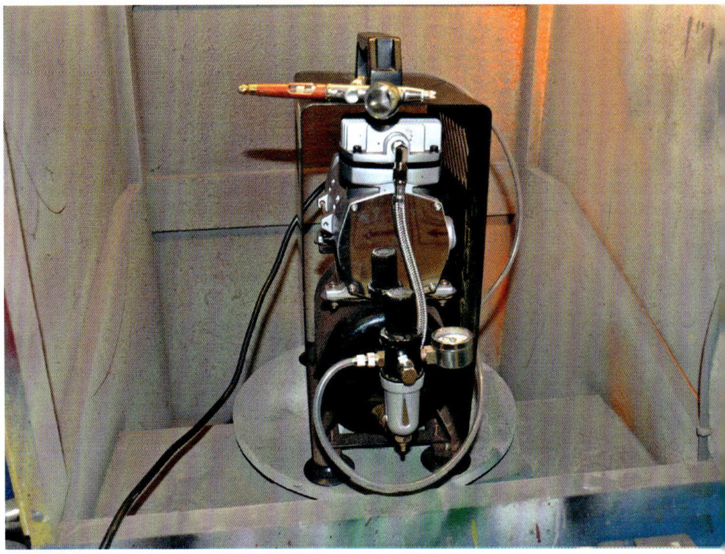

ABOVE LEFT Specialist paints, intended for airbrushing. These types of paints can only be airbrushed – they are far too thin to hand paint with a brush.

ABOVE RIGHT An airbrush, with a compressor, itself sitting in a home-made spray booth. This has lighting and an extractor fan built in.

RIGHT Airbrushing, using a piece of bent wire as a ‘hand hold’, taped to the component.

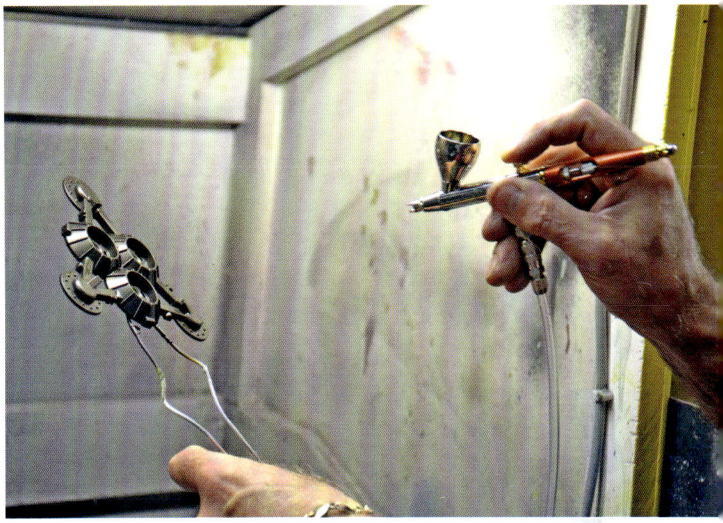

ABOVE A commercially-made spray booth. This is obviously somewhat limited in terms of the size of components that can be sprayed, but has a filter and dust extractor to direct the air outside.

LEFT If there is room, some sort of drying cabinet comes in very useful. This is home-made, with an old airing-cupboard tubular heater to provide a gentle updraft of heat to aid drying.

If you have a dedicated modelling area (even if you are not using it for spraying paint) good ventilation is important.

Specialist paints and mixes for weathering, including 'rust'!

The ideal solution for allowing paint drying is a dedicated drying area, though this of course is also down to individual conditions. Dedicated drying cabinets aren't really produced for the home hobbyist, so you will have to devise some method of your own. Warmth helps with drying paint. The example illustrated shows a simple box structure, with rails (made from small-diameter rails, such as those intended for towels) to hold the paint hangers or clothes pegs. A tubular airing-cupboard heater is fitted to the base, which allows warm air to rise upwards by convection.

If such a 'drying cupboard' device is not possible, ensure drying parts are out of the way of other work, as moving air is going to carry small particles you don't want on the paint surface while it is drying. If there is an unpainted 'inner surface' to the painted part (such as the previously mentioned car body or hull of a ship), try and dry it upside down – if any dust does fall it will then collect on the inner surface.

DRILLING

For drilling, there is the choice between a hand-operated pin-vice (pin-vise), or an electric drill. The pin-vice is more precise, especially when using very small drill bits to drill very small holes. However, electric drills, besides being faster and time-saving, can also be fitted with other tools, such as sanding discs, cutting discs and polishers.

Electric drills can be mains or low-voltage, and most will come with a speed control, as it will be vital to control the speed of the operation in most cases. There are even small drills that are charged via a USB socket. Electric drill controllers often have the option to use companion tools that plug into the same transformer, such as a small jig-saw, which can be invaluable for some tasks.

STICKING TOGETHER

In the early days of plastic kits there was just the one glue option – the tube of cement. This consisted of a styrene filler in liquid form in a carrier solution, but it had 'bulk', and you usually had some residue left over which squeezed out between the joints, and – once thoroughly dry – the excess had to be trimmed and sanded.

These problems were solved with the introduction of liquid cement. This is purely a liquid, which dissolves the styrene and in effect allows the surfaces to 'weld' together. It works much faster than the cement in a tube, and will not leave a residue of filler, as there is no filler.

The liquids used can vary, as many chemical compounds will dissolve styrene, but most are based around an aromatic hydrocarbon solvent base. The majority of these liquids evaporate quickly, and if not actually poisonous, can be unpleasant. Consequently, although relatively small qualities

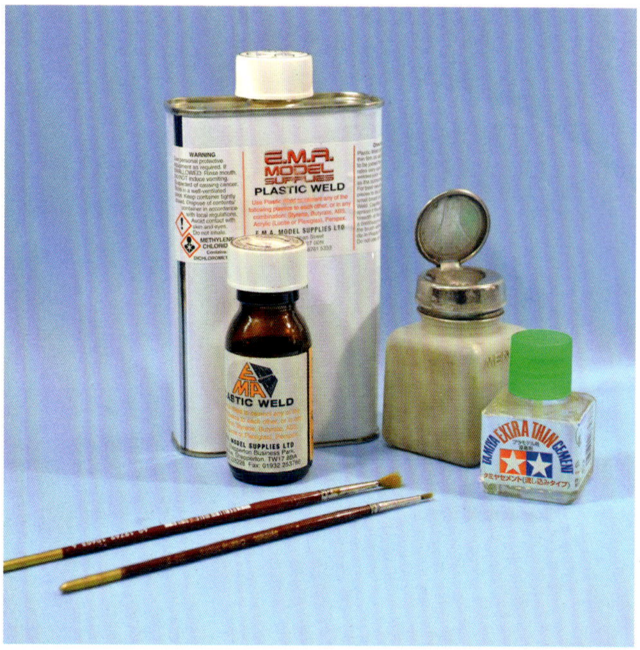

Liquid cements, mainly used today on plastic kits. Note the dispenser (centre right) and old paint brushes colour-coded with yellow paint on their ends, so they don't get muddled up with new brushes.

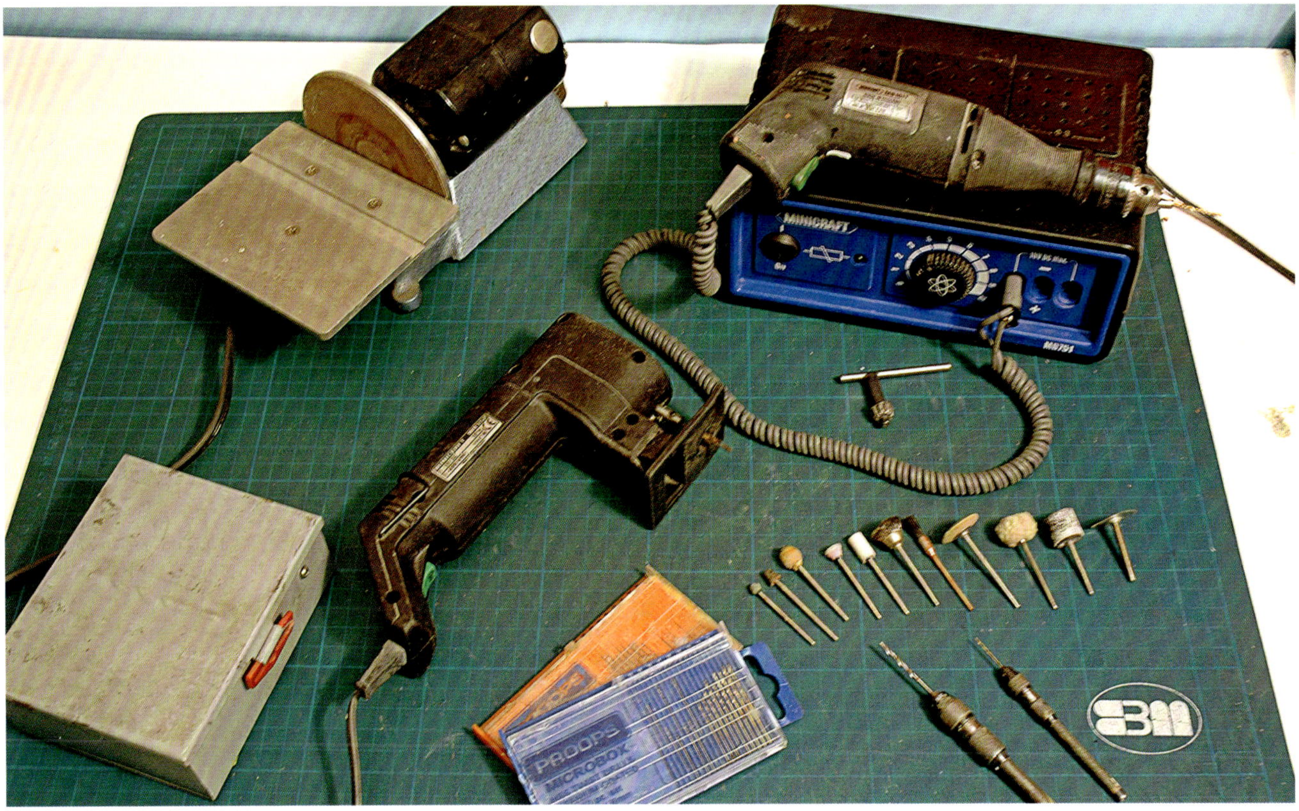

Electrical tools, including a small sander (upper left), an electric drill, and a controller (upper right), which will also run a jig-saw (centre). Also shown are some of the various tools for use with the drill, and two sizes of hand-operated pin vices (lower right).

Hot-glue guns in two sizes. These melt the glue sticks (centre), and although they can't be used to glue a kit together, will be extremely useful when it comes to constructing large structures and bases for dioramas.

A wide range of glues (left) and fillers (right).

are being used for model-making, it is vital to ensure the work area is well ventilated, and if you are particularly worried, wear a mask with a suitable filter. Also, keep the liquid in a sealed container when not in use, otherwise it can get expensive, as you will find it has all evaporated!

If you have a dedicated workshop area, you may even be able to fit an extractor fan, though ensure it is of an adequate size to shift a reasonable amount of air. Those sold as kitchen or bathroom fans rarely have sufficient through-flow, so you may have to move up to something intended for commercial use.

Liquid cement will cover the vast majority of plastic-kit construction needs but, as mentioned previously, many kits these days are 'multi-material' in that they come with additional parts made from materials such as resin, white-metal, photo-etch, or even flexible materials used as seat belts in aircraft and car kits. Consequently other gluing methods are required.

This requirement is likely to apply even more when it comes to the construction of a diorama, and the main adhesive commonly used here is cyanoacrylate, or CA, otherwise known as 'superglue'.

Superglue comes in various viscosities – thin, medium and thick – and keeping a bottle of each in stock is sensible, though if storage space is limited opt for the medium. These glues are available in various sizes of bottles, but frankly the amount a modeller will use is not that great, so it is better to go for the smaller sizes. The reasoning behind going for smaller pack sizes is that superglue has a limited shelf-life when opened, and you'll find that with the larger-size bottles most of the contents will harden over time and the bottle will have to be consigned to the waste-bin.

With superglue, the adage is 'less is more'. Use the smallest amount possible, as it will cure faster. The curing can be speeded up by the use of accelerator, or 'kicker', available in a hand-pumped spray bottle, but the resulting chemical reaction gets hot – in some cases, very hot – so be careful to keep fingers away from the parts! The use of kicker also weakens the join, not that this is usually a prime consideration when building a model kit. Superglue is also excellent for gluing skin together, but bottles of 'de-bonder' are also available.

Superglue is extremely useful, as it will glue the vast majority of modelling materials, and can be used to glue dissimilar materials together. However, it is not really suitable for gluing clear styrene or acrylic (as used for parts such as cockpit canopies, car windscreens and headlamp lenses). This is because when curing, it gives off fumes which can affect and cloud the clear surface. For clear components, it is best to use what is usually called 'watchmaker's cement'. This is a thin, clear adhesive in a tube that does not have the volatility of liquid cement or superglue. Contact-adhesive glues in general will also be useful for many aspects of diorama construction, such as sticking card to wood, while PVA glues can usually be used to stick wood to wood, as it is specifically designed for that purpose.

There is one other gluing method that can be invaluable for diorama modellers – the glue gun. A glue gun uses low-temperature-melting glue sticks, and the guns are powered from

Using commercial card boxes for storing reasonably large parts.

the mains (though really powerful ones use a gas canister). The 'gun' section heats the stick sufficiently to enable the glue to flow, and the glue is directed out of the nozzle by applying pressure on the trigger, which also pushes the stick forward. This technique is obviously not suitable for gluing a kit together – the glue is far too thick and uses too hot a temperature, but for large-scale gluing of diorama parts, it is ideal. More on glue guns in later chapters.

FILLERS

When building the actual models, fillers are available to fill those small gaps, the odd hole that has been drilled in the wrong place, or areas where the surface isn't quite as smooth as it should be.

For dioramas, fillers of all types are going to be very useful. Large-scale dioramas with ground sculpting will need 'bulk' fillers, and more will be found in the relevant chapters.

STORAGE

Storage considerations will depend on your overall circumstances. If you are fortunate enough to have a dedicated area for model-making, most tools and glues will likely have their own trays that are kept within reach and don't need to be packed away after every session. If you do need to pack things away, storage boxes for paint, glues and tools will almost certainly be necessary. The most straightforward options are the type sold for small tools, screws and nails that can be bought from DIY stores, or even boxes for fishing accessories. These of course can also be used by those with dedicated modelling areas to keep benches neat and tidy.

Small sets of plastic drawers, available from office suppliers and DIY stores, can hold spares, knife blades, drill bits and other paraphernalia. Recycled food containers can hold tools for easy access, and old mugs are handy for storing paint brushes – upside down of course, so the bristles are not wrecked. Mugs can also hold pens, pencils and rulers.

Older paint brushes, once past their best, can be re-used one further time as the applicator for liquid cement – though mark them to distinguish them from brushes that are still being used for paint!

Old glass jars can be recycled to hold cleaning fluids – and if you are using a mix of paint types, such as acrylic and enamel, you will need thinner/cleaners for both types.

You will likely find for diorama building that larger tools and equipment may be necessary, as the parts could very well be a lot larger than any model. This brings us to tools designed for general household and DIY use – drills, jig-saws, sanders, etc, all of which can be cordless, not necessarily mains-powered. Larger tools, such as band and circular saws and sanders could all be gainfully employed when you need to cut out a large base, or when building a floor-mounted stand.

A small multi-drawer cabinet can hold smaller parts.

ABOVE Good lighting is important wherever you do you modelling. Here, the work bench is next to a window. With blinds if the Sun is too dazzling!

RIGHT Magnification can come from a lens with built in light, and a head-set with interchangeable magnifying lenses can also be useful.

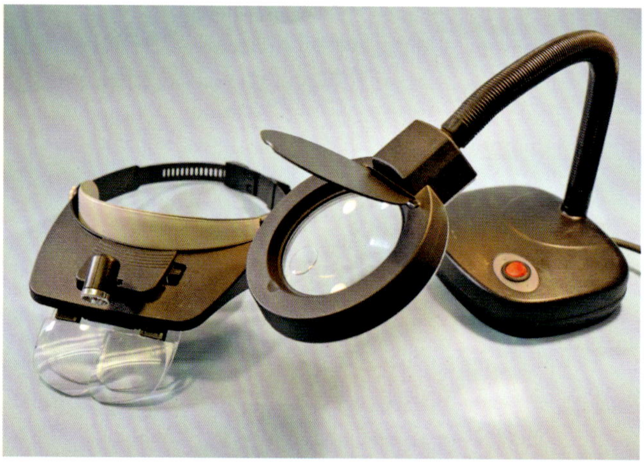

LIGHTING

Wherever you do your model making and diorama building, it is very important to have adequate lighting. If working on the kitchen table, ideally make sure it is near a window or a good light source.

If you are lucky enough to have a dedicated work area, and that has a window, position the main work bench under it. If there is no window (or when it is night!) artificial light sources will have to be used. What classes as a good light source is really down to the individual, but workshops or 'garden offices' tend to have fluorescent tubes fitted by default, although LED replacement 'baton lights' are now commonplace. Old-style filament light bulbs are still around, but in many cases have been replaced by LED equivalents. LED lighting can be obtained in various degrees of 'temperature', mimicking the light spectrum – from the 'warmer' (red) end to 'colder' blue (closer to daylight).

For close-up work, you may need specialist 'modelling lamps' (though sold for anything that requires close work), usually on some sort of adjustable stand. Some have magnifiers built in, and you can buy headsets with lights and similar close-up lenses.

ABOVE You could use old kit runners to build a *Star Trek* Borg Cube. *Model by Andy Preston*

LEFT The future? Small 3D printers are readily available, and not expensive, so could become a natural part of any modeller's workshop.

RECYCLING RUNNERS

One question that does come up quite often is: 'Can I recycle the runners, when all the parts are removed?' Here, unfortunately the answer is generally no – but that isn't down to the material. Ironically, polystyrene is a perfectly recyclable plastic, but that does not mean that any local recycling centre will, or can, actually do this. Also, the amount any hobbyist is likely to generate is unlikely to make it worthwhile. However, there are various uses to which old runners can be put. They can be cut down and used as paint stirrers. They can be gently heated over a small flame and stretched into, maybe, the wires for aircraft antennae, even rigging for ships. (It's actually where the modelling term 'stretching a sprue' came from – although that is really wrong, as you are 'stretching a runner'.) Then there is the case of modellers who scratch-build spaceships, and have used parts of the runner, or whole runners, as detailing parts for their latest build. The ultimate is to use runners to build a Borg Cube from *Star Trek* – yes, this has actually been done and, yes, it does use up a lot of runners!

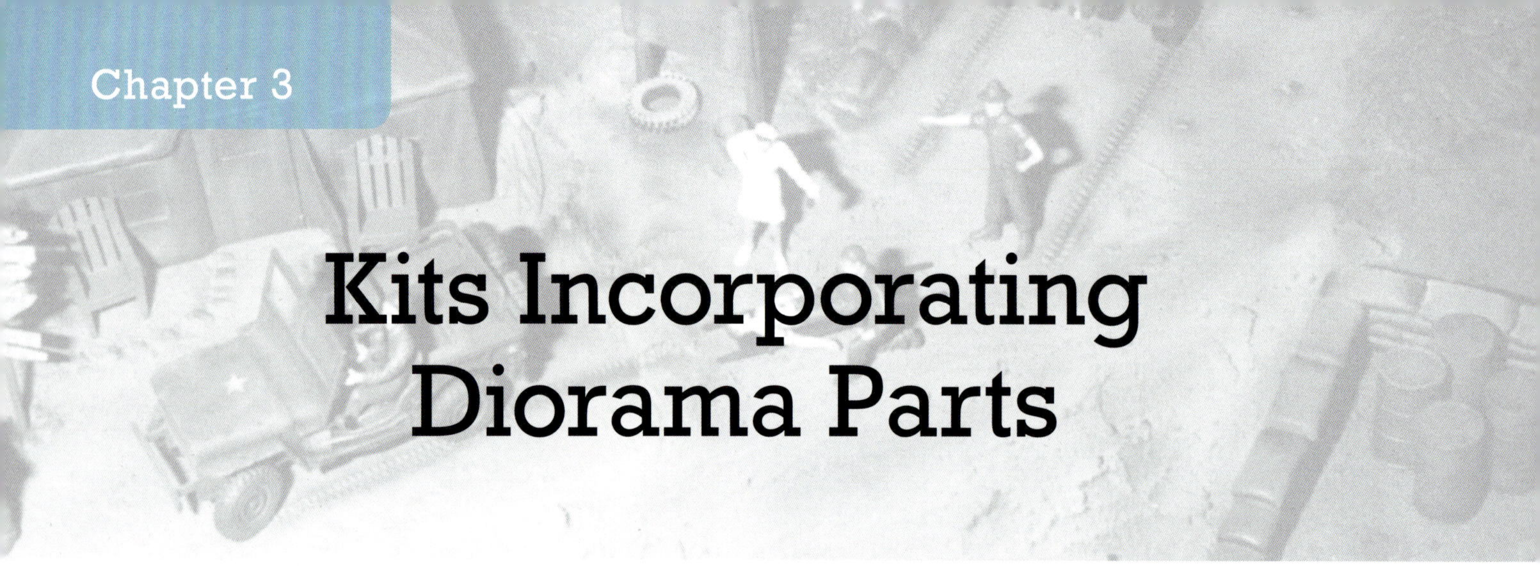

Chapter 3

Kits Incorporating Diorama Parts

Ever since the modern plastic construction kit arrived on the scene – and here we are really talking the early 1950s onwards – along with the main subject of the kit, the manufacturers started to put parts in the box that could be classed as 'elements for dioramas'.

These can be split into two basic types – firstly kits that came with parts and a base, therefore forming an 'all supplied, ready-to-build' diorama, and secondly kits in which all the parts were included, but there was no actual base, so to complete a diorama, you would have to find parts and materials for a base and build it yourself.

STANDING FIGURES

For the first example of kits incorporating elements of dioramas, let's turn to figures. In the vast majority of cases, kits of figures involve a human figure standing upright, so a base is handy, frankly, to stop them falling over! An aircraft is stable on its undercarriage, a car on its four wheels, but a figure – a human figure that is, with two legs – is far more prone to toppling over. This is possibly less of a problem with four-legged animals, but with human figures this is why, in the vast majority of cases, a base is included. As there is a base, there are often some diorama elements added for decoration. Many of the original model companies – the ones that started in the 1950s – produced model kits of figures, including Airfix, Pyro and Revell, though the most famous has to be Aurora.

The Aurora range of figures was legion, and although some included purely a base to keep them upright, maybe with a name plate, many included some more interesting features.

The classic series from Aurora was the Universal Monsters series – the creatures that starred in the Universal Pictures movies of the 1930s, including Dracula, the Mummy, the Creature from the Black Lagoon, the Wolfman and, of course, Frankenstein's Monster. All came with bases depicting a suitable setting – including Dracula with dead trees and bats, the Mummy with snakes and broken Egyptian columns, and Frankenstein's Monster in a graveyard. Of course, as a bonus when compared to the black-and-white movies, the model could be finished in colour.

The classic Aurora 'Monster' figures, each on a base with a semblance of diorama elements.

The Aurora-style figure was mimicked in more recent years when Monarch Models made Nosferatu, produced in a similar setting to the old Aurora kits.

PRESIDENTS, MONSTERS AND OTHER CREATURES

However, Aurora was not producing purely 'monsters', it made historical figures – President John F. Kennedy in his library, sitting, legs crossed, in a seat by the fireplace. George Washington in the boat crossing the Delaware followed, and although there were plans to produce eight President figures, only these two were ever issued.

One 'single-issue' kit also involved more 'American heroes', though these had more of a connection to the Universal Monsters than the US Presidents. The characters in question were The Munsters, with Aurora issuing a kit of their living room, complete with four of the family – Herman, Lilly, Grandpa and Eddie. Only Marilyn – the normal one to us, the freak to the rest of the family – was omitted. However, this did form a genuine diorama, in exactly the same sense as President Kennedy in his library. Interestingly kit manufacturer Moebius continued this theme many decade later with individual 1:10-scale figures of Herman and Grandpa, both at their respective work stations in the basement of 1313 Mockingbird Lane – Grandpa by the electrical distribution board, and Herman by a workbench full of equipment. The bases of both could be fitted together, though whether you would legitimately term these true dioramas, is debatable. Add a background to provide the walls of the workshop, and it would definitely class as diorama, though without, maybe we are indeed in 'vignette' territory (see Chapter 1).

ABOVE Not all Aurora figure kits fell into the 'monster' category. It started a series of US Presidents, but only produced two, one of which was John F. Kennedy.

ABOVE A true diorama from Aurora came in the form of the Munster's living room, with four of the family in typical poses.

RIGHT Moebius Models continued the Munster theme with larger figures of both Grandpa and Herman. Again both kit contained diorama elements.

Then there were Aurora's sports sets, heroes and wild creatures, all of which featured a base and some extras, though whether you would class them as full dioramas or vignettes, is down to individual opinions and interpretations.

Airfix also issued its series of 1:12-scale figures, and although they did all have a base (again, primarily to keep them upright), most additions provided would probably limit them to being classed as a vignette rather that a full-blown diorama. This followed through to the Airfix six 1:1-scale bird kits, and with these you did tend to get slightly more of a diorama feel, as most had branches or twigs to sit on, even a dead mouse for the owl, and a fish for the kingfisher!

LEFT Aurora planned to produce more dioramas in the form of two dungeon scenes. These were never issued by Aurora, but the tooling existed, and so DennCom issued both for a short time. This is the Animal Pit, and it was originally intended for Aurora's smaller Dracula figure (which was issued) to be walking down the stairs.

ABOVE The Airfix Robins came with a small base, which could fall within vignette territory.

LEFT Some kits are made full size – or 1:1 scale. This was the case with the Airfix series of birds, which all had some diorama touches.

Early airliner models from Revell contained a lot of diorama elements. The 'United Flight 707' had baggage carts, stairs, stanchions and a posing Hollywood starlet.

FREE-STANDING PARTS

The idea of producing some parts that enabled a diorama in basic form, but didn't include an actual base, appears to have begun with airliner kits from both Revell and Monogram – still at that time of course, the 1950s, independent, and rival, companies. (The two names joined forces in 1986.)

Perhaps because airliners were generally simpler in construction than military planes and were without weapons and armament, the company bosses may have thought that they should offer the builder of civilian plane kits a bit more. Revell's airliner kits actually culminated with the 'Airport Scene', featuring a Douglas DC-7 Mainliner. The kit was, perhaps slightly confusingly, called 'United Flight 707', which might suggest that the airliner was a Boeing 707, but it was a DC-7. It did, however, include a host of diorama accessories. These included a refuelling truck, baggage carts and truck, towing tractor, and boarding stairs (we are talking of a time before jet bridges). There was even a red carpet with stanchions, for the Hollywood starlet with paparazzo! Just add a suitable base, which being an airport, would not be a problem, as it would be flat. Oddly, apart from our wannabe starlet, there were no passengers, just a stewardess and drivers for the tow-trucks. Maybe the flight was just for the red-carpet lady?

The kit was issued in two different versions – the United Airlines version was the standard kit, but rarer is the Pan-Am version, made exclusively for that airline to sell through its airport desks.

Monogram was not to be left out, and its airliners came with at least boarding stairs, if no other equipment. However it went further for its more-individual civilian planes. For the second issue of its Ford Trimotor, it supplied the marking for the C.W. Byrd expedition to the Antarctic in the 1930s, and for this you got not only the markings, but two suitably-clothed figures and a dog-sled team of huskies. However, once again no base, so you had to add you own snow.

Monogram's Antarctic Expedition Ford Tri-Motor had two figures, three dogs and the sled included

FIRST FLIGHT

The world's first crewed, powered and controlled flight, from Kill Devil Hills, Kittyhawk, North Carolina, in 1903, was captured in a classic photograph that shows the just-airborne plane. There is Wilbur at the controls, with Orville running alongside and a selection of equipment scattered around. All these elements visible in the photograph are included in Monogram's kit of the Wright Brothers biplane – but still no base. However, as with the Antarctic Expedition Trimotor, creating a flat base for the Kill Devil Hills somewhat flat landscape was hardly going to tax modellers.

Many kits of smaller civilian planes also came with diorama accessories. The Monogram Cessna 180 Sport Plane with floats came with a water-skiing female figure and pilot, though it was also a time of slightly misleading box-art, as this shows the plane and pilot flying somewhat too close to the actual skier on the water – presumably being pulled by a boat, not the plane. However, the kit does not depict that scenario, as it comes with both figures standing, the girl holding her skis.

Even 'lighter-than-air' craft had their diorama elements. ITC originally issued the US Navy Blimp, reissued in more recent times by Glencoe Models. That came with mooring tower, tractor and crew. The scales of the elements were somewhat miss-matched, but when completed and fitted to its supplied base, you did have some idea of how these blimps were handled on the ground.

ABOVE Monogram's Cessna 180 sports plane has a water-skier and skies, though not in the position seen in the box-art.

LEFT Monogram's Wright Brothers' Flyer has, besides the aircraft, both brothers and all the small details seen in the original historic photograph.

BELOW ITC's US Navy Blimp makes a small diorama 'out of the box', with the mooring tower, tractor and ground crew. The kit was reissued in recent years by Glencoe Models.

LEFT The Matchbox Monty's Caravan makes up into a small, but very detailed diorama in its own right.

BELOW Revell's 105mm howitzer included a small diorama base and four figures.

THE MILITARY

Military subjects really do demand dioramas, but here it took some time for anything approaching a diorama base to be introduced. Some small models in the early years did include a semblance of a diorama. Revell's 105mm Howitzer came with four figures, ammo boxes and spent shell casings, all on a small emplacement base, with 'built-in' tyre tracks and footprints. Again, it is debatable whether these fitted into the diorama or vignette categories, but they certainly have many elements of a small diorama. Kit manufacturer Adams interestingly produced a similar kit of a howitzer with a small diorama base and five figures, and Adams and Revell, if not officially connected at the time, did work together on various projects, so it is slightly odd that these two kits covered the same subject, but were totally different kits.

Many early military models were, however, reasonably large in size. For example, Renwal's Atomic Cannon in 1:32-scale was nearly 1m (3ft) long, so providing a base in the kit, in addition to the object itself, would have been impractical. Consequently, in the vast majority of these early Renwal military vehicle kits, figures were supplied, but no base.

The smaller scale for military Armoured Fighting Vehicles (AFVs) had also been introduced by Airfix – 1:76 scale – which matches the UK model-railway 00 gauge. For these models, including a base would have been, one might have thought, a natural extension, but no Airfix AFV kit ever included a base. However, when the rival model company Lesney – most famous for its range of Matchbox toys (though few, if any, ever fitted in a conventional matchbox), decided to start a kit division in 1974, also called Matchbox, it began a complimentary range of military kits – and these did include bases. Some of these were fairly small and simple – much like the Revell 105mm Howitzer – but some were more complex, forming what could legitimately be termed a diorama.

One example of these kits was the Matchbox kit of Monty's Caravan – the workstation for General Bernard Montgomery. It was a Leyland Retriever lorry with an Italian-built 'caravan' mounted on the back. The kit also contained a Daimler MkII Scout Car, and a base with three figures, a table built from a plank sitting on two barrels, two wooden road barriers, plus a section of a street. All of this builds into a very convincing diorama – small, but emphasising that overall size does not necessarily limit what is possible.

CATALOGUE DIORAMAS

Intriguingly, some manufactures were now showing military dioramas in their catalogues, particularly Monogram, Aurora and Revell. At the time, none were manufacturing the diorama parts, but the companies were becoming aware that military AFVs were the one subject where dioramas were a natural – and were showing what could be done with their kits. Precise step-by-step instructions were not provided in the catalogues, but finished results were shown, and a few details were included in the instructions for the kits.

One military kit series that did fall under the umbrella of dioramas, was when Revell obtained the license for the movie, and later TV series *M*A*S*H*. Three kits were issued, and although one – the classic Bell H-13 Helicopter – included just the helicopter, the Swamp Scene and Medical Scene provided a Jeep and a six-wheeled US Army truck respectively, they also

ABOVE The Revell M*A*S*H kits in a larger diorama made by Revell itself for one of the iHobby trade shows in Chicago.

LEFT Revell's M*A*S*H kits did contain diorama elements, including a base.

MONOGRAM®

DIORAMAS

Creating dioramas for displaying models has become a popular extension of the model building hobby. Monogram kits are highly detailed, and the assembled model can be painted with a "weathered" appearance and mounted in an appropriate setting with artificial landscaping and "battle-scarred" structures.

A detailed diorama can show your model in a realistic situation.

Vehicles in combat take a terrific beating.

Mounting your vehicle on a landscaped base adds interest to the model.

Imagination is a key ingredient in building dioramas.

Clever little touches can do much to enhance the fascination of your model.

Tarpaulins, ammo boxes and bedrolls add realism.

40

Monogram – even though it wasn't making any diorama accessories itself – went to great pains in its 1970 catalogue to show what could be achieved with it military kits.

As early as 1957, Revell had a page in its catalogue showing its military items being used not only to create dioramas, but also how they could be used for photography.

came with diorama features. The Jeep is arguably the better example, as besides the vehicle, the kit included a typical army tent, two wooden seats, signpost and three figures plus a base. Intriguingly, it isn't the base that is vacuum-formed, it is the tent – the base is injection-moulded styrene. The truck scene lacks a building structure, but has four figures and also an injection-moulded base. It would be a simple matter to build a larger base, and to incorporate the three main elements to create a much larger scene, which Revell itself did for displays at model shows.

The practice of including dioramas with kits faded somewhat in intervening years, though this may be due to companies issuing diorama accessory kits of their own, alongside the main kits.

ABOVE AMT reintroduced card diorama background for many of its kits. Here, the card garage (that first appeared with a 1934 Ford pickup) has been re-assigned to a garage for The Three Stooges – it isn't advisable to take your car there!

LEFT The short-lived Addar company (basically a spin-off run by ex-Aurora employees) made three kits of daredevil Evel Knievel. One was his Sky Cycle that jumped the Snake River Canyon. The kit has a foreshortened backdrop of the Canyon, made from injection-moulded polystyrene, not vacuum-formed or card.

TIME FOR CARD

One diorama element has been reintroduced with some kits in more recent years – that of a diorama setting made from card. This has mainly come about with the current owner of the AMT and MPC brands – Round 2 Corporation. AMT in particular used to issue some of its car kits with card diorama backdrops. Card was used as it was far cheaper than producing a tool to make an injection-moulded version, though that was occasionally done. For example, Addar produced a plastic backdrop diorama for its Evel Knievel kit of the rider with his Skycycle X-2, the backdrop being the Snake River Canyon in Idaho, which Knievel jumped in 1974. However, a backdrop in plastic was unusual, doubly so as the backing was forced-perspective, the distances involved having to be considerably foreshortened.

The majority of these kit dioramas however have been in card, which besides being far cheaper to produce, packs flat and so would fit standard boxes. Card can be reasonably

ABOVE A card diorama backing used to great effect with AMT's own AMTtronic car design.

RIGHT One of Revell's car dioramas that combined one of the company's existing car kits, in this case the 1960 Corvette, with a section of a famous (some would say 'infamous') hotel on Route 66 – the Coral Court. It was demolished in 1995, though a small section – that more or less matches the kit – was rescued and re-built at the National Museum of Transport in St Louis, Missouri. These card dioramas were designed by Dean Milano when he worked for Revell-Monogram.

LEFT Designer of the Revell kit, Dean Milano points to its inspiration, the only remaining section of the Coral Court Motel, rebuilt at the Museum of Transportation in St Louis, Missouri. The car is a 1941 Cadillac.

AMT's Man in Space set of all five of the original space rockets with crews – with its Kennedy Space Center diorama backdrop.

detailed, and the idea has been reintroduced by Round-2 in recent years. Some kits have been recreations of the originals. AMT's own 'futuristic car', the AMTronic, was first issued in 1969 with a comprehensive diorama backdrop, produced in pre-cut card. This comprised several layers, so although each layer was flat, the final result definitely gave a 3D look. The kit was reissued in 2000 in the Millennium Range, but without the card diorama, which definitely lessened the overall appeal, although the kit itself is excellent. Fortunately, this situation was rectified in 2012, when the basic original kit was reissued with the original box-art and the card diorama was now reintroduced.

Revell briefly entered the card diorama scene in 1988 with four kits of its existing cars that included new three-dimensional buildings. Designed by Dean Milano, these included a gas station, a diner, a drive-in and a section of the Coral Court Motel, a famous location once found along Route 66.

It wasn't all automotive. AMT provided a similar card diorama set-up with its Man in Space set, with (at that time) all five crewed rockets of the American space programme – Mercury Redstone, Mercury Atlas, Gemini-Titan, Saturn 1B and Saturn V. These all sat on a diorama base depicting the Kennedy Space Center at Cape Canaveral, including the Launch Umbilical Tower (LUT) for the Saturn V. This was reissued in 1999, again without the card parts, but instead including a flat black plastic base. The set was reissued yet again in 2011, now including all the card parts once more. This does conveniently demonstrate how the exact same model – or models in this case, as there are five rockets – just sitting on a plain base, couldn't really be termed a diorama, (or even a

ABOVE Interestingly, the Man in Space kit was reissued in the 'Pro Shop' range, but without the card backdrop. So although the plastic parts were exactly the same, because it now lacked the backdrop, it turned the kit from a diorama to a model on a base.

LEFT Monogram made its Earth Satellite kit of both of Americas first artificial satellite launchers. As the launch pad and figures were included, it produced a simple diorama.

ABOVE LEFT Arguably, the American Bison – originally from Aurora, but later from Atlantis – couldn't really be considered a diorama, but with the inclusion of two prairie dogs, it starts to take on a diorama feel.

ABOVE RIGHT None of Renwal's military kits had any diorama-type accessories, just figures, though here a few details have been added from Italeri accessory kits.

LEFT The Revell (later Atlantis) Mercury Atlas launch pad was classed as a diorama kit, as although it lacked a base, it featured a truck, trailers, the rocket carrier and (originally) several crew figures. Adding a flat base to turn it into a more extensive diorama was therefore fairly straightforward.

vignette), but the exact same model, against the backing – even if the backing is card – certainly fulfils the diorama definition.

One of these rockets – the Mercury Atlas – was issued as an earlier kit by Revell in 1963 with a highly-complex launch platform. This itself was first issued when the kit was the Convair Atlas missile (issued in 1958), and the number of extra pieces, including a truck, three trailers – one for the rocket itself – and two fuel bowsers, plus figures in the early kit (unfortunately omitted in recent reissues) really did make for a complete diorama in box. The launch pad matched the actual one at Cape Kennedy Air Force Station (not Kennedy Space Center itself) extremely accurately. You just need to sit the rocket on a flat base – and ideally double the length of the ramp – and you have a pretty good representation. (It lacks the bright red service tower, though you can't have everything, and that was actually made for a time as a photo-etched kit by LVM Studios.)

MAN ON THE MOON

Kits of real spacecraft rarely have diorama elements as what would they be? Yes, a Saturn V is fine on the launch pad – as AMT did with the card backdrop – but that really only qualifies as a diorama as it has the background. The launch pad alone – which Revell produced in the form of its Shuttle Launch Pad – although highly complex, isn't really a diorama without anything else. However, one the craft that the Saturn V carried – the Apollo Lunar Module – certainly was when it landed on the Moon. Even the very earliest issue (first issued in 1970) of the Airfix 1:72-scale Lunar Module kit came with a small circular Moon base, and some of the items of equipment carried for the 'One Small Step'. It was later reissued with a large, vacuum-formed base, and the set of astronaut figures that was issued separately. Monogram went one stage further with its 1:48-scale model of the Apollo 11 on the Moon kit, as it included a reasonably large base, all six pieces of equipment carried by the mission, and even the sharp shadows of the equipment and astronauts were 'etched' into the base. Dragon

ABOVE Monogram's 1:48-scale Apollo Lunar Module came with a base, the two astronauts and all six pieces of equipment carried by Apollo 11. The base even had the sharp shadow on the lunar surface, etched in, making it a true diorama.

LEFT MPC issued four large insects and arachnids, each rampaging in some downtown American location. Most of the parts were made in styrene, but the backdrop and base were card. This is the Airfix issue of the Gigantic praying mantis, but apart from the logo, the kits are identical.

The card-backing idea originated with 'store displays' made by many of the American kit companies, particularly in the 1960s. This is a small sample of them, showing that they covered all subjects. *From the Mark Mattei collection*

also joined in with its 1:72-scale Apollo 17 diorama with Lunar Module, two astronauts, and equipment, including a minutely-detailed 1:72-scale Lunar Roving Vehicle (LRV), all positioned on an oval-shaped lunar-surface base.

Combination kits, those that included both injection-moulded styrene diorama elements and a card background, were typified by MPC when it issued a series of four 'Gigantics' kits. These were generally known as the 'giant insect series', but biologically that only correctly applied to two – a praying mantis and a wasp. The others were a tarantula and a scorpion, so more correctly, two giant insects, and two giant arachnids – all attacking buildings and people. The vast majority of the kit components were injected-moulded plastic, but the backdrop in each case was card.

STORE DISPLAYS

The use of card in model-kit dioramas almost certainly developed from the practice of the model companies making special shop displays, used to promote the new kits in hobby stores' window displays. These covered the full range of models – cars, ships, aircraft, military, etc – and were only supplied to shops and stores. There was a built-up model at the centre, but all the surroundings were card. Maybe these, and the card dioramas in kits, are not true dioramas, in that the card somewhat limits the amount of three-dimensional detail that can be produced, but it also can be argued they fulfil exactly the same role as the original 'theatrical dioramas' of Daguerre and Bouton, back in the 1820s (see Chapter 1).

PREHISTORIC SCENES

One model-making subject that has always been popular – and popular in every aspect – is dinosaurs. It is also ideal for the model companies in that precise accuracy is not that important – get the rivet pattern 5mm out on an F-14 Tomcat model, and aircraft modellers will never forgive you, but who is really going to say if that the line of back plates on a stegosaurus is out by 5mm? Even palaeontologists are continually arguing, changing their minds and redefining species. Ideas on the colours of dinosaurs also keep changing, and it's thought that some may even have been adorned with feathers! So, ideal subjects for a model company, and for the modeller, where they can really exploit their freedom of choice. Hence, many early kit companies took the dinosaur route – and long before *Jurassic Park*. These included Airfix, Aurora and Pyro and many examples can still be found in catalogues, although some are now under different names. Tamiya also got in on the act somewhat later, but it went one stage further and issued some of its dinosaurs on diorama bases. These were very cleverly designed, with non-styrene items, such as pre-coloured, thin, corrugated paper for items such as the leaves for prehistoric plants, adding to the general feel of the scene.

Tamiya make a whole range of dinosaurs as dioramas, complete with base, other small creatures and vegetation. This is a parasaurolophus with a figure of a modern-day anthropologist for scale.

FAR, FAR AWAY

Commercial kit production was well established, when kits were introduced that were not purely stand-alone, but fulfil the description of a complete diorama, including the individual stand-alone models. This was assisted by the introduction of bases produced as vacuum-formed mouldings, enabling far larger bases, where the use of injection-moulded plastic would be impractical. MPC exploited this more than others, especially when it became the first company to offer a range of models from the *Star Wars* movies. The *Star Wars* franchise has since grown exponentially to include several other model manufacturers, but the MPC kits came first.

MPC launched a range of what were truly complete dioramas in a box, invoking scenes from the first three movies, today known as Episodes 4, 5 and 6. So you could build Ice Planet Hoth, with snowspeeders, ATATs, and numerous figures, or The Palace of Jabba the Hutt. Both consisted of numerous small items and a large vacuum-formed base. Scales were therefore correspondingly fairly small, and although not listed officially, it could be worked out that Hoth was around 1:144-scale, and Jabba's Palace somewhat larger, around 1:96. An even larger-scale model was produced in the form of Luke's meeting with Yoda on Dagobah, though here the base was fully injection-moulded styrene, though the scaling was somewhat compromised, as Yoda was almost as large at Luke!

This overall idea of these *Star Wars* diorama kits may have been prompted by wargaming, where figures, equipment and a large base were commonplace. MPC even made its own wargaming-type kits, under the Historama name, using Airfix figures and equipment (the two brands were part of the General Mills conglomerate at the time), and MPC's own vacuum-formed base. There was even a Dungeons and Dragons-type kit, and one from the first Indiana Jones movie, *Raiders of the Lost Ark*, both with vacuum-formed bases. MPC also took some of its car kits and gave them diorama bases in its Autorama series.

And MPC returned to this scenario in far more recent years, the name now owned by the Round-2 company. The Gerry Anderson live-action (as opposed to puppet) TV series *Space: 1999*, had regained popularity – though probably safe

One of MPC's *Star Wars* dioramas – Jabba the Hutt's Palace, featuring a vacuum-formed base with injection-moulded styrene figures.

ABOVE Jeep Commando – one of several MPC car kits with a very basic diorama setting, using a vac-formed base and card backdrop.

ABOVE MPC added to the *Space 1999* kits from decades ago with new diorama-style models. Here, the Nuclear Waste Disposal Area has injection-moulded parts, a vacuum-formed base and lighting to create a full diorama.

to say, it had never been lost – and for the first time in many decades, there were brand-new kits. One of these is the Atomic Waste Disposal area on the Moon, with standard styrene structures and figures, and even the ATV six-wheeled vehicles, all sitting on a vacuum-formed base. Overall, MPC probably issued more of these diorama-based kits than any other manufacturer, so if you want a basis to start you own diorama model, one of these MPC kits could very well be a good place to begin.

SHADOW BOXES

Few companies made complete diorama kits presented with a full display case, as you might see in a museum, but there were two companies that did take this route.

In the early 1970s, Tonka (yes the same company that makes the large toy vehicles), made six dioramas kits in conjunction with the Smithsonian Institute. These came with a complete display case, in effect a shadow box. The first four consisted of one car example, one loco, and two aircraft scenes – the latter the Wright Brothers Flyer at Kill Devil Hills, and Lindbergh's Spirit of St Louis landing at Paris. Later two similar, but smaller, kits were added. One other company with a similar approach was Eldon, which made several dioramas, again, with full display cases, and a 'picture frame', including one on the Moon – the Moon Survey.

THE SCENE TODAY

There are still models today that follow these early ideas of issuing individual kits incorporating diorama ideas, although these days many more concentrate purely on the model itself, and many aircraft kits can even lack a pilot figure! Consequently, if the modeller intends to build such a kit into a diorama setting, they will rely on the multitude of aftermarket diorama accessories that are now available.

RIGHT One of several Tonka dioramas – in fact shadow boxes, as you get the complete display box. This example features the Ford Model T.

Chapter 4

Aftermarket Diorama Elements

Mention has been made in the previous chapter of model companies such as Airfix, Aurora, Monogram and Revell including diorama elements in early kits. Some of these manufacturers even made stand-alone kits that contained purely the dioramas elements.

EARLY DIORAMA/ACCESSORY KITS

Many of these early kits were associated with model cars, as these were the prime subjects where 'customising' came into play. To this end, AMT, Revell, and Aurora all issued stand-alone accessory packs containing customising parts. However, these were not all diorama parts, they were mostly parts to customise an existing car kit. There were a few exceptions however, one of which was AMT's Drag Strip Accessories pack, which contained genuine diorama items to build a drag strip – you just needed to add the dragster and driver.

With the exception of railways – more of which in Chapters 6 and 7 – the idea of producing separate diorama accessory kits had a long way to go, and arguably it wasn't until the 1980s that individual diorama accessory kits came to the fore.

ABOVE One of the earliest accessory sets that included diorama elements came from AMT back in the 1960s. The Drag Strip Accessories set can be seen bottom right. *From the Mark Mattei Collection*

LEFT AMT's Drag Strip Accessories 'in action'. The set includes most of the items in the background and the 'classic' TV camera on the left. The Dragster is from MPC and the Chevy pick-up from AMT.

LEFT Just a few of the many Airfix 'trackside accessories', in their original poly-bag packaging, plus later boxes, and some built examples. The tooling for these now resides with Dapol.

Consequently, it wasn't until around then that the one model subject that does scream 'Put me in a diorama!', got its way. This was subject of 'land-based military', or put another way – tanks. So companies began to manufacture diorama accessories for the armies of the world, primarily in the two 'military scales'. Although there are of course exceptions to the rule, the main military scales are the combined 1:72/1:76 scales, and 1:35-scale. Although there are other military scales, such as 1:48 and 1:16, the vast majority of military Armoured Fighting Vehicle (AFV) kits are today produced in 1:72/1:76 or 1:35 scales.

Although not by design, the smaller scales were actually already reasonably well catered for, in the UK at least. When Airfix began producing its range of smaller-scale AFVs, it used 1:72-scale. It also had a range of buildings and structures intended for use in model-railway layouts in 00 gauge, which equates to 1:76-scale. At this physical size, 1:72 and 1:76 can conveniently be considered much the same – especially when it comes to buildings. The buildings produced for model railways were not in the destroyed state invariably seen in military dioramas, but with some modification they could be used as a starting point. These 'Trackside Accessories' (as they were generally termed) also featured useful structures such as water towers, engine sheds and the ubiquitous girder bridge, and so not only provided the structures themselves, but also a useful range of materials – roofing, piping and all those girders. Additionally, the scales almost matched the same traditional scale as aircraft, ie, 1:72, so diorama accessories were introduced for airfields, including refuelling bowsers and recovery vehicles. One Airfix building was a World War II airfield control tower, based on a generic design seen across the UK during the war, many of which still survive in use today.

BELOW Modern accessory packs from MiniArt. These are almost exclusively in 1:35-scale, and as can be seem from these examples, cover a very wide range of parts. Although they are 1:35-scale, many can be adapted to other scales – after all a wooden box is a wooden box!

1:72 vs 1:76

Meanwhile, other small-scale AFVs were being introduced by Japanese companies, primarily Hasegawa and Fujimi, and these tended to be 1:76-scale. In these cases, it was the buildings that were already available – those initially produced for model railways, as previously mentioned, and in the UK these were, again, produced to the same scale – 00 gauge, or 1:76. This doesn't necessarily apply outside the UK, as in many countries the main model rail gauge is H0, or 1:87. There is actually a 10 per cent difference in scales between 1:87 and 1:76, although with buildings it perhaps mattered less than with vehicles or aircraft.

However, and with apologies to those 1:72 and 1:76 military builders, arguably now the main military scale is 1:35, and in terms of diorama accessories at this scale, there was really nothing until we got into the 1980s – it was scratch-build structures or go without. Admittedly, many of the buildings in such dioramas are in damaged/derelict condition, so the task was slightly simpler – a pristine paint finish for a house was not really relevant if it didn't have a roof and was missing a couple of walls.

Interestingly, Aurora, Monogram and Revell had been illustrating battlefield dioramas in their catalogues as long ago as the 1970s (see Chapter 3), and in Revell's case, as far back as the 1950s. None produced the actual structures, or the battle-damaged tanks, but provided photographic examples, many from well-known modellers. The images were there basically to give the builder inspiration for how to go about the conversions to create the scenes.

Tamiya, in Japan, also took this approach at around the same time. It would show in its catalogue model dioramas photographed at that year's Shizoka Model Show, and also highlighted detailed accessory kits produced by Francois Verlinden.

VERLINDEN

Francois Verlinden created, and for many years ran, the Verlinden model company in his native Belgium. He was perhaps the forerunner of such garage companies that specialised in supplying detailed accessory parts, primarily in resin, for building military dioramas.

Verlinden had identified that AFVs were a popular subject for dioramas, and if anything demanded diorama accessories, it was a battlefield. The company was founded in 1988 (and closed in 2016, due to his retirement), and although the company dabbled with aircraft aftermarket parts, and also some car-related 1:24-scale figures, its main speciality was always with the AFV side of things. By the mid-1980s, the military scale of 1:35 was well-established, so the vast majority of Verlinden diorama accessories were to this scale.

Verlinden produced a vast range of damaged buildings and other structures, most of them World War II-specific, such as bombed-out shops and street scenes, barns and mansions, farms and town halls, plus pill-boxes, dug-outs, and gun positions. Later on, structures from more recent

The cover of one of the Verlinden's catalogues, in this case for Summer 1989.

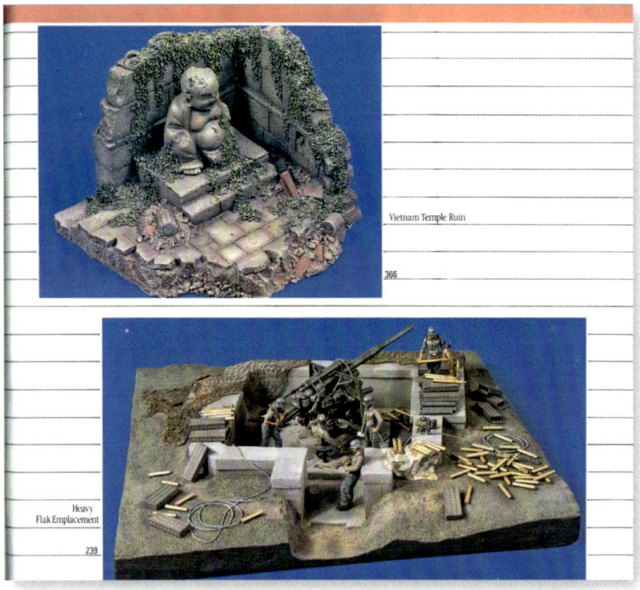

One of the pages from Verlinden's 1989 catalogue. These two images show the wide range of parts offered, from military diorama parts (bottom) to the Buddha figure (top), suitable for dioramas set during the Vietnam conflict.

More from the Verlinden catalogue, showing just a few of the buildings available in a 'wrecked' state.

conflicts were introduced, such as Middle Eastern buildings. These were produced almost exclusively in resin, and with the basic structures available, Verlinden added all the accessories needed for a diorama – not only the obligatory ammunition and weapons, but crates and bottles, military provisions, jerry cans, rucksacks, tents and bedrolls and, of course, figures. Many military kits already came with figures – at one point Monogram issued a kit that comprised just GIs – but battle scenes would need a lot more soldiers, and Verlinden obliged. He was also among those who pioneered the use of combining a foreground model scene with a real photographic backdrop, so putting the model into context.

STYRENE vs RESIN

The idea of producing kits in resin was not something the mainstream companies originally contemplated. They were, after all, set up to use injection-moulded styrene in large, expensive and heavy steel tooling, running at high temperatures, putting out a complete kit in thirty seconds, and with production runs of many thousands. Resin casting can be done at home, in short-run rubber moulds, at room temperature – but, and unlike injection moulding – it is highly labour intensive. However, two mainstream companies in particular have toyed with resin castings for military dioramas. One is Italeri, the other Airfix. Airfix had ironically sold off the vast majority of its 'trackside accessories' to Dapol in the early 1980s. This became even more ironic, as Airfix was then acquired by Hornby in 2006 – and

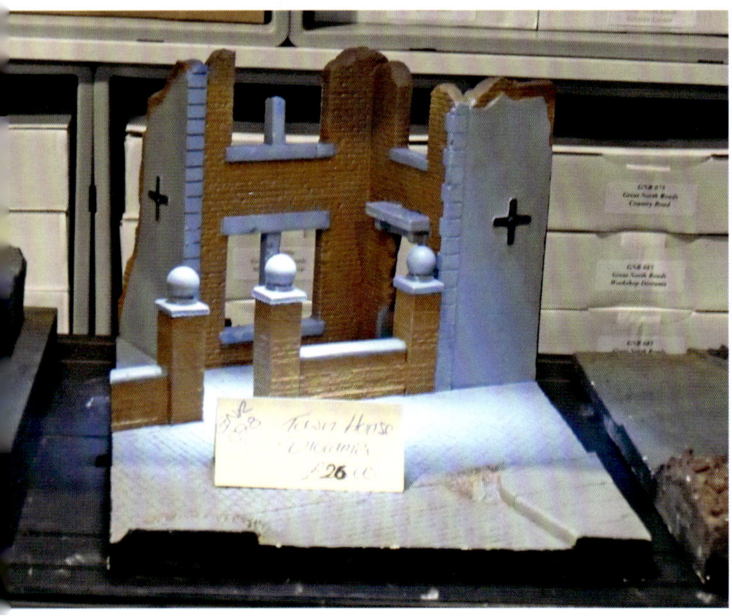

ABOVE One of Italeri's examples of its 'wrecked buildings'. This is in 1:72-scale and, as the label indicates, suitable for wargaming.

LEFT The 'wrecked buildings' approach still continues, with many specialist companies producing useful models. This is one example from Great North Roads, cast from plaster.

A few of the very wide range of accessory packs available from a number of kit manufacturers. Many are 1:35, though there are increasing ranges in 1:48-scale, as the Tamiya set in the centre (a common scale for aircraft, but becoming popular with military vehicles).

what does Hornby specialise in? Railways! As a result, Airfix increased its very low output in the larger scale. Originally, Airfix produced kits to 1:32-scale, but introduced 1:35, not only reissuing military kits from other manufactures, but also producing brand-new examples of its own. It then added to its range with diorama buildings in resin, in both military scales. Most have few parts, but provide the basic structure to incorporate into a military diorama – indeed they are specifically made for this purpose, and frankly they are not really any use for anything else!

The only other mainstream manufacturer to produce resin structures in significant numbers has been Italeri, although, unlike Airfix, it has also made many military-style wrecked structures in injection-moulded styrene.

Regardless of manufacturer, these resin building kits are invariably one-piece, or restricted to a few pieces, and can be turned out faster on a production line than is possible at home, but the production runs are still shorter than those for a complete, injection-moulded styrene kit.

As the decades passed, other mainstream kit companies caught on, and also began to add conventionally injection-moulded-styrene diorama packs to their catalogues.

STREET FURNITURE

Much of the commercial diorama-accessory output is still aimed at military modelling, though 'street furniture' – such as road signs, telegraph poles, pillar-boxes, gates and fencing – also became available and can sometimes be adapted to other subjects.

As time went on, 'civilian' accessories were produced, though here there was a change of scale. The main scale for model cars, and many other vehicles, is the joint scale of 1:24 and 1:25 (usually written 1:24/5), and civilian figures were made mostly to match these scales. The slight difference – 1:24 vs 1:25 – hardly mattered for figures, but it certainly did when comparing 1:35-scale models with 1:24/5-scale. It's possible to get away with some 'non-human' items – a large fence at 1:35 would make a small fence at 1:24/5. This often also worked with animals. Tamiya made an interesting farm-animal set, which is intended for military dioramas, so is in 1:35-scale. The Tamiya set features a large (actually a very large) pig in 1:35-scale, but that makes a perfectly passable smaller – but still quite large – porker in 1:24/5.

A small diorama showing that kits in one scale can be adapted to another. The main diorama scale is 1:24, with the Airfix-Heller Citroën 2CV Dolly. The figures are from Tamiya Campus Friends and Miniature Autobits. However, the well and fountain are Italeri items in 1:35-scale – but they fit in perfectly with the 1:24-scale items.

Tamiya's 1:35-scale 'livestock' set, includes a sow and her piglets. The diorama however is 1:24-scale. The figures are from ICM and Scale Production, but the pigs still fit in.

LEFT A small selection of MasterBox 1:24-scale figures, ranging from Greek mythology, the 'old west' and modern-day through to science-fiction.

BELOW LEFT Sometimes you just need a 'day-to-day' figure for your dioramas. Over the years, several sets have been available, and here two examples are shown produced by JTT and distributed by MRC.

BELOW RIGHT For the 'Wild West', several 1:48-scale dioramas were issued by Adams in the 1950s. The Covered Wagon seen here (top) has been reissued by Glencoe Models (bottom).

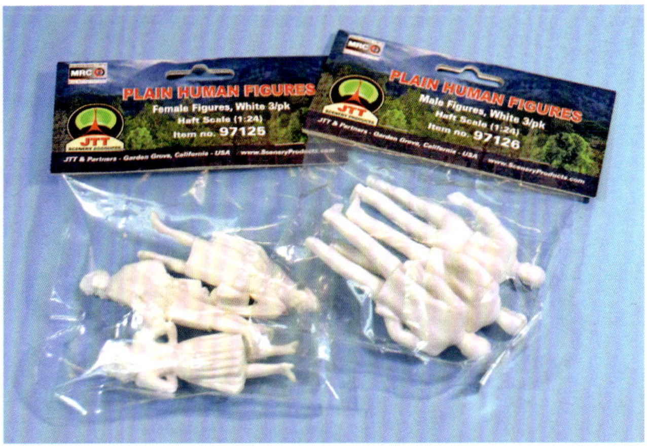

MASTER FIGURES

Master Box is a relatively new company based in Ukraine, and has produced animal-themed figure sets in 1:35-scale, along with human figure sets. It also makes a wide range of civilian and police figures in 1:24-scale, in addition to a range of science-fiction and mythical figures, plus figures from the early days in North America, colloquially the 'Wild West'. Actually, the Wild West had been catered for in previous years by Adams, which produced not only four typical western wagons – such as a stage-coach, covered-wagon and the like – but also a series of western figures as well. These were all in 1:48-scale, so conveniently matching the US '0' model-railway gauge, and could be used in dioramas with suitable early locos. The moulds were also used by manufacturers such as UPC and Revell, and some of this tooling has recently been acquired by Glencoe Models.

Revell went one stage further with what were originally the Adams sets of Wild West kits, by combining all four wagons, plus the figure sets into one kit – a ready-made diorama.

ABOVE Fujimi has made several versions of its garage workshop, capable – as here – of being extended with extra kits. Fujimi also makes ranges of model tools, including the hoist, welders and cabinets. The van is the Ebbro adaptation of the Tamiya Citroën 2CV, to produce the van version.

LEFT SceneARama makes a wide range of model sets that can be incorporated into dioramas. Staying with the Wild West theme, this set included tepees (or are they wigwams?), in card. They are nominally 1:48-scale, but could be adapted.

Glencoe has reissued some of the original kits, though much of the tooling was missing, so it is very unlikely that the full set will see the light of day again.

Many of the figures – being 1:24/5-scale – were obviously aimed at car and vehicle modellers, and other manufacturers joined the party. More set of tools and equipment were issued, including the types of machinery seen in repair garages, such as hoists, welders and cabinets, and even full garages themselves (or sections of them) made by Fujimi.

PLANE CATERING

Next, airfield diorama accessories started to be produced, a lot, conveniently, as flat card sheets – airfields being mostly flat – with runway markings and similar pre-printed on them. Airfield buildings were also made, and Revell makes an aircraft hangar – termed a 'Shelter and Ground Plate' – that could fit many eras of planes. Airfix's World War II control tower that was initially part of its 'trackside accessories' range for railways, but of course that scale is 1:76, while Airfix's – and many other companies' – primary aircraft scale is 1:72, but the two are close enough.

In addition to background scenery, other items to compliment the focal point of the airfield diorama began to appear. Again, Airfix was at the forefront, realising that aircraft were its main subject, and that airfield dioramas needed the associated vehicles and equipment, especially for World War II scenarios. It produced accessory kits such as the RAF Refuelling Set, RAF Recovery Set and RAF Emergency Set, suitable for wartime scenes, though such

RIGHT Revell issue its aircraft Shelter & Ground Plate, here partially constructed. The base plate is in three vacuum-formed sections, fitted to a thin MDF base.

BELOW The 'trackside accessory' that Airfix retained – the Airfield Control Tower. Over its lifetime, figures have been included, though more could be added from the many sets available.

vehicles remained in use for many years after hostilities ceased, so the models could be used in other more up-to-date scenarios. More recently, Airfix has returned to this idea, and has issued brand-new sets such as the WWII RAF Bomber Re-supply Set and an equivalent USAAF set.

PLAY TIME

Airfix boosted the market when it started making Play Sets. This was likely inspired by the American idea of play sets, which proliferated in the 1950s and actually continues in various forms to this day. The buyer was given a set with a theme – maybe based on a current TV series, or an everyday scene such as a garage or store. Along with a building came figures and other accessories, providing the ability for a child to create their own world.

The one thing the American play sets were not, was to accurate scales – figures, buildings and vehicles, were invariably approximations. The Airfix Play Sets differed in that they were true scale, even if that scale did encompass 1:76 through to 1:87! There was also a slight problem with the Airfix figure sets included with the Play Sets – they were not moulded in polystyrene, but in polythene, which is a softer plastic. This was done because the parts would release from the tooling more

ABOVE Airfix's airfield accessories – the Emergency Set, Refuelling Set and an older issue of the Recovery Set.

LEFT An example of an American 'Play Set', here with a 'Western Town' theme.

BELOW Airfix did move to all-styrene plastic for other sets, such as the Waterloo Farmhouse.

easily, and they were more forgiving when it came to play – being flexible, any thin parts were less likely to snap off. However, this did make the parts very difficult to paint, as in the early days, the only modelling paints generally available were enamel, and enamels would not dry on these types of plastics. Various methods of persuading the paint to stick were tried, though none particularly successfully. A favourite method was to cover the figures with soap before painting, but this resulted in – literally – mixed and messy results. It was only in more recent times, with the introduction of acrylic paint, which will dry on these plastics, that the problem was solved.

ZOO TIME

All the components supplied in these early Airfix Play Sets were made from the same polythene material – even the buildings. For example, the Zoo Play set contains the two Zoo Animals sets, along with a vacuumed-formed base with three enclosures and several small buildings. Ironically, the vacuum-formed base was produced from polystyrene, so took enamel paint fine, but everything else was made from polythene. Over the years, Airfix has continued with the diorama sets, though thankfully moving to styrene. The Battle of Waterloo Farmhouse, although intended to be used with its various Waterloo figures sets – still moulded

ABOVE One of the Airfix equivalents of a 'play set'. This used the company's existing Zoo Animal sets, with new enclosures and a base.

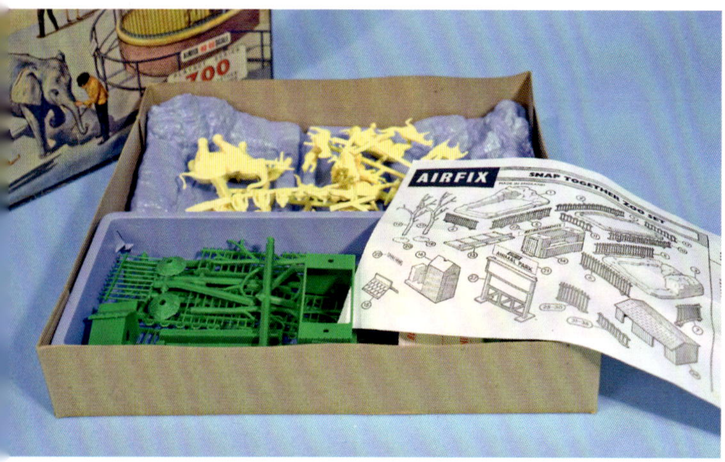

LEFT The Airfix Zoo set, with the existing animals set (top, in yellow), and new buildings in green. These are all soft plastic, the only styrene parts being the pale-blue vacuum-formed base.

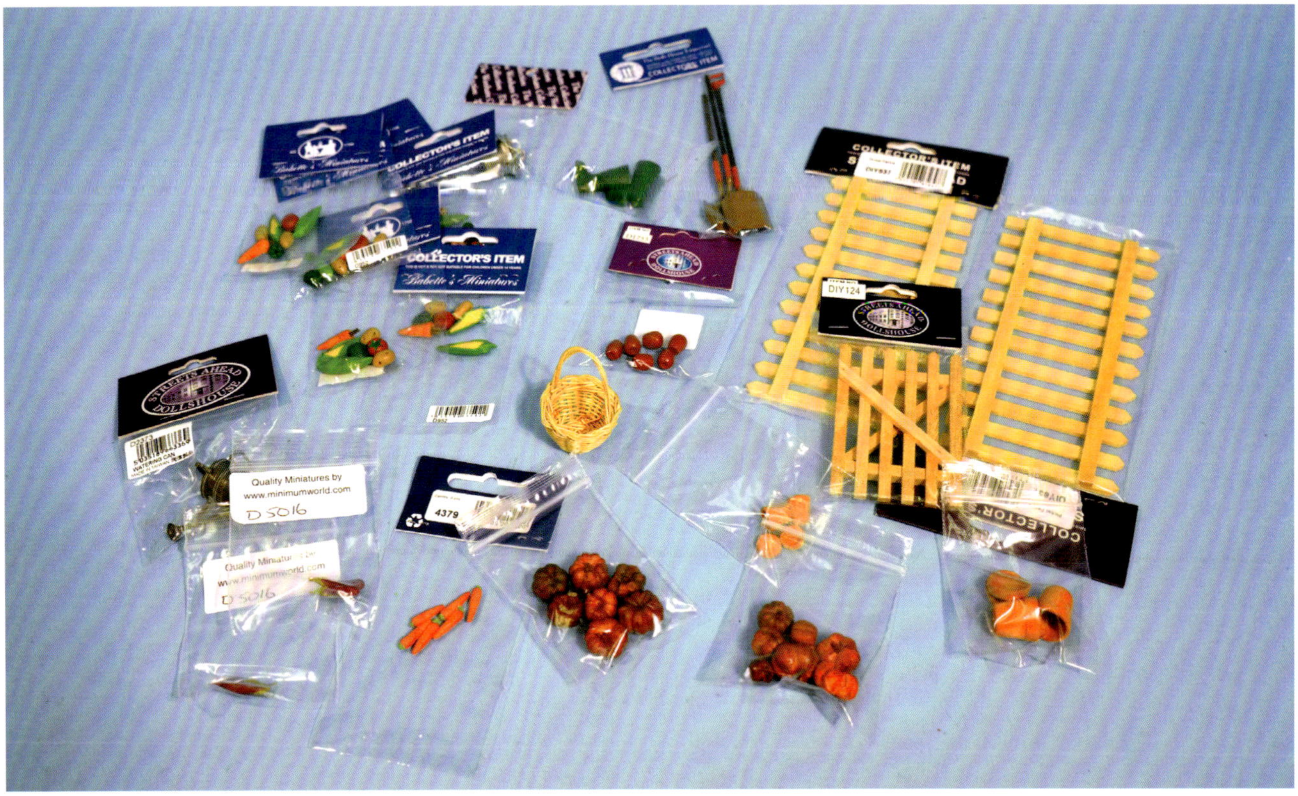

ABOVE There are many, many doll's house accessories available, usually in either 1:24-scale or 1:12-scale.

RIGHT Doll's Houses are a popular modelling subject. Here is one of many on display at the amazing The House on the Rock in Wisconsin, USA.

in soft plastic – is actually moulded in polystyrene, making assembly and painting far easier. Airfix continued with these sets – later called 'Gift Sets' – with various military scenes, including a quartet of sets based around D-Day.

DOLL'S HOUSES AND A MOTORISED WHEELBARROW!

Aftermarket products used for dioramas do not necessarily have to have been manufactured specifically for the modelling hobby, but can be adapted. This includes doll's houses. Yes they are models in the wider sense, but are invariably thought of as being part of a completely separate hobby. However, the two mains scales for doll's houses are 1:24 and 1:12, and both match traditional model-kit scales. 1:24 scale is of course a major model-car scale, and various items intended for doll's-house builders and collectors could be adapted, both for individual models and into dioramas. 1:12-scale also fits in with cars, and many have been made in this scale.

One bizarre custom car – one could almost say 'the most bizarre custom car ever', (a statement fraught with problems!) – was the Elegant Farmer, a customised wheelbarrow with a V4 Lancia engine! It was built for real (from a real wheelbarrow and a real Lancia V4), and was made as a kit by MPC. With dioramas in mind, and as it's a wheelbarrow, adding fruit and veg, plus a range of garden tools, from various doll's-house catalogues, was a natural progression.

MPC's Elegant Farmer custom car (or more correctly 'wheelbarrow') is in 1:12-scale, so provides an ideal opportunity to create a small diorama combining it with a selection of doll's-house gardening accessories, including the white picket fences.

Modelling with a water-based theme usually has to rely on other accessories and scratch-building, as seen here with a Supermarine Walrus amphibian and vehicles including an RAF Austin Tilly. *Model and photo by Patrick Pycke*

ON THE WATER

In terms of dioramas, aircraft, tanks and cars have been reasonably well catered for over the years, but the same cannot be said for ships. Here of course, the main problem is one of size – ships tend to be the largest 'vehicles' made on Earth, and although arguably they do run in size from a rowing boat, canoe or inflatable raft at one end of the scale, to an ocean liner, container ship, or an aircraft carrier at the other, the vast majority of ship kits are of very large subjects and consequently most ship models are available in smaller scales than other vehicles. Accessory kits to create dioramas are therefore few and far between. However, Skywave made kits of harbour quaysides, docks, buildings and equipment, to one of the standard ship scales, 1:700, and so very close to another – 1:600. So with scratch-built quayside and water, you can at least find items to populate the rest of the scene, but figures might be a little more difficult. For ships in larger scales – and there are some at 1:35, 1:72 and 1:144 – figures are generally obtainable. It gets slightly more tricky as the scale number increases – the most common scales for ships being 1:350, 1:600 and 1:700, though even here some tiny scale figures are obtainable as photo-etch sets.

Ship modellers are not very well catered for with regard to accessory packs, but SkyWave has issued several in 1:700 scale, including a dry dock.

Space and science-fiction is beginning to be catered for as far as accessories and dioramas are concerned. Here, the Monogram *Battlestar Galactica* Viper diorama has accessories provided as 3D-printed parts from Cozmic Scale Models.

OUT INTO SPACE

Intriguingly, the one model subject where it is rare to find manufacturers making dedicated specialist diorama accessories is the one that might be assumed to be a natural – science fiction and fantasy. There are many aftermarket sets providing new and improved decals for the latest *Star Trek USS Enterprise*, or lighting and photo-etched sets for adding the minutest details to the Moebius 1:8-scale Discovery Pod from *2001: A Space Odyssey*, but they are for the models themselves.

One very logical reason is that deep-space ships – such as the *Enterprise* or the Discovery Pod – are just that, intended for deep space, where diorama elements are few and far between. So, that begs the question as to whether 'space' can be a diorama, to which the answer is in many cases, 'yes', but apart from the craft and some background (even if the background is purely stars), a diorama with very few elements.

However, science-fiction – and real spacecraft for that matter – do land on solid surfaces. Real Apollo craft have landed on the Moon, and a variety of space-probes and rovers on other planets. Science fiction has an even wider range, where the background material can be a wide as your imagination, or even beyond your imagination! Sir Arthur C. Clarke was fond of quoting the earlier scientist and writer, J.B.S. Haldane, who had postulated the thought: 'The Universe is not only stranger than we imagine – it is stranger than we *can* imagine.' So maybe the reason there are few aftermarket science-fiction diorama accessories is down to the question of just what would you make? However, new specialist companies, such as Cozmic Scale Models and Giblet Creations in the UK, both using 3D printing methods, are producing ranges of figures, accessory and diorama parts, and there are few other companies doing so, such as Red Planet in the US. Otherwise, when it comes to dioramas, science-fiction and fantasy subjects are ideal for scratch-building.

Chapter 5

Material World

You don't need that much to build a simple diorama – decide what you want to display – find the components, and then put them onto a base. Overall it can be as simple as that. It is of course at this stage that looking at exactly what sort of materials could be used to build bases comes into the discussion.

A typical diorama on a flat wooden base, here 19mm MDF. The Me-163 Komet is the Hasegawa kit in 1:32. All the accessories – vehicles and figures from Italeri and Tamiya – are 1:35-scale, but the slight difference is hardly noticeable.

WOOD

One of the most widely-used materials in the world is wood in some form or another. One of the oldest modelling materials – carved wooden figures, boats and other artefacts have been discovered in the Egyptian tombs – wood itself of course is available in a multitude of varieties. In terms of use as a material by humans, originally wood would have been just that – the original stuff that at one point was growing as a tree, felled and cut into useable planks. Basically it was either hard wood, from deciduous trees, or soft wood from conifers. There is slightly more to it than that, but using a

A selection of wood, including (from the top): block-board, two thicknesses of plywood and two thicknesses of MDF.

piece of wood a century ago, it was basically going to be one or the other. So it would really have been either hard wood for detailed carving, or soft wood for supports and bases.

Wood can be cut easily with saws – hand or mechanical – and screws and nails can be used for fixing. Wood joins well with many types of glues, and many types carve and sand to shape very well. Finally, wood can be finished with a variety of paint. Consequently, wood is likely to be the starting point for many dioramas. In most cases, you just need a base that is going to be covered, so the type of wood isn't really relevant, it just needs to be strong enough to support everything.

Sheets of wood come in a variety of types. However the size of any sheet of wood is initially dictated by the size of the tree. Generally speaking, the larger the tree, the more expensive the wood; there is after all (thankfully) a limit to the number of Californian Redwoods that can be felled! Consequently, the vast majority of large sheets of wood are built up from layers. Plywood is one of the most common composite woods, and it built up of several layers, with the grain of the wood running in alternate directions, and the layers glued together. Hence '5-ply' comprises five thin sheets, 7-ply seven sheets, and so on. The greater the number of layers, the better the quality – and the less prone the sheet is to warping, though of course as the number of layers increases, so does the price.

There is an alternative to plywood, and that is block-board. Here though you only have two plywood layers. The two plywood layers are on the outside of a sandwich, with thicker blocks of cheap, soft-wood in the middle, so it could be made thicker and cheaper than traditional plywood. Block-board is very useful when it comes to basic structures, as it is strong and reasonably cheap, though it seems to have fallen out of favour with wood merchants these days.

However, from a modeller's point of view, there is a finishing problem with both. The top and bottom layers are fine, but the cut edges, needed much more work – especially with the thicker sheets of block-board. This invariably requires a lot of wood filler, then a lot of sanding, and then finishing with a lot of primer. Not impossible, or that difficult, but can be very time-consuming. Alternatively, and especially with the thicker block-board bases, thin strips of wood veneer may be used for the edging, glued or nailed in place, or alternatively strips of plastic glued on.

Here, an old kitchen drawer is being dismantled. The sides are plastic, the base hardboard, but the front is hard wood, suitable for a base – just remove the knob!

MDF

During the 1980s, to the delight of home DIYers everywhere, MDF (Medium Density Fibreboard) appeared. This is wood, pulped, with resin added and then the whole mixture is pressed into sheets of varying thicknesses. The advantage over 'genuine' wood is that the finish on the main outside surfaces is far smoother than most other woods (and therefore does not requiring a lot of sanding), and the cut edges need far less finishing – usually a light sanding and priming are all that is required.

Any of these woods – ply, block-board or MDF – can usually be obtained from wood yards or DIY stores, and if you have suitable equipment yourself, can be cut to size. If you are intending to build a large number of dioramas, and

Other woods, including (top) chipboard with both back and white laminate coverings. Note the black has one side with iron-on edging, which is available in both colours to trim the sides and end. Underneath are two examples of hardwood from a shelf and (bottom) a door panel.

ABOVE LEFT A circular saw is ideal for cutting wood – any wood. MDF, as here, benefits from being cut with a power-saw as, being compressed board where the density can vary, power-cutting tends to give a more accurate and cleaner cut.

ABOVE RIGHT Pre-made wood bases can be bought, leaving more time for the actual build of this vignette of Captain America and foe. *Model by Andy Yanchus; photo by Pat Yanchus*

will need a large number of bases, it will be far cheaper to buy a whole sheet of whichever wood you will be using. However, take into account that you then have to transport it, and then cut it into suitable sizes. Most wood yards and DIY stores, also have selections of off-cuts that may be exactly the right size for your needs, or larger sheets can be cut to size.

A base for your diorama however can be obtained from other sources however, and ingenuity is the key here. Dismantling old kitchen cabinets can provide a supply of wood – soft wood composites for the backs and sides, but the doors are usually hard wood. Here, you could find that old drawer front is a ready-made base. Off-cuts from other DIY jobs can be used – shelves for instance – and many of these have the top and bottom surfaces already finished in a laminate, and you can buy iron-on strips to cover the edges.

Ready-made

Some specialist model suppliers sell small, ready-made model bases, usually in wood. Maybe for many modellers, who are used to making everything themselves, buying a standard ready-made square base isn't quite the done thing, but round bases and plinths are also available, ideal for figures and the like. These are far less easy to manufacture yourself, unless you have access to a wood-turning lathe, and these ready-made bases can be an easy short cut. They will invariably be turned from hardwood, so could be stained and varnished and left as a wooden base, or primed, sanded and painted in any colour of your choosing.

Here is a simple diorama on a square wood base – 'The Rescue', featuring Airfix Aardman Animation characters Gromit, Shawn the Sheep and the three naughty pigs. *Model by Nick Allen*

A very simple base (the top of a medicine bottle) for this alien doing some maintenance. *Model by Andy Yanchus, photo by Pat Yanchus*

Examples of types of foam. On the left, EPS (Expanded PolyStyrene), showing the crumbly nature of its texture. On the right, XPS (eXtruded PolyStyrene) in blue and black. Note the texture is far more dense and even the thinner sheets don't have a tendency to crumble.

BASE RECYCLING

Bases can also be made out of everyday objects. Modellers have used the plastic lids off of such as coffee jars. Being plastic they are usually produced from some form of thermoplastic, maybe even polystyrene – the main model-kit material – so will cement with standard model-kit glues. They will also take standard model finishes, both fillers and paints. Some may also have some ribbed pattern round the outside, which gives a built-in decorative pattern. So, if you want a standardised base for a series of figures, this could be an ideal solution – just drink a lot of coffee!

Many other containers, boxes, packing and non-modelling materials can be recycled and used to help create structures for bases. Boxes such as plastic take-away containers can bulk out areas where you may want hills or slopes, or can be incorporated into building structures in their own right, and odd plastic shapes can be used to create different structures, especially if you are building a science-fiction or fantasy diorama.

FOAMED POLYSTYRENE

Another extremely useful material for making diorama bases, and many other aspects of a model landscape, is EPS (Expanded PolyStyrene). This is also sometime generically known by the trade name Styrofoam, though strictly speaking that is purely for products from Dow Chemicals and specifically a slightly different foam polystyrene, that of XPS (eXtruded PolyStyrene). However, for modelling purposes, most of these 'foamed polystyrene products' can be dealt with in a similar manner.

THE FOAMED-POLYSTYRENE STORY

This book is not intended to be a detailed examination of all types of foamed expanded polystyrene, and they way that they are manufactured, but it may be useful to look at the very general details.

All these 'foamed' versions of polystyrene have the same chemical formula as standard polystyrene – $[(C_8H_8)_n]$ – the type used in the vast majority of model kits (and a great deal else besides.) However, these have been foamed to make them very light in weight, in fact most contain over 95 per cent air.

The foam can come in several forms (and colours) but, as mentioned previously, there are two main types – Expanded PolyStyrene (EPS), and eXtruded PolyStyrene (XPS). Both were initially developed as building materials – primarily as insulation – and also for packing around electrical goods, but today they find themselves used for many other purposes, including model-making.

The primary difference between the two types is that EPS is made from already-formed polystyrene beads that are pressed into a mould and heated, which causes the beads to fuse together. The result is a sheet of expanded polystyrene – almost exclusively white in colour – which is relatively strong and rigid, and very light. However, because of the beads, it can be somewhat crumbly in texture, as the beads can start breaking away at the edges. This is a particular problem with thin sheets, as the beads can get everywhere!

XPS, has the chemicals directly injected into a mould, so although they are still foamed and full of air, this method produces sheets that are more rigid in structure, have smoother surfaces, and do not tend to crumble as easily as EPS.

Unlikely to be used this thick by amateur modellers, but expanded polystyrene (EPS) can be obtained in thicknesses up to 1ft, as seen here on the right. These are for a miniature landscape for a filming session, but amateur modellers could build up similar thicknesses in layers from thinner sheets.

Cutting EPS with a hand saw. Not difficult, as it saws very easily, but this does generate a lot of 'beads'. They are not toxic, but a definite nuisance and possibly an irritant, as they get everywhere and stick to anything due to static!

Unless you are a house builder using it for insulation, expanded polystyrene will most usually be seen as packing. Buy any piece of modern electronic equipment, white goods or flat-packed furniture, and it will almost certainly come packed in expanded polystyrene packaging, which of course is then immediately discarded. In theory it could be recycled, but most recycling centres don't do this, so reusing this packing for a diorama project at least means you are doing your, admittedly tiny, bit for recycling. Plus – as an important bonus – it's free!

Although free, expanded polystyrene used for packing can be somewhat limiting in that you get what the manufacture deemed necessary for the packing requirement, and the sections will have been manufactured to fit round whatever is being packed. So, in many ways, this source is down to pot luck – though as a bonus you can come up with some interesting shapes, particularly if you a building a base for a science-fiction or fantasy scene.

However if you need specific sizes, and a reasonably large amount of EPS, buying the source material (that used for insulation) could be the better option. Expanded polystyrene sheets comes in regular sizes, and a variety of thicknesses. But of course, these will cost, and the sheets are usually large – in the UK many still in the imperial sizes of 4ft by 8ft – so there could be a problem moving, transporting and handling. EPS is also made in thicker sizes, up to 12in (330mm), which again is an excellent starting point for features such as mountain ranges, but you will have to saw through 12in of polystyrene!

Extruded polystyrene (XPS) tends to generically known as 'blue foam', as initially it was made in a blue colour. Ironically, it is now rarely made in blue, and is now most often supplied in a black or grey colour, though many still refer to it as 'blue foam'! It is also available in yellow, and even white is made in a very dense form – the latter specially designed for model-making, as it carves very easily, without crumbling.

Consequently, modellers have a choice – the cheaper and, if it is from packing, free – EPS, or buying sheets of XPS. Very generally, landscapes can be constructed perfectly well with EPS, but more precise structures, such as buildings can benefit from the denser and smoother XPS.

When it comes to building more complex bases for dioramas, your best friend is likely to be large block of expanded polystyrene. Any landscape that is anything other than flat needs contours, and the easiest way to produce these is to carve them from EPS, and as you will be covering it with a finishing surface, any tendency to crumble will be contained.

Much will be dictated by exactly how high or thick the landscape needs to be. As mentioned previously, EPS can be obtained in quite thick sections, but unless you need these thicknesses, you will probably be dealing with thinner sheets. There is another problem with the thicker sheets, in that they are less easy to cut. Unless you have access to commercial band-saws, you will need to use a standard hand saw and a lot of elbow-grease. Of course, you can build up thicknesses by gluing together several thinner layers.

Once cut to manageable sizes, any of the EPS/XPS products are easily cut with a sharp knife, or modelling razor-saw, though you may still need a conventional hand-saw for larger sections. Foamed polystyrene can also be sanded with coarse glass-paper, files or even a wire brush, but any of these methods creates a lot of debris – especially with EPS – and being extremely light they float everywhere, and due to static electricity, stick to everything. The particles are not toxic as such, but can be an irritant, so the wearing of face masks, carrying out the work in a well-ventilated area, and ideally using extractor devices, are recommended. For the amateur modeller, without access to professional extractors, laying the nozzle of a vacuum cleaner near to the sanding will help.

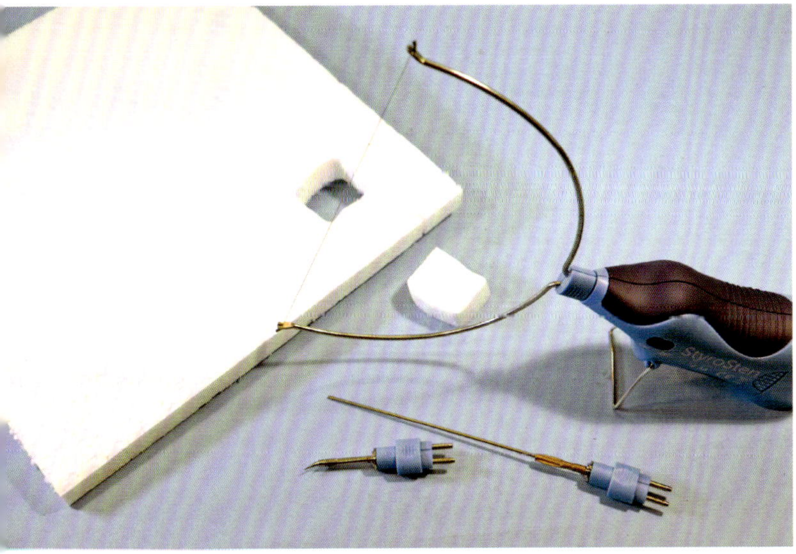

ABOVE LEFT A simple, battery-powered, hot-wire cutter. This one also comes with optional sculpting tools.

ABOVE RIGHT Painting EPS with a thickish plaster mix. When dry, this will prevent any tendency for the EPS to crumble.

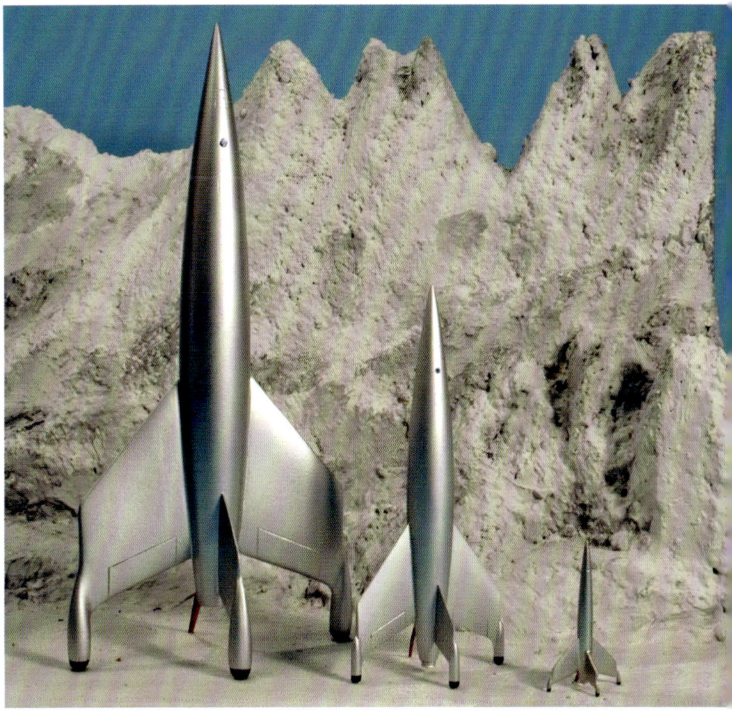

RIGHT Using the finished EPS 'lunar' background for a display of space rocket Luna from the movie *Destination Moon*. Left to right: – Lunar Models, Pegasus and Comet Miniatures 'Mini-Metals'.

Hot-wire cutters

Both forms of foamed polystyrene can also be cut with a hot-wire cutter. These are a little like a fret-saw designed for foamed polystyrene, where a low electrical current passes through a thin wire, which then melts its way through the plastic, and can cut intricate patterns. These devices range from small, child-friendly devices powered by a battery, to more professional tools that can cut through large thicknesses. When using a hot-wire cutter, the wire burns the polystyrene to a degree, and this will give of noxious fumes, so again masks and adequate ventilation are a must.

Ironically, if polystyrene (in any form) is burnt at over 1,000°C, it completely combusts, and will only give off water and carbon dioxide (plus a few trace elements). However, if the temperature is below this, which it will be in most general circumstances – hot-wire, mechanical cutting, even heavy-handed sanding – the burning is incomplete, and unpleasant hydrocarbons will be produced, in the form of a dense black smoke – which should *not* be breathed in!

Although all these varieties of foam are indeed 'polystyrene', they will not cement with conventional polystyrene cement, especially the liquid variety – it will just melt its way through the plastic (though, as an aside, that can produce interesting effects for strange landscapes, or even stranger figures). Instead of polystyrene cement, a non-volatile cement has to be used, usually one with a PVA (latex) base. Depending on the specific instructions, one, or both surfaces should be coated with the glue, which should be allowed to partially dry for a few minutes, before the two surfaces are pressed together. In most cases the bond is immediate, so it's important to get the positioning correct before that final contact.

Alternatively, given that these surfaces will – usually – be finished and painted, the paint itself can be used as a 'glue', and if water-based paints are being used, some PVA glue mixed in will help with bonding.

Foam-board

When it comes to buildings and structures, another form of foam can be introduced – foam-board. Here, a thin sheet of XPS foam is sandwiched between two layers of card. This has the advantages over both basic EPS and XPS, in that the main surfaces are not foam, they are very smooth, and the surfaces can be painted and drawn on.

Foam-board also cuts very easily and cleanly with a sharp blade, and can be glued more easily than either of the two other

Sheet foam-board and off-cuts, in two thicknesses. Note the scalpel blade points to the foam layer sandwiched between two layers of card.

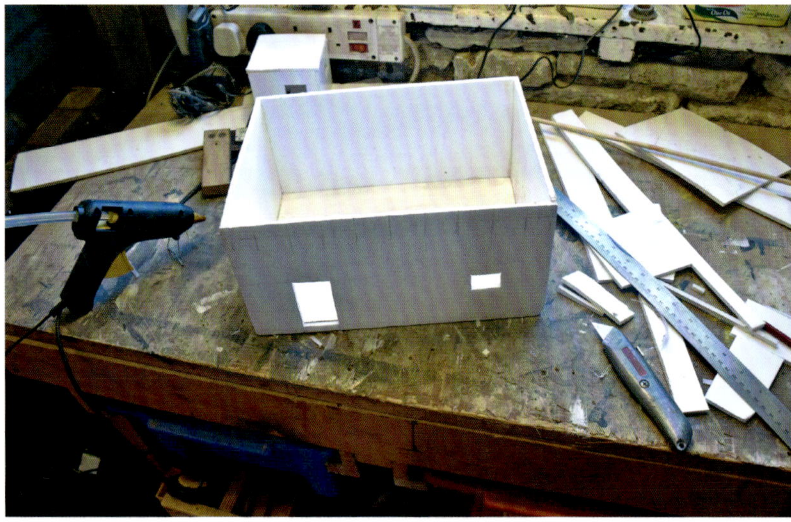

Foam-board is also ideal for the basic structure of buildings.

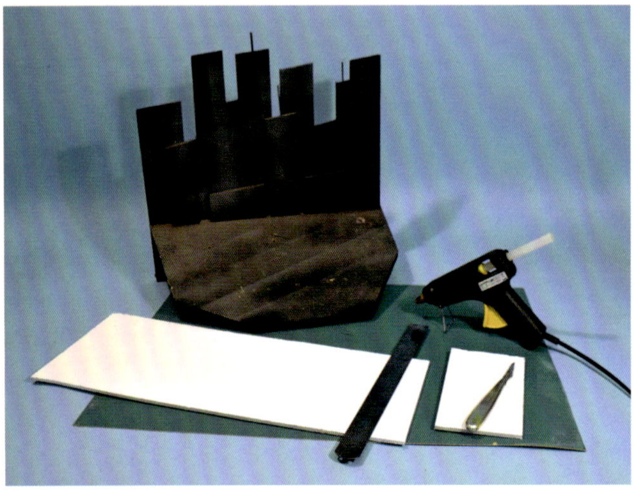

Foam-board cut very easily with a sharp knife or scalpel, ideally using a metal straight-edge. It also glues very easily with a hot-glue gun. Here, it is used to build a simple 'silhouette' background...

... for a Revell *Batman Forever* Batmobile.

'foams', as a contact adhesive or even a hot-glue gun can be used, which would melt the expanded version. Admittedly there is foam at the edges of the board, which could melt slightly, but the major surfaces are card, so will take the heat of a hot-glue gun without too many detrimental effects.

ALTERNATIVES TO POLYSTYRENE

The oldest type of 'diorama' for the hobbyist – though the term was not really used – was when building model railways. A favourite method used to form landscapes for railway layouts was using chicken-wire, formed into suitable 'hill side' shapes, and nailed in place on a base. Plaster bandage was applied over the wire, with the whole ensemble pushed into final place while the plaster set. A specific model version was made, called ModRoc (Model Rocks), usually sold through

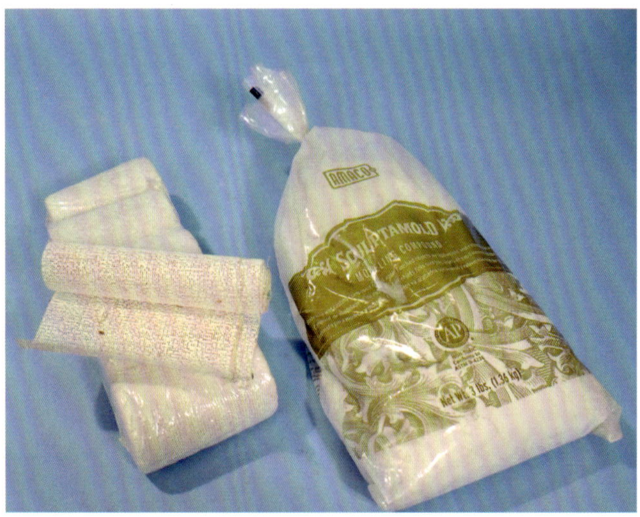

Other sculpting materials include plaster bandage, generically known as ModRoc (left), and Sculptamold (right).

model-railway shops, but this was still plaster bandage with a fancy label, and if you could get the original bandage from a chemist (drug store), it was far cheaper. It was soon realised that handfuls of crumpled newspaper would do the job just as well as chicken-wire, it was even cheaper, and avoided the nicks and cuts you invariably got on the skin with the sharp edges of the wire! The newspaper version was perfect adequate if the landscape was solid, and you didn't need to get underneath, but if tunnels were being built, where access to the track would of course be necessary, the chicken-wire method was preferable, or even supports cut from plywood or similar..

Both methods have fallen out of favour with the introduction of polystyrene, though both are still practical alternatives.

With the basic structure of the diorama base built – it then comes to finishing. Bare polystyrene is hardly likely to be used 'as is' – except possibly for a snow scene or a setting on the Moon, and even them it could do with a dusting of a top surface.

This also brings in an interesting question as to whether the top surface should be finished 'solid' or left loose. The latter is the normal position with special-effects miniature sets (see Chapter 11), as the sets are a usually used 'one time only'. The set is then broken down and the materials re-used for the next set-up. However, for the amateur model maker, usually a diorama is 'for life', not just for the most recent model show, so best to avoid scenic material blowing away when a window is opened!

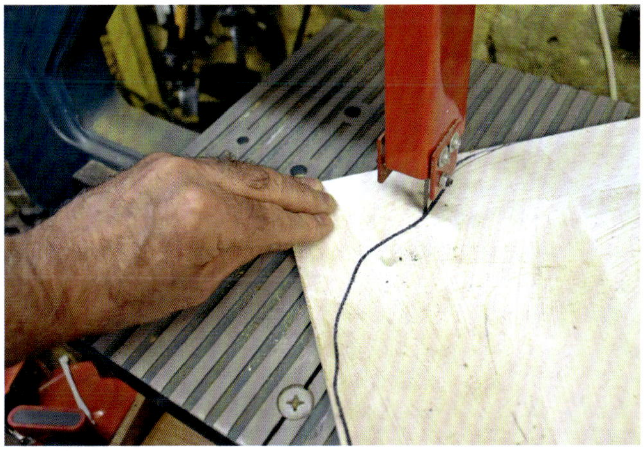

TOP LEFT The base for dioramas doesn't have to be square, or even regular. A bandsaw is being used to cut an irregular base from MDF.

TOP RIGHT Shaping some EPS with glass-paper to create rocks.

CENTRE LEFT Gluing the EPS with a PVA (latex-based) glue, that will not dissolve it.

CENTRE RIGHT Adding structure using plaster, with paint added to pre-colour it. For this diorama, this will represent the sea bed.

LEFT Adding fine sand to the base while the plaster is still wet. This is shaken on using an old kitchen sieve.

LEFT The finished base for a diorama centred on the AMT Aqua Rod show car. The sea creatures are from a toy set, and the background object is intended for an aquarium.

BELOW LEFT A range of 'non model' paints useful for dioramas. Household paints – white and black – and fine-art acrylics, which can be used 'as is', or to tint the white paint.

FINISHING MATERIALS

Ideally, the materials used for the top surface need to be fixed solid, and this brings in the finishing materials, primarily paint. For anything other than a very small diorama, a lot of paint will be required. Because of this, you will soon find that the classic model kit paints, in tinlets or bottles, although very cost-effective for the models themselves, can prove disproportionately expensive for a metre-long base. So, an alternative source of paints is advisable.

This 'moving up' in quantity comes in two stages. First there are the 'art supplies' paints – the type of paint used by fine artists for their canvases. Available at art and craft stores, these paints come in various pack sizes from small tubes to larger bottles, and in all colours. The vast majority of these paints are acrylics, which have the advantage that they thin (and can be cleaned up) with water. Compared with oil paints, they dry reasonably fast – traditional artists' oil paints can sometime take days, or even longer, to dry, though they still find favour with some model-figure builders.

For even larger surfaces, household paints are going to be the cheapest option. Again, the vast majority these days are acrylic, and many DIY stores have mixing machinery, so you can get a very precise custom colour, or match. Of course you are buying a lot of paint for a diorama – it may not seem so much when it comes to painting the dining room wall, but for diorama bases one can of paint could last several years. If well sealed after each use (make sure the lid is firmly fitted, and briefly invert the container so the paint forms a seal), it should last a considerable time. Where large quantities of paint are required, a very basic selection of colours would probably suffice – maybe a black, a white, a green, a blue and a brown. Different colours can be made by mixing the other paints, and given that they are all water-based, this should not cause any compatibility problems. Alternatively, a large quantity of white could be bought, and smaller quantities of colours, such as artist's paints, could be mixed in when required.

TEXTURE

Then there is texture. Very little in the way of landscapes is a smooth finish – a calm sea is possible the only example, and even here the calmest of oceans is going to have some ripples. So, fillers are required to give the surface some texture.

One of the most easily obtained and cheapest forms of filler is sawdust. Bags can be bought (usually as pet bedding), but cheaper still, collect sawdust from a power-saw. Even general sawing – circular-saw, jig-saw, band-saw – can produce a sizable amount, just make sure you put a container under the saw to catch the dust, or vacuum it up and empty into a container.

Sawdust can be sprinkled over wet paint, though then itself will need painting, so it is easier just to mix the sawdust directly into the paint in the first place.

Another useful material is plaster, and here it is not dental or 'plaster of Paris', as they dry and set too fast. The best option is decorators' plaster mainly used for ceilings – it is usually just referred to as 'ceiling plaster' – and this type of plaster has a supreme advantage in that it does not dry fast. Consequently, it is ideal for landscaping where you want to continuously mould and re-form areas – maybe add vegetation – without worrying that the plaster is about to set hard. These plasters also take paint extremely well – use it as part of the water you would add to the plaster anyway – and it can bulked out and textured with sawdust. This plaster can be moulded with your fingers, or a brush, or a wooden spatula for larger areas.

Because this type of plaster will remain soft for some time, it allows other items to be pushed into the surface – either other components, or effects such as tracks from tyres made by rolling the tyres across the surface, leaving the imprint.

There are other commercially-made forms of plaster, produced especially for model-making. One example is Sculptamold, which is available in smaller bags than 'building' plasters, so may be more convenient for storage, depending on how much you need.

This is mixed well with water (usually 2 parts water, 1 part Sculptamold), and then moulded or sculpted into shape. It dries reasonably fast, and is light in weight, so does not result in a base too heavy to lift.

Building a simple base, using thin EPS sheet to build up a grassy roadside.

Sanding the road to shape, with fairly coarse glass-paper.

Sealing and painting the polystyrene with plaster.

Painting on the top coats.

With some vegetation detail added, the finished diorama – a scene from *Supernatural* with 'Baby', the 1965 Chevy Impala, as made by AMT.

Chapter 6

Base Decisions

The vast majority of dioramas that the home hobbyist is going to attempt are not going to be particularly large, because you have to have space to work on it in the first place, and you have to put it somewhere when it is finished. If you are building much larger scenes, you are almost certainly a professional modeller working on larger displays, or building for a temporary show. This is really beyond the scope of this book, though elements are included in Chapters 10 and 11.

Larger bases are dealt with in passing in the next chapter, and this deals in more detail with the actual landscaping materials that would be used for any size of base. Here we look more at the type of diorama scene that can be built up on a small base.

AFVs still seem to still dominate model dioramas, and this example incorporates a photographic background. *Model and photo by Spencer Pollard*

A simple diorama to show the old Airfix Scammell Scarab three-wheeler lorry. The kit allowed two optional versions – one for the brewer Watneys, with its beer-barrel-shaped containers, and the other in British Railways markings. To keep the three-wheeler theme, a very early Reliant three-wheeler is in the background, built from a white-metal kit.

DECIDING ON WHAT TO DISPLAY

First, you have to have some idea of what you are intending to depict. Maybe you have a model itself built, or are about to start the build, which provides inspiration for setting it in a diorama, or may the idea of a scene comes first – re-creating a scene from a book or movie, or even a photograph of an historic event in a magazine – and you then have to find the parts to suit. It may be just a single model – for instance aircraft, car, or tank – with minimal diorama elements, or it may be more, with more figures, some landscaping, maybe a building. Or something even more adventurous, with a multitude of vehicles and figures?

There is also the matter of size and scale. A 3ft^2 base would take very few items that are, say, 1:12-scale, but a vast number if they were 1:144-scale, so choose accordingly. The choice also depends on whether you are using an existing model kit that is already built, or starting from scratch.

The most straightforward way to take an existing kit that already contains the diorama elements as part of the kit, and build a suitable the base, and the most straightforward modelling subject here is going to be aircraft, working on the principle that aircraft require a flat runway for take-off and landing, which greatly simplifies the construction of the base.

As an example, the 1950s American television series *Sky King* featured a Cessna T-50 – a twin-engine, four- to-five-seater plane – used in both military and civilian environments, and was Cessna's first twin-engined plane. Squadron Products re-vamped the 1:48-scale Czech Model kit of the T-50, to include the *Sky King* Cessna – named *Songbird* – and the company also issued resin figures of both the main character, Sky, and his niece, Penny. Atlantis Models later reissued the original Revell Chevy Stake Truck, also in 1:48 scale, and so, bearing in mind that *Sky King* was set in a farming community,

The diorama structure itself doesn't automatically need to 'contain' all the elements. Here, a version of Gotham City has been built from foam-board and a lot of spares from the 'bits and pieces' boxes, that can take two Batmobiles on its elevated roadway – here the Polar Lights original Barris TV version, and the far-newer Tumbler from Moebius. Other Bat cars, from AMT and Revell, can sit in front, so adding to the overall feel.

RIGHT The Squadron Productions modified Czech model kit of a Cessna T-50, built as *Songbird* from the *Sky King* TV series. Resin figures of Sky and Penny have been added, and the Atlantis Models reissue of the Revell Chevy Stake Truck is seen unloading goods.

BELOW The Monogram Antarctic Expedition Ford Tri-Motor, with the supplied diorama accessories – two explorers, three dogs and the sled. The base is a simply a square of block-board, covered in plaster.

what could be more natural than combining the two, having goods delivered by the truck, maybe to be loaded onto the Cessna. So the two kits and figures were combined into a simple diorama, built up on a flat MDF base.

Another example, already mentioned in a previous chapter, is Monogram's Antarctic Expedition Ford Tri-Motor. This kit can be built with wheels or skis, and for a snow-based scene, the latter is more appropriate. In addition, the plane would have landed on a clear, flat stretch of snow and ice.

Consequently, a flat piece of wood of suitable size is a good starting point, purely adding a thin sprinkling of ceiling plaster for the 'snow'.

BASE INSTINCT

Referring back to Chapter 5, choose what material you are going to use – these days it is likely to be MDF – and cut to size. Unless you need exact sizes for several bases that will match, a 'random' size is likely better, as when displaying dioramas of different subjects, a 'mix and match' approach is likely to be more aesthetically pleasing.

With any diorama there is also the question how to finish the base. Is the whole of the base part of the diorama, and therefore should any landscaping goes right up to the edge of the base? Or is the base precisely that – purely something the diorama is displayed on? For the former, the edge of the base will need to be incorporated into the whole scene, so the grass, desert, snow or whatever, has to be taken up to the very edge, in effect becoming the edge. If your base is made from foamed polystyrene sheet, some thought will have to go into protecting the edge – as previously mentioned, expanded polystyrene, especially EPS, can get very crumbly at the edges. It may be that a tougher edge has to be used, maybe wood, or XPS, that is less likely to break up if the edge is knocked. If it necessary to alter the material for the edges, it can still be finished in the same way as the main base, so in effect the transition becomes invisible.

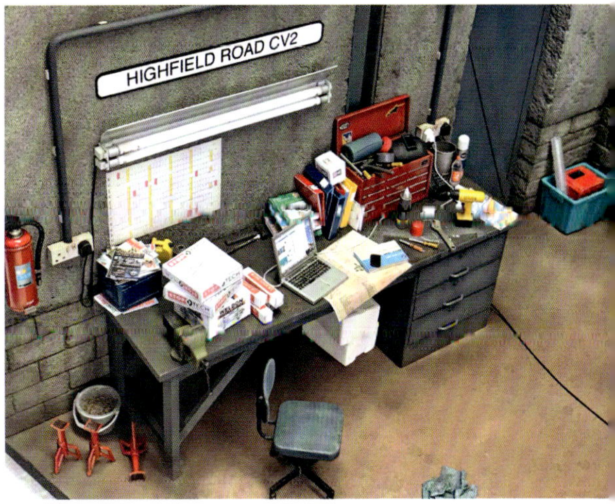

ABOVE LEFT Sometimes modelling doesn't need to take itself too seriously. RMS *Titanic* was after all warned about an 'iceberg'… *Model by Cris Simmonds*

ABOVE RIGHT Details count – here a bench in some workshop with a mix of car parts and modern niceties such as a laptop. Note the aerosol cans, one with the top off; the Haynes Manuals, and boxes of car parts. Even the plugs and sockets on the wall are the correct UK 'G' type. *Model and photo by Spencer Pollard*

ABOVE A lot can be told in a small space. Here, the 'Aerobatic School' T-28 Trojan (the Monogram kit) sits outside the 'school house'. Note the detail touches such as the three dogs, the parked Ford pick up (a dio cast model), the fact that the windsock and US flag are not waving, so there no wind, plus the vulture perched on the aircraft's tail! *Model by Tory Mucaro*

LEFT Modelling also looks into the future – or some future. Here, an Alternative Universe German fighter has knocked over Trafalgar Square's Nelson's Column! *Model and photo by Cris Simmonds*

If the model is going to be moved a lot, and maybe displayed where it can't be monitored, a clear acrylic case can be built to protect it. Here a Perspex case has been fitted over a Moebius Space Chariot from *Lost in Space*, on display at a show.

If the base is intended to be just a support, and the focus is on what sits on it, things could be slightly more straightforward. On the assumption that the base here will be likely be a different material to the landscaping, it is probably going to be wood, so there is then the choice between either sanding, priming and painting it to give an alternative finish, or accepting that it is wood and making a feature of it. If the base is to be painted, always try to prime and paint both sides, especially in the case of plywood. Although warping is unlikely, unless the material is very thin ply (though very thin ply is not really a suitable material for a base), painting both sides should eliminate any likelihood of this. If the wood is going to be a feature in itself, a hard wood is the best choice – oak or beech work well. It can be staining and varnished far better than soft woods, and the finished result will look better. Then the addition of a plaque explaining the scene will set it all off.

CLEAR CHOICE

Other materials for the base could be used. Acrylic plastic (also known by the trade names of Perspex in the UK and Plexiglas in the US) would make a distinctive base especially, say, in a dark colour, even maybe black for a futuristic diorama. Acrylic plastic is not the easiest of materials to work with at home, especially if using thicker sheets, but specialist companies can usually cut the material to your requirements. The edges can remain matt where they have been cut, but polishing will give a better finish – this can be done at home, with a polishing pad in an electric drill, and special Perspex-polishing liquid, but it is time-consuming. It is also easy to 'burn' acrylic plastic, by getting it too hot, so it starts to char and even melt if you are polishing it too enthusiastically. So, if you are buying from a specialist supplier, it may be best to ask them to finish the edges for you. Acrylic plastics are also necessary if you wish to build a clear display case to go over your creation.

BASE METAL

Another possible material for a base could be metal. Here, working with the material is going to be even more difficult, unless you are set up specifically for metal work. However, aluminium sheet could be used, and this is relatively light and reasonably easy to cut. A jig-saw can be used and there are blades available specifically for metals (it is advisable to wear goggles and ear-defenders when sawing metal – it will get very noisy!). Metal will almost certainly need more finishing at the edges, filing and sanding to ensure all sharp burrs are removed and all sharp edges smoothed. If a 'metal' base is required, it may be easier to use wood and finish it with a metallic paint finish.

LARGE DIORAMAS

For a major diorama such as a model-railway layout or a slot-car track, it is traditional that such a project is built either in the basement or the attic, primarily as if it is being as a permanent set-up – or even semi-permanent – you don't want

Structures to build bases and rostrums for railways can be bought, as per the Mod-U-Rail system devised by Woodland Scenics. Note the waterfall and river in the centre of the layout!

About the largest (non-railway) set-up built for the home – and occasional display – is father and son, Rod and Ian Knott's 'The Motor Museum'. Several 'exhibition rooms' have been made over the years. This shows just one display out of three that are usually set up. *Models by Rod and Ian Knott*

have to dismantle everything to clear, say, the dining table, every time a meal is served. This situation of course depends entirely on domestic circumstances. A dedicated space also allows the layout to grow, and allows work space to build the models in the first place.

Model-railway layouts in particular – unlike a lot of slot car circuits – are usually built off the floor, as not only is it a lot easier to deal with the intricacies of planning loco movements, but access will almost certainly be required underneath the layout for electrical wiring and mechanical connections. The wiring is not only for taking power to the rails, but maybe signalling, and even lights in buildings or street lighting. All of this wiring needs to be built into the base at this stage, although if such bases are built 'off the ground', these can be run underneath. Alternatively, if the scene is only viewed from the front, it may be possible to build the electrics into the scenery, to be hidden by landscaping or buildings.

ABOVE When building a railway layout, consideration must be given to access in wiring, and any mechanical connections. *Layout by Elmhurst Model Railroad Club*

RIGHT A range of ready-formed, expanded polystyrene shapes has been used here to create all types of landscapes. This display runs left to right form the bare bones (or polystyrene) to a finished layout. It sits on the Mod-U-Rail rostrum.

A diorama depicting the return of the first 'space' flight of SpaceShipOne (SS1), in 2004 in the Mohave Desert, California. SS1 is followed by its launcher aircraft, White Knight One. The resin kits are from Anigrand Craftswork to 1:72-scale. The Hummer is a die-cast.

SUPPORTING LARGE BASES

For a large diorama/layout built 'off the floor', some sort of support is going to be required to support the base board. Some companies offer a series of trestles supplied as kits of wooden parts, enabling modellers to build a growing scene – Woodland Scenics is one such company, producing the Model-U-Rail system. Although intended for use with model-railways layouts, these parts can be used to support any large diorama. The layout can be started with one section, and when time, space, budget – and inclination – allows, another section can be added, continuing the build. It should not be beyond the expertise of any competent modeller to build such a structure themselves. Alternatively, buy ready-made trestles from a DIY store or builders' merchant – even an old table or chest of drawers could be used as a base for one section, and that – with the drawers – would provide built-in storage.

Unless you are working with Z-Gauge (1:220 scale) railways – which can be fitted into a suitcase – most railway layouts are going to be of a certain size, and if permanent (or semi-permanent), you are looking at a base that is probably at least 2m^2 (6ft^2) in size, and possibly a lot larger. Many 'built-in' rail layouts have custom-made supports, fitted around the room, with access to the centre of the room either via a lift-up section, or by just crawling underneath! It is beyond the scope of this book to go into intricate details on building the structures to support a room-sized rail layout, but with the supports and the main base built, you will have the starting point to add the landscape and diorama elements.

Even stranded aliens in *Third Rock from the Sun* needed transport, so they acquired a 'normal' piece of American automobilia – a 1960 Rambler American! Perhaps they also thought they had an affinity with a certain place in Nevada? The Rambler is an old Jo-Han kit, and the figure of Dick Solomon is modified from one of the generic human figure sets.

KEEPING IT FLUID

The vast majority of hobby dioramas are going to be made 'fixed' – ie, all materials, especially landscaping, earth, grass, vegetation etc, are fixed in place. This is likely, because once the model is completed, you will not re-use the materials or modify the diorama and, more to the point, you don't want all the loose material blowing around when a door or window is opened!

There may be occasions where the diorama remains 'soft', in that the materials are not fixed down permanently to the base. This is certainly the case with special-effects miniature sets – see Chapter 11 – but could apply to the hobbyist. If you do a lot of photography of the models, there could very well be a case for building up a base that isn't permanent, and which can be modified depending on the shoot. In this situation, it is also an idea to build everything on a large sheet of disposable material – say a large sheet of card – that is not seen in the image, but is there when it comes to clearing everything up! Given that the landscaping materials will be loose, once the photography is completed, the materials need clearing away. Unless any of the materials are to be recycled, if a sheet of card has been used, it is probably best to carefully remove it from the photo area, bend into a 'chute' and pour the material into the dustbin.

However, if you do a lot of photography, you will almost certainly retain the material for future use, so instead of disposing of it, pour it into a dedicated container.

If a diorama is only used once, in this case for photography, it can be built 'soft', so the components do not need to be fixed down…

…so here the (real) sand is spread out on a card. The palm trees (from Britains) were then added, plus the 1970 Nova (built from a 1972 AMT kit), as the car from *Beverley Hills Cop*. After the shoot, the scene was broken up and the components returned to storage.

You can tell a lot in a small space. Here, a US Army recovery truck is pulling an FW-190 out of a ditch. *Model and photo by Suresh Nathan*

MATERIAL STORAGE

Having a range of containers for a variety of landscaping materials is advantageous – for example sand and other landscaping materials, plus 'bits and pieces'. Storage boxes are made in plastic in many sizes, available from DIY and office stores and aren't expensive. After all you don't want sand mixed in with plaster, or with sawdust, as all could be used again in different scenarios.

Many kits contain extra parts, in order to build alternative versions, and not all will be used in one finished model. Early American car kits were famous for this with their '3 in 1' approach – build the car in 'stock' form, competition or custom. So, particularly when building the stock version, a lot of parts would be left over. Other subject matter followed, with tanks with optional turrets, or aircraft with optional armament or auxiliary fuel tanks. This consequently left the modeller with an ever-growing supply of spare parts. Most modellers tend to hang on to these parts 'just in case', and this can be very useful when building a diorama. In a diorama, a car garage needs spare parts for the shelves, or just scattered around, while an aircraft hangar may need additional armament, or fuel tanks, ready to be fitted to the waiting fighter. If you only ever build one or two kits, the spares will be correspondingly small, but you will be surprised how quickly the supply can build up. Of course, these parts will then need to be stored. A lot depends on your situation and exactly what sort of spare parts you have, but invariably the spares are going to be of various sizes, will need categorising, and will need to be stored in such a way you can find the parts if you need them in the future. Logically, small parts are going to need small containers, and small sets of drawers (again available from office suppliers and DIY stores) could serve the purpose. Larger parts can be stored in the box the kit came in. In the longer run, though this solution may not be practical, depending on how many kits you have built. Alternatively, recycled food containers or proprietary storage boxes can be used. Whatever the storage solution, it is vital to make sure that containers are adequately labelled – you really don't what to spend precious time going through all the boxes, only the find the part you want is in the last one to be checked!

Storage boxes for diorama-building materials, including tinted sawdust, sand and even coal dust.

Another simple build using diverse components. The Italeri F-117 flies over a location that we assume is somewhere near Nellis Air Force Base in Nevada. The clue is the infamous 'white mail box'. An Army officer in a Jeep has been added to the scene. The base is simply a slab of expanded polystyrene on an MDF base.

An existing kit with a semblance of being a diorama can be extended by adding a larger base. Here, the Revell 105 Howitzer is test-fitted into a new expanded polystyrene base.

The Revell 105mm Howitzer in position in its extended base, with the base now painted, and debris added. If the model was intended to be permanent, the gaps could be filled, and the two bases blended together.

Two farmers admire their presumably new Ferguson tractor (the Heller kit), with a range of Tamiya animals, old twigs turned into frees and hedges, and various added accessories. Those that know their BBC radio *The Archers* will realise that the setting is Tony Archer's Bridge Farm – given away by the sign. Figures are Tony (in cap) made from the mechanic from ICM's Henry Ford & Co, and John Archer, a modified 'Lucas' figure from Scale Production.

The same basic setting can be re-used, here to display three 1:24-scale tractors. Not only the Heller 'Little Grey Fergi', centre, but also the red Porsche and green Deutz tractors from Revell.

The same base can often be adapted to different models. Here a Moon Base (expanded polystyrene and plaster), has two Dragon Apollo astronaut figures and the MPC Moonscope (that was actually a serious design by George Barris for a Lunar Rover).

The same Moon Base, here with the two Apollo astronauts now examining an 'alternative' Lunar Rover – actually the MPC Luna tricycle!

The Tamiya Kawasaki Ki-61 Hien in a simple diorama setting. As it is 1:48-scale, it also uses Tamiya's Kurogane light vehicle and figures, all on a simple grass mat. *Model and photo by Keng Leong Ng*

Another example of combining two separate kits into one scene. Both are Revell – the US Army truck has been issued a number of times, and the Aerobe-Hi sounding rocket at least twice. Both are 1:40-scale. Figures from both kits were employed and the base features real sand and few model rocks.

An Airfix 1:24-scale Junkers Ju-87 Stuka being serviced. *Model and photo by Patrick Pycke*

Here, a simple change has been made to an existing supplied diorama scene. Round-2 reissued the MPC Jeep as used in the Godzilla movie *Invasion of the Astro Monster* (it sounds better in Japanese!). The diorama elements were supplied as card, including Godzilla.

However, a simple improvement can be made by replacing the card Godzilla with a kit version – here an Aurora original, though he has been made in several forms by several manufacturers. The next stage would be to build this into a proper diorama on a base board.

An ingenious adaptation of the Airfix Aardman Animation kit, here Wallace and Gromit have turned their Austin A-35 van into something somewhat older – a creation of Leonardo da Vinci. *Model by David Hart*

The Airfix Aardman kits lend themselves to an extremely wide range of modifications. Here, the A-35 van is posing as the Galileo Shuttlecraft from *Star Trek*. *Model by David Hart*

ABOVE No harm in the occasional bit of model humour. Rommel is saying: 'Don't be afraid boys, it's just one of Monty's tricks.' Rommel and his Sd.Kfz. 250 half-track are from the Airfix kit, the T-Rex is from Aurora.

RIGHT A Tamiya Honda S600 sports cars being serviced in a scale garage. Besides the more obvious garage tools and equipment, note also the details such as the posters on the wall and the scale model glider! *Model and photo by Spencer Pollard*

Of all the German World War II 'Luftwaffe 46' projects, this was definitely the most bizarre – Die Glocke (The Bell). It was supposedly a mix of an anti-gravity device, a time machine, a source of unlimited power, and heaven knows what else. This is a resin kit and built into a diorama setting 'somewhere underground'. Dioramas need not be 'fixed', they can 'grow' with time, and this went though several incarnations.

RIGHT Some of the components that went into building the Die Glocke diorama, including: the base; the 1:35-scale resin kit from Silesian Models, that includes a figure; a framework built from EMA girders; a Heller Kübelwagen and a variety of accessories.

The latest incarnation of the Die Glocke diorama, with more details added, and these may change in the future – whenever that is. Maybe The Bell's 'time-travelling abilities', will get involved...

Chapter 7

Landscaping

Building the base is one thing, but adding the detail is another matter. Some detailing can come from existing models and accessory packs, though this tends to be objects such as boxes, tools, carts, trolleys and the like. However, what about the surrounding landscape?

SUBJECT MATTER

Landscaping once again brings in the one model subject that is likely to be the largest diorama built by an amateur modeller – that of a railway layout. Firstly, the subject of railway modelling is extremely wide, and there are many books on the subject and a great number of magazines. This chapter is in no way intended to duplicate these, so you will not find the answers to such as 'which is the best gauge?'; 'running digitally-controlled trains'; or 'authentic signalling', here. Instead, we concentrate purely on the diorama aspects of a layout – the general principles of which are similar to many other modelling subjects – military, cars, aircraft, maybe even space and science fiction!

A large railway layout, part of the Elmhurst Model Railroad Club layout. Note the demarcation line between the 3D model trees and the photographic background of trees and sky.

A smaller railway layout that would be more appropriate for a home – basement or attic.

A railway layout that showcased the Airfix trackside accessories – part of the Classic British Kits display at the 2015 Scale Model World show.

A slot car track that has a few diorama elements – in the form of buildings and a few bushes, but the emphasis is on the actual track.

Two other large diorama subject areas that could be tackled by the amateur – either at home, or in one case, more likely at a club – are model slot-car racing layouts, and wargaming. Both can involve large layouts, though whether these are permanent or temporary set-ups can be down to individual circumstances.

Slot car racers will usually set up the track at home, invariably on the floor, unless there is access to a very large table and the layout is relatively compact, and although in general terms slot-car layouts are comparable to model-railway layouts – mainly in that both subjects move – the details are quite different. The movement of trains mimics real life: passenger trains; goods trains; shunting in a siding. Yes, slot-car racing mimics full-size motor racing on a basic level, but that is really the only comparison. Model-railway layouts usually involve a landscaped setting, with trains having a view outside their scale windows, whereas slot cars are there to win races, not to admire the scenery – do that and you crash. Consequently, a slot-car layout may have a grandstand or two, but this hardly constitutes a diorama. In the 1960s especially, there was a proliferation in commercial slot-car tracks set up in large model shops, but the interest died away by the time the 1970s was reached. There has been a rekindling of interest in recent years, but nothing to match the 1960s. Rarely does a slot-car layout rely on a scenic diorama to provide the racing vista – it more often involves the odd grandstand and a scoreboard (though the latter these days will usually be digital).

Wargaming is really a subject in its own right, with books and magazines and even companies – such as the well-known Games Workshop – dealing purely with this aspect of modelling. It is arguable whether wargaming can really be termed 'modelling' in the tradition sense, as many such games use pre-made and pre-painted figures and vehicles, in much the same way as a Monopoly board may use 'pieces' that replicate familiar items, but in no way can they be termed scale models. The games are usually played on a flat board, so no landscaping is involved. On the other hand, some gamers do build intricate armies – real and fictional – for their gaming, and so that can involve building individual models, for 'gaming' on something resembling a diorama base. So most of the techniques described here will apply to that scenario.

The fundamental principles of landscaping a diorama are similar regardless of the subject matter – whether a model railway, a military scene, a wild-west scene with classic cowboys, Indians and a stage coach, an English country village in the 1930s, or for that matter some futuristic Moon city set in the far future – maybe with a monorail for transport!

So, having taken care of your base, what goes on top that everyone will see? Unless your diorama is complete flat – though this could very well be the case for say a rail layout in a town or city, or an airport scene – there is usually some sort of landscaping, and various techniques come into play here.

An airport could make a diorama. This is part of the Gulliver's Gate model show in New York City.

Can a war-gaming layout be classed as a diorama? Possibly, but although the road and trees are 'landscaped' and don't move, everything else does, and certain elements are combined together in groups, so they can be moved around.

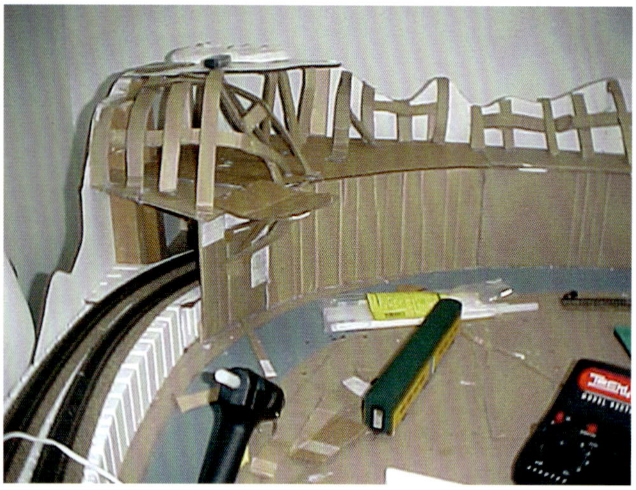

Building a rail tunnel from strips of wood, hot-glue gunned into place. *Build by Bill Lastovich*

The finished tunnel structure, now covered with plaster bandage to give a solid structure. *Build by Bill Lastovich*

The finished tunnel structure, now with trees and buildings, and fitting into the overall layout. *Layout by Dean Milano*

TUNNEL VISION

Firstly, almost exclusively when dealing with railway layouts, there is the perennial favourite of the tunnel.

To make a tunnel, it should be perfectly possible to take one large sheet of thick, extruded polystyrene (XPS – see Chapter 5), fix it to the base, and go to town with a saw and plenty of sanding materials. Alternatively, contours could be built up using chicken wire pushed into shape and covered with plaster bandage.

There is a third option – especially if you want a tunnel through which a train can travel. Formers can be cut from plywood, or MDF, to the desired tunnel-opening dimensions and shape, to fit in place on the board, maybe with stringers in between (made from, say, 1in²/25mm² soft wood) and the structure can then be covered with plaster bandage.

Many scenarios will likely use a mix of these methods.

ABOVE LEFT A larger tunnel structure built using expanded polystyrene, part of the Elmhurst Model Railroad Club layout.

ABOVE RIGHT Building basics for a large-size layout – again, part of the Elmhurst Model Railroad Club layout.

RIGHT Another example of an Elmhurst Model Railroad Club layout, where landscape shapes have been smoothed to shape, and are being covered with 'grass'.

LANDSCAPING

There are a number of companies that produce landscaping materials – from earth, gravel and sand, to grass, flowers and plants, and on to bushes, hedges and trees. Many of these products are primarily intended for rail layouts, but a tree is a tree, is a tree, whether there is a train in the scene, or a truck or a tank. One the largest specialist manufacturers of these products is the American company Woodland Scenics, which make a very wide range of such materials. Other such companies in the UK include Peco, Treemendous and WWScenics. Many of the model-railway manufactures have their own catalogues with similar materials, such as Hornby, Faller and Walthers.

ABOVE Work on a river and bridge of the Elmhust Club layout. Wood had been used for the bridge to carry the tracks over the river, and the ply base has yet to be filled with 'water'.

LEFT Adding the landscaping material on any baseboard is easier with an old sieve. Here 'grass' is being added over 'soil'.

LEFT Large rail layouts, invariably built by clubs in a permanent set-up, can indulge the size by having tracks with more authentic shallow curves than is possible with the layouts built at home. *Layout by Elmhurst Model Railroad Club*

BELOW Classic materials for general ground effects, such as the pre-tinted material in the packs; 'rocks' of all sizes and dried lichen, all of which was used to make the base shown here. Not all the bits will 'stick' to this base – but don't throw them away, keep them in a box, as on the left (an old food take-away container) for re-use.

PACKS OF MATERIALS

These materials can be difficult to describe using one all-encompassing term – it really is the classic case of 'you know it when you see it'. Packs of materials are produced to finish off bases to resemble green fields, flower meadows, scrubland, brownfield sites, sand – and a host of other scenarios. Perhaps 'landscaping materials' is a suitable term. To these 'ground' materials, you can add bushes and trees, and then structures such as walls, fences, gates, and buildings (see Chapter 8).

ABOVE General supplies of 'greenery' that can be bought. There are separate packs of flowers and bushes. The 'Forest in a Box' has actual dried plants that, with added 'leaves', take on the appearance of trees.

RIGHT Trees can be bought ready-made, and in various seasons. Here summer and winter from Woodland Scenics

RIGHT Ready-made trees, and othor accessories, from Hornby, in place on a layout. There are intended for Hornby's own trains and layouts, but of course can be adapted to any scenario.

BELOW Trees can also be made from scratch, or in this case, using supplied 'real foliage', with the leaves added by giving the tree a coat of spray-glue, and dipping it in green landscaping materials. Here, it is half-done, alongside a yet-to-be-sprayed example on the right.

ABOVE Individual leaves are available, both as paper 'stamps' (left), to scatter around as if they have fallen, and as brass photo-etched leaves and plants. Time-consuming to build, but gives a very effective final result.

GREENERY AND VEGETATION

Ground-coverage vegetation (such as grass) is one thing, large plants, bushes and trees are something else. Many options are available ready-made, but can be expensive. So, it's cheaper to make your own. Many types of trees can be made from twisted wire to build up the intricate structures of trunk, branches, and even twigs. Assuming you don't want a deciduous tree in mid-winter without leaves, photo-etched sheets of leaves are available, and even punches that will produce a single leaf from a sheet of material – very time-consuming to cut out, prepare and finish, but the final results can look amazing. It is easier and quicker is to spray the branches with spray-glue, or dip them in a liquid glue, then sprinkle 'green vegetation' to represent the leaves, and shake of the excess, which can be re-used.

Bushes and hedges can be made in a similar way, although as they will generally be bulkier, you can use materials such as wire-wool to create the main structure, then add spray-on greenery. Even torn up pieces of sponge can be used to make hedges.

RIGHT Tree kits are also available from several manufactures – these are example from Treemendus.

With vegetation, you are not working to exact dimensions, so odd scraps can be used up, and cut from a larger lump of material. Unless you are recreating the precision garden layouts of Capability Brown, or The Gardens at Versailles, the lines need not be that precise and – in the vast majority of cases – should not be.

Grass materials can come from various sources. Again, commercial model landscape companies produce a wide range of 'grass' in all shades and textures. Some of this is made from flock – the same loose material that is used in materials from flock wallpaper to full-size car interiors. For landscaping, flock forms a good base, though will only be single colour. This is somewhat unrealistic, unless you are modelling a manicured lawn, so 'details' will need to be shaken over the top – slightly different shades of green, or maybe colours for meadow flowers.

WATER

Creating water is interesting, as from a modelling point of view, even if the diorama is static, the water should usually appear to be moving. Water in a diorama can range from oceans supporting an aircraft carrier or liner, to a river running through a meadow, a waterfall, a pond, rainfall in a gutter, or even water in a bird-bath or bucket. Each scenario may involve a different approach to the way the modeller tackles the challenge.

Water is – in the main – clear, but the scenario of open seas or oceans invariably looks opaque, the water effect being achieved with modelling textures and paint techniques. The textures can be modelled with one of the plasters previously mentioned (see Chapter 5 and Chapter 9), with waves moulded in, depending on the scale.

Several modelling companies produce 'water' that can be poured out of a bottle and allowed to set. This only works in reasonably thin layers, though of course can be built up in stages.

Water can also be made from a sheet of thin, clear acrylic (Perspex, or Plexiglass). This works very well for small ponds in fields, where the depression for the pond can be made, and finished with whatever mud, plants, etc, suit the scene. The acrylic can be roughly cut to the shape – allowing for an overlap – then the pond bank can be carved out of the

LEFT Bottled water! Very useful where only small amounts are required. Pour out of the bottle, allow to dry, and repeat if required.

BELOW Larger expanses of water can by produced using clear acrylic sheet, tinted if necessary. The boats are cut off at the waterline and glued in place. This is part of the Egypt display at Gulliver's Gate in New York City.

ABOVE A waterfall created at Gulliver's Gate, New York City. Most of the effect here has been achieved using poured 'waterfall' liquid.

RIGHT More water created from pouring. As the notice indicates, this is a two-part resin that is mixed and poured, and sets within 24 hours. However, these materials need to be carefully covered while curing, as they are prone to dust falling on top – which you then can't remove!

base (perhaps from filler, applied first), the acrylic put in place, and the bank can be built up with filler, before applying whatever top surface you are using. You could perhaps add a few ducks, by cutting off the 'underwater' section and gluing the top half in place. Alternatively, before fitting the acrylic, you could also glue the bottom half of the duck on the opposite side of the acrylic to the top half, though this could be noticeable if the scale is quite large. Water plants could then be added to the top of the water surface.

Running water

Rivers can be made in a similar way, though here, the length of the river (or rather the size of the diorama), will dictate the size of the piece of acrylic required, though two pieces butted together could probably be made to work by judicial placement of more plants – or ducks – to hide the join. Either way, additional details could be added to the top of the clear acrylic using paint, to represent small plants, weeds and similar.

Waterfalls can also be modelled, but here of course the water – whatever the scenario – is fast-flowing (frozen in mid-winter is the only exception). As with rivers, waterfalls can be produced using a piece of clear acrylic as a base. Fix the acrylic in position at the top and bottom, perhaps using heat to bend the top and bottom edges – to simulate water flowing over the top edge of the waterfall, and then flowing into the continuing river at the bottom. A hot-air gun, or even a powerful hairdryer, would help here, with the usual warning – it gets hot! Once the acrylic is in place, some clear resin gel, with the catalyst (hardener) added so that it begins to cure, can then be poured down the waterfall. It can take some practice to get the precise amount of hardener correct – aim not to use more catalyst than recommended, as this will start the curing too early, the resin will get hot (and could catch fire) and the 'clear' nature of the resin will be wrecked, as it will turn opaque. Other materials, such as silicone sealant used in bathrooms to seal the edges of baths and sinks, will work, though use the clear version, not white. In reality, a waterfall will have a certain amount of 'white' colouring, due to the foam produced, but this is most easily recreated by starting with a clear material and adding the white with paint.

A snow scene produced on a simple flat base. Here, the Beetle won't start, and the diorama element is helped with the addition of a few fir trees.

SNOW BUSINESS

Snow scenes seem to be a favourite with modellers, perhaps because it can be used to cover a multitude of sins! If that pathway isn't correct, the building isn't completed, or the scene lacks general details, a gentle layer of snow can provide a comforting layer of camouflage!

'Snow' is available from the specialist diorama-material suppliers, though the old favourite of white plaster powder or ceiling plaster works very well, and it can be sprinkled in place (use a kitchen sieve to get the 'snow' to fall correctly). This method will really work best if the surface is left 'loose' – ie, the plaster does not have water added. Of course, if the model is to be moved (or is in a constant draught), you may find that making the surface solid is a better option. One way to do this is to create the snow as before – shaking into place, but then put some water in a hand-pumped spray, and gently 'mist' the water over the 'snow'. This does remove some of the natural snow look, but is safer if the model has to be moved.

SAND

The best material to represent sand in a diorama is… sand! Sand can be bought in various grades from builders' merchants, though in larger quantities than in likely to be needed, unless you have some leftover materials from a building job. This sand can be relatively course, though you can also buy the sand intended for children's sand-pits that is finer. Even finer sand can be bought from aquarium suppliers, and here you'll probably find different grades, and even different colours available. One thing to bear in mind when using real sand is that it is likely to be damp, especially the builders'-grade type, so for model use, it is best to let it thoroughly dry out first. This can be done by spreading in thin layers on a tray and placing somewhere warm, such as in an airing cupboard, for several days.

WALLS AND FENCES

Walls

Walls range from those used in buildings, to dry-stone walls in fields. Here, extruded polystyrene (XPS – see Chapter 5), generally known as 'Blue Styrofoam' (even if it isn't blue!), is the most straightforward option.

This can be easily cut and shaped, though a sharp scalpel blade should be used, as a blunt one will tend to tear the edges. A steel straight-edge is useful – assuming you want a straight edge – though watch the fingers! Shaping the foam is best done with modeller's scribers. This is generic term for a number of tools that have been adopted from a variety of sources. Some are intended to sculpt clay, some have different tips that fit into scalpel-blade handles, and some are even the tools dentists use to clean your teeth! Consequently, most of

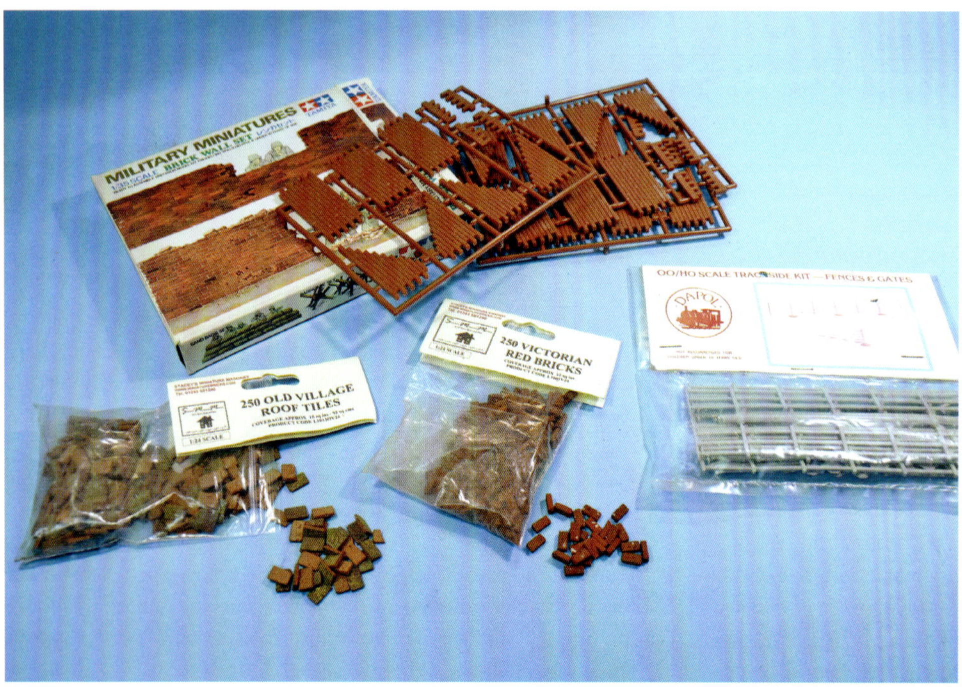

Fences and walls can be obtained from commercially available parts, included brick wall sections in this Tamiya set – top; fencings – right - from Dapol (the old Airfix set) and individual slates and bricks – centre and right.

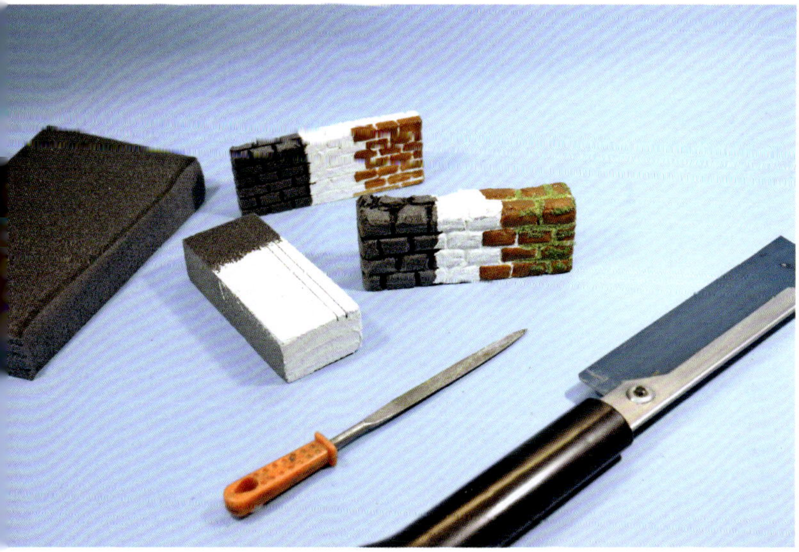

LEFT Stone walls built from rigid foam. The foam cuts easily with a razor saw – right – and can be shaped with many types of tools, here a small file was used. Then painted with a thin plaster mix, and finished with various paints and some 'lichen'.

BELOW Making you own fencing from wood strip. Here the lining up is done with a piece of square plastic tubing, seen at the bottom. Water-based PVA glue – right – is used to cement the parts.

these tools will be metal, though a very tough plastic tool could also work. Regardless, the tool needs to have a handle, with a hard point at the 'tool' end that can scribe into the EPS surface, creating the lines between bricks or rocks. Alternatively, heated tools are available for such sculpting.

Fences

Fencing can be bought ready-made. One of Airfix's early Trackside Accessory packs was fencing, so in 00 gauge/scale, and other manufacturers make fencing in larger sizes, particularly 1:35. Even doll's-house companies make it up to 1:12 scale. The classic 'picket fence' can easily be constructed with strips of wood. Balsa is usually the easiest to deal with, as it cuts so easily, but other modelling wood, such as spruce will be stronger. Depending on the scale required, sort out a suitable width and cut into suitable lengths. These can be glued with a wood glue, though on this scale you will find a drop of superglue will be quicker. Gates and stiles can be built in a similar manner, and then everything either stained a suitable wood colour, using actual wood-stain, or thinned model paint, or painted 'traditional white'.

Other types of fencing, such as iron railings, are found in other accessory packs (most in 1:35-scale), or photo-etched sheets. Or, if you feel so inclined, these could be built-up from metal rod, soldered together.

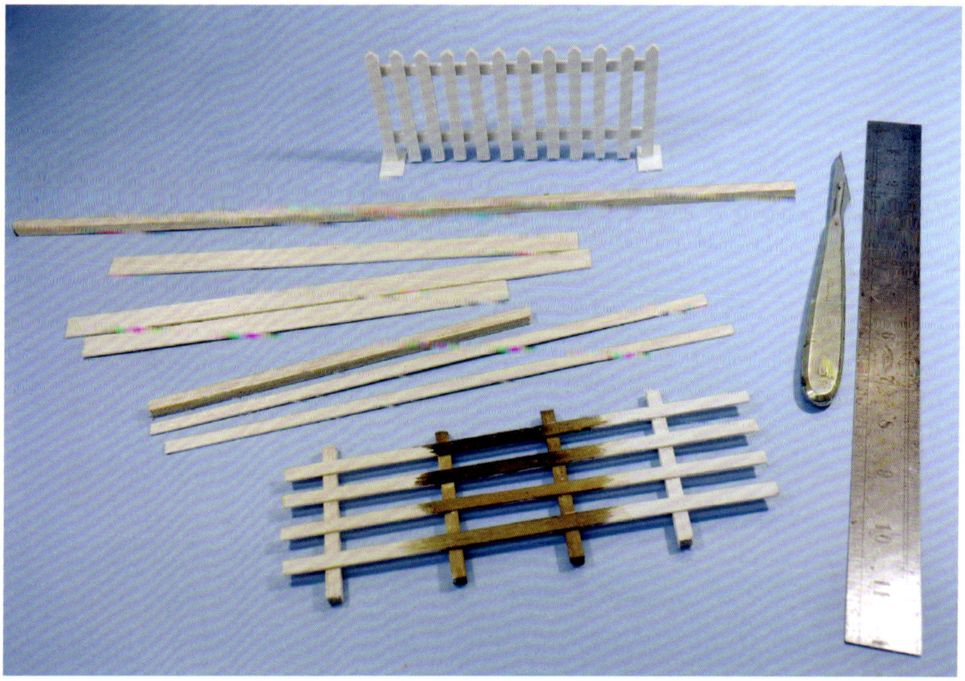

A section of fencing built from the balsa strips, middle, here painted – wood stain (centre) and white (right). Top is a pre-built picket fence from dolls house fittings.

Backdrops can be plain, or can have simple patterns, such as clouds airbrushed on. *Layout by the Elmhurst Model Railroad Club*

BACKDROP

One thing invariably missing from a model diorama, is a backdrop. Backdrops are not totally unknown, but the question is, how can you create it to be in scale with the main diorama? The easy answer is 'you can't', as distance, and therefore perspective, is involved. However, some elements could be added to create a semblance of what is in the background. As mentioned previously, some card dioramas are included with kits – mostly from AMT and MPC, but also some from Atlantis Models. Most involve artwork, though Atlantis Models uses a photographic background, admittedly fairly small, for some of its Flying Saucer kits such as the saucer from 'Earth vs the Flying Saucers', parked on the lawn with the White House in the background, or the saucer supposedly seen over Monument Valley, where a suitable backdrop accompanies the model.

Atlantis supplied a simple but evocative background for its Monument Valley flying-saucer kit. This is small, but the idea could certainly be enlarged.

Backdrops can also incorporate other distant scenery – such as the sea. *Layout by the Elmhurst Model Railroad Club*

A small railway layout, with fluffy cumulus clouds painted on the background.

ABOVE Lighting can definitely set the mood for a diorama – large or small. Here a night scene for the Elmhurst Model Railroad Club layout.

RIGHT Dioramas (of any size) can benefit from lighting, and special modelling light packs are made.

More out of this world for some alien city, with an alien sky. The stars are holes punched in the black background, and lit from behind. The nebulae are produced from white spray paint – but lit with colours, to make them far more vivid that could be achieved with pure paint.

Revell supplied card backdrops with some of its display cases to hold model cars. Other aftermarket companies make separate backdrops, though again most are intended for model cars. These also tend to be on the small size, as they are intended for a single car.

For the larger landscape we are discussing here, if a backdrop is added, it is usually going to be painted. A decision then has to be made as to the material to use for the painted backdrop. If the diorama is displayed against a wall, and that wall is flat – that could be an answer, though not if the diorama is likely to be moved in the near future. Alternatively, photographic 'backdrop' paper is produced in a variety of colours. It is available in long rolls (Colorama is one of the major makes) – up to 2.72m (9ft) wide, and most rolls are 11m (36ft) long, so big enough for most layouts! Unless you just want a plain-colour background (maybe black for a space scene) the paper will then need to be painted. Items such as clouds are straightforward to produce, even from a spray can.

For smaller dioramas, a sheet of thin plywood, or even a sheet of plastic, can be curved round. Styrene sheets are available in reasonably large sizes, around 4ft x 6ft (1.2m x 1.8m) and in both black and white. You would, however, need to go to commercial suppliers to obtain this size, it is not something a model shop would stock.

If you are building a space diorama, anything goes! Paper backings can be punched with holes and back-lit, to produce stars. Nebulae and star clusters can be created by spraying paint on the front of the card, though first spray white and then spray whatever colour you want on top. For even more startling effects, leave the white paint and – to produce the colours – use lights. This really can be 'out of this world'.

Chapter 8

Buildings

Many dioramas, regardless of subject, include buildings. Full-size buildings can vary hugely, covering a vast range of shapes and sizes and built from a vast range of materials – from a mud hut or a tent at one end of the spectrum, to a castle or skyscraper at the other.

Model buildings were produced from the very early days of the commercial kit companies, and were even available with wood as the primary material before plastic came along. Originally, model buildings were inexorably linked to model railways.

PROMINENT BUILDINGS

There were exceptions to kits of buildings produced for model railways – and model kits of buildings and similar structures were not automatically intended for railway layouts. There have been kits of The White House and The Capitol in Washington DC; structures such as the Statue of Liberty in New York and the Eiffel Tower in Paris; there is even a kit made of a lighthouse.

RAILWAY BUILDINGS

Exactly the same techniques used to create a modern diorama were there in those early days. When building a model railway, if you had room, a baseboard was built, and sometimes the railway layout grew and grew. To this end, buildings and accessories were required, and the model companies around the world realised this could be a large market. In the UK, Airfix was one of the first with its 'Trackside Accessories'. In the US, Revell started its own line of buildings and accessories, but it wasn't the only one, Aurora and Renwal also had lines of accessory kits for model railways. While these kit companies dealt with other modelling subject matter, some model companies were established to specialise purely in model railways – such as Atlas, Athern, Bachmann and Walthers. In Continental Europe, Faller was starting to make what could be termed classic German architectural structures in H0-gauge, for use in layouts depicting 'Central European' scenes, and today the company retains this dominant hold on the whole hobby. (Though it is not often remembered, Faller originally used to produce models of other subjects, such as aircraft and missiles!)

1600 Pennsylvania Avenue, otherwise known as the White House. This is a detailed kit issued by Marx, later by Glencoe Models. *Model and photo by Dean Milano*

ABOVE LEFT A small range of continental European buildings from Faller, Heljan and Revell-Germany.

ABOVE RIGHT A highly detailed kit from Faller – St Katherine's Hospital. The kit includes all the items, people and vehicles seen here and also – not shown – a medical helicopter landing on the roof! *Model and photo by Dean Milano*

RIGHT Buildings on a railway layout. The vast majority here come from US model companies such as Walther and Bachmann, though there are few European interlopers. *Model layout by Dean Milano*

BELOW Care is needed to ensure the buildings and general infrastructure fits the location. This is 'New England', part of the Gulliver's Gate display in New York City.

These kits of buildings aimed at railway modelling naturally include buildings directly related to trains – station platforms, signal boxes, engine sheds and similar, but also other day-to-day structures, such as houses, shops, service stations and churches.

ABOVE More typical American city buildings, used in the Elmhurst Model Railroad Club layout.

CENTRE RIGHT A typical American suburban house from Revell in 1961. It is – being US – 1:87/H0-scale.

BELOW RIGHT One of Aurora's 1:87-scale railroad buildings from the 1960s.

SCALES vs GAUGES

For most rail layouts, buildings are made in the appropriate scale for the trains, and if modelling scales overall can be difficult, railway scales worldwide can be even more complicated, as not only the 'scale' of the object has to be taken into consideration, but so does the gauge (width) of the track – and the two may not necessarily match. The best example is the most common railway scale worldwide of H0 ('half 0'), which corresponds to 1:87 scale. All countries use this – except one of the pioneers of model railways – Britain. Although the British model-railway gauge is H0 (so will run on H0 track), the overall scale is not – it is 00 ('double 0'), which is 1:76. Consequently, UK-based model companies make buildings intended for rail layouts in 1:76-scale, whereas everyone else worldwide makes them in 1:87-scale. In reality, as previously mentioned, this probably doesn't make too much of a difference size-wise, whether you are using H0 or 00.

Quite why the difference is lost in the mists of time, but Britain originated 1:72-scale for aircraft recognition models in the 1930s (hence the very first 'plastic' aircraft construction kits – though not moulded in polystyrene, they were in cellulose acetate) – the Frog Penguins. These were produced in 1:72 scale, which is an imperial engineering scale (1in to 6ft), and became the first 'standard' scale for aircraft models. However, as mentioned in Chapter 4 when discussing diorama accessory kits, 1:72-scale is very close to 1:76-scale.

So, you had railways at 1:76-scale and aircraft at 1:72, and unless you are an absolute scale-model purist (though admittedly some are…), putting 1:76 and 1:72 in the same

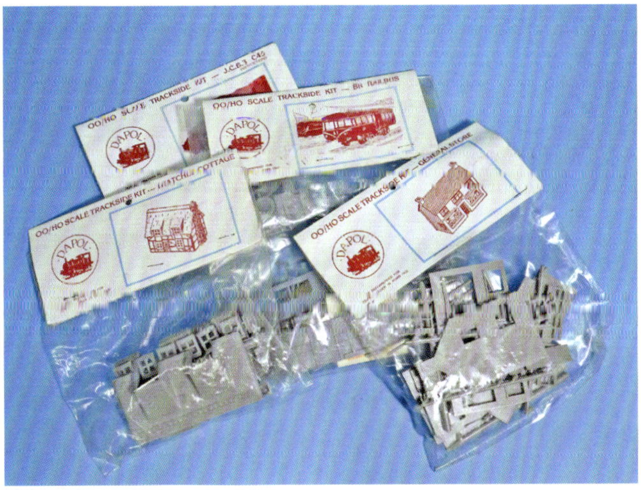

ABOVE These kits were originally in the Airfix trackside accessories range, later available under the Dapol name. The series included actual rail vehicles, as well as buildings.

ABOVE RIGHT The church, from the Airfix trackside accessories range, here used for a different purpose, to create a diorama for a Christmas card.

RIGHT Making a change from completed buildings, this layout has one under construction. The wood is real wood.

scene can work perfectly well. Putting 1:76 and 1:87 in the same scene, however, isn't quite so clear-cut. Here there is a 10 per cent scale difference, though you may get away with it for many buildings and street furniture.

BRITAIN vs THE WORLD

As it is only been produced for the British market, the 00/1:76 range of buildings is somewhat limited. Airfix used to produce a fine range of building kits, though these were sold to Dapol during one of Airfix's various take-overs. Even taking these into account, along with the smaller specialist companies, the range is still relatively limited and very British-specific. The current owners of Airfix, Hornby – itself of course primarily a manufacture of model railways – also makes its own ready-built rail buildings and structures, while there are many other smaller companies making other kits and ready-builts in a variety of materials. However, again they are mainly 00/1:76 and again very British-centric.

In 1:87-scale however, there is a very wide range – though as the vast majority come from the US, Germany, Denmark and Japan, they tend to reflect their geographical location, although some more anonymous buildings, such as sheds and industrial buildings could work in a British context. Vast ranges of cars and trucks are also produced, but of course at 1:87-scale, they are really too small to be compatible with 1:76/00.

As the UK uses 1:76/00, employing what was the Airfix range of 'trackside accessories' will work in many 1:72 aircraft dioramas, where buildings – especially many countryside buildings – have not really changed over the centuries. Probably the only sign your thatched cottage is in the 21st century, not the 18th, is that there is a car in the driveway, not a horse and cart, and there is a satellite dish on the roof!

The most relevant building for any airfield is the control tower, an example of which was produced by Airfix which, interestingly was retained by the company, and did not go to Dapol. This is the type that was typical of those used during World War II. It became such an icon of the British war effort,

ABOVE The three 'Ghoul Houses'. Left– the Bates' Mansion, from Psycho, by Polar Lights; centre – 1313 Mockingbird Lane, home of those 'just plain folks', the Munsters; right – the Addams' Family house, originally an Aurora kit, then recreated by Polar Lights. These are all in H0/1:87 scale.

LEFT Here, the Bates' Mansion is incorporated into a rail layout, seen at one of the Chicago iHobby fairs. The motel was converted from an existing kit, and the rail lines have been moved a lot closer than was the case in the movie – artistic license.

BELOW Mel's Drive-In from *American Graffiti*, without its roof to show the interior details. The H0 kit was produced by Moebius Models.

that there is even a replica in the grounds of the United States Air Force Museum in Dayton Ohio, that could almost be a full-size Airfix kit! Revell also makes some aircraft-orientated buildings such as a European 'Shelter' hangar in 1:72-scale.

US ARCHITECTURE

Looking at the range of buildings available as kits in the US, the number is vast. Walthers, using its Cornerstone name, produces approaching 1,000 kits of buildings and associated structures. Bachmann, under the Plasticville name, produces a similar range. A kit for any type of building you can probably think of is produced by at least one of these manufactures. Most are specifically (and naturally) American in style and they are all H0/1:87, or the smaller N-gauge (1:150), but some could certainly be adapted to more 'international' use. Occasionally, the mainstream, 'non-railway' kit companies provide some buildings, though they are invariably tied into another subject – usually film and television. For example, over the years all three of what could be termed the major 'ghoul houses' were made in

1:87-scale by Aurora, Polar Lights and Moebius Models. These are the Addams Family House, the Bates Mansion from *Psycho*, and 1313 Mockingbird Lane, home to the Munsters. Moebius even made Mel's Drive-In, in 1:87 scale, as featured in *American Graffiti*, although the main scale for all the relevant car kits is 1:25 scale, so it is difficult to display them together.

LEFT A diorama made from a Fujimi garage, here two kits joined together. Fujimi also made most of the equipment, while a Monogram Cobra is being serviced.

CENTRE LEFT In 1:35-scale, most buildings that are commercially available are in a wrecked state. These are Italeri buildings, supplying a backdrop for the Revell Halo Warthog armoured car.

BELOW A scratch-built garage workshop, with many intricate details. *Model and photo by Spencer Pollard*

Some of these 1:87-scale structures, would also certainly work in 1:72 for aircraft and AFVs, (and British 00 gauge rail), but there are many other scales for dioramas, besides those used for railways, so what happens here?

A case could be made that – after railways – the next most common scale for dioramas is 1:35, used for military models. Suitable kits of building structures have been produced (especially by Verlinden – see Chapter 4), and this continued with buildings from Airfix and Italeri. As these kits are primarily intended for military dioramas, and military dioramas tend to concentrate on fighting scenarios, consequently the vast majority of such buildings are in a wrecked condition.

SCRATCH-BUILDING FROM FOAMED-POLYSTYRENE

If your required building is not already available in kit form, it will be necessary to scratch-build, and here we go back to some of the basic materials discussed in Chapter 5, many of which revolve around 'foam' in its various forms. The white expanded polystyrene (EPS) is the least useful here, mainly because of its 'crumbliness' – though that aspect could be useful for some damaged or destroyed structures. Far more useful is extruded 'blue foam' (XPS), which is denser. This can be scribed to produce brick patterns, primed and then the individual colours and cement lines picked out. Given the material is comparatively soft, there are a variety of ways the lines can be scribed. There are special 'hot tools' made for such a job, but 'cold' scribers, designed for purposes such as sculpting clay, will work, as will almost any pointed object, such as a cut-down kebab stick, small slotted screwdriver, needle files, or even abrasive paper folded so you get a sanding edge on both sides.

Using a carving tool that uses heat to scribe outlines for stones and bricks in buildings. The window frames are simple strips of balsa wood.

However, although XPS is reasonably strong, especially in the thicker versions, another technique can come into play – building the basic shape of the building from foam board (again, see Chapter 5).

The foam board itself comes in various thickness, though the 6mm (¼in) variety is probably the best choice for most structures. If it is to represent an actual building, or a typical building structure, you may find you need to draw up plans, depending on the scale. Because the outer surfaces of foam-board are card, you can draw directly onto this with a soft pencil. The foam board can then be cut with a sharp scalpel. At this stage, also cut out any windows and doors, and then the various parts can be joined together. If the building interior is not going to be seen – or a wrecked building is being built – a hot-glue gun is the quickest way of joining the pieces. Run a bead of the hot glue along the mating edges and hold together long enough for the glue to 'grab'. Ensure glue cools with the foam-board panels in the correct orientation, and then add the any further panels. Once completed, place on a flat surface to ensure it all sets in the correct orientation. Hot glue stays hot for a short time, while it is still malleable, but of course will start to cool and solidify fairly quickly, so this whole process has to be done as fast as is practical, so ensure all the parts to be joined are cut, trimmed and ready to go.

WOODWORK

If the building has conventional window and doors, the frames, glazing and doors will need to be made. Here, wood in many forms can be used. Balsa wood is a favourite, as it cuts and glues in place easily, but does have quite prominent grain. This may be what you need, but some harder woods, such as spruce, are available in model-making sizes, which may be more suitable.

Doors can be cut from balsa sheet, or again, maybe something harder. A traditional door built from planks of wood can have the edges of the planks scribed with many of the tools used for scribing foam, and any door furniture – letter box, door handle, etc – added later. Make these from scrap plastic or metal rod. If you are working in 1:12 or 1:24/5-scale, doors and windows can be bought from doll's-house suppliers, as these are the two traditional scales. This saves work on building these items, and means you have more time to concentrate on other work.

ROOFING AND BRICKWORK

If the roof is intended to be slates or tiles, as with the brick-work, patterned sheets of plastic are available, which again saves time and effort. An alternative is to cut individual tiles from plastic sheet, and fix individually. This is far more time-consuming, but it means you can build in your own style, and maybe even miss out a slate or two, making the finished result totally individual. For buildings that have been wrecked, this will also allow loose tiles to be scattered around. The same applies to bricks, and here packs of individual bricks – in various scales – are produce, to allow them to join the tiles on the ground, adding to the wreckage (see Chapter 7, page 110).

The exterior-surfaces bricks can be added using a thin sheet of XPS, say 2mm, stuck on the outside of the foam-board 'shell', on which can be scribed the brick pattern, as described earlier. Alternatively, exterior – and interior for that matter – patterns can be added using pre-formed, embossed plastic sheets. These are available a wide range of patterns, from regular brick, stone and corrugations, to irregular patterns.

DROP BY THE DINER

As an example, several embossed styrene sheets were used for most of the exterior the Cadillac Café diner, a building required as the backdrop for photographing model cars.

As world-wide, the major car scale is 1:24 (and by default, that includes the US 1:25), the café was built to that scale.

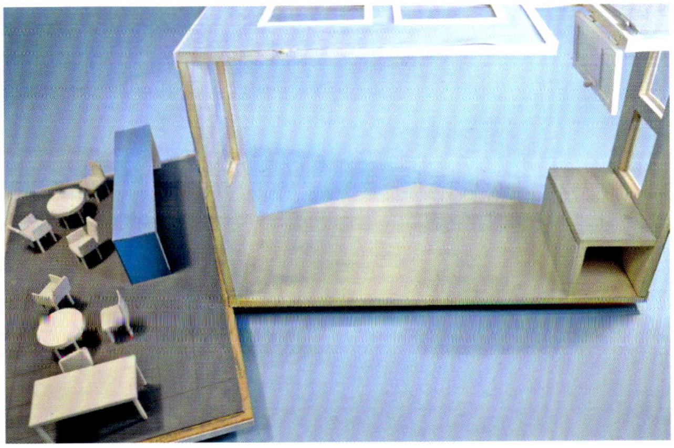

The structure for the Cadillac Café. The whole building is built around foam-board, with an MDF floor. Because the interior could be seen, this was not glued with a hot-glue gun, and instead superglue was used.

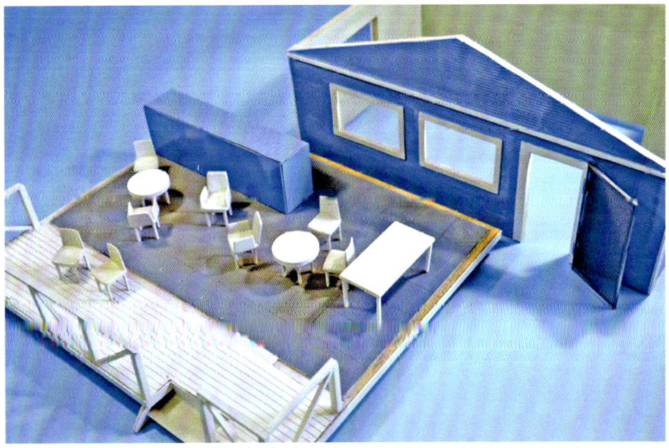

Setting out the interior. The chairs and tables are EMA architectural items.

ABOVE The completed building with the roof sign added

BELOW The Cadillac Café with visitors. The custom Ford is an AMT kit, the figures are Tamiya's Campus Friends, and the Coke machine is from Jimmy Flintstone.

RIGHT The Coke machine and Wurlitzer have been delivered. Both are Jimmy Flintstone Production items. The '59 Caddy is from Monogram.

Based on an MDF base as the floor, everything else was constructed from foam board covered with embossed styrene sheets. The wall structure is foam board, though as the interior can be seen, hot-glue wasn't used, and instead the board was cemented with superglue. The window and door openings were cut out with a sharp scalpel blade. The windows then had strip-plastic frames added, while the door was stock polystyrene, and a 'screen door' (made from metal mesh) was added, as we are presuming this diner is in the mid-west! The floor tiles were scribed onto plastic sheet, while the exterior of the walls, and the roof, came from pre-embossed sheets.

When fitting the pre-embossed sheets, it is purely a matter of cutting the embossed styrene sheet to shape, and fixing in place. A contact adhesive is best here, and if the surface is large, a spray contact adhesive is quicker. The standard embossed sheets are usually around 12in x 8in (30cm x 20cm), so you may find you need several for one wall, and you may find it necessary to 'juggle' the edges so they match bricks or stonework with no obvious join. As they are made from standard polystyrene, these patterned sheets take any standard modelling putty to fill gaps, and any modelling paints – enamel or acrylic – can be used.

The whole café structure was then raised off the ground, using girders from manufacturer EMA, and steps were built to reach the veranda. Inside, and on the veranda, the chairs and tables came from EMA's architectural range, and the Coke machine and Wurlitzer from Jimmy Flintstone Productions.

ADOBE AND DESERTS

One type of building that can be built from foam board and finished more-or-less 'as is', is the adobe-type structure found in the south-west Americas. All this basically needs is an exterior coat of plaster.

Building a simple adobe-type house from foam board. Here the main-structure sides have been cut out, and stuck together with a hot-glue gun.

A smaller building structure added on the roof, and the whole covered with a rough coat of tinted plaster.

Close-up of the adobe house roof structures. The pots and bases are doll's-house items.

Details include cutting short lengths of thin dowel and gluing them into holes to represent the tree trunks that would be used to support the roof.

Doors and windows frames have been cut from balsa wood.

The completed adobe house with some accessories. Most are designed for doll's houses, while the snake is from a zoo animal set!

The adobe house in a desert setting. The trike is an MPC kit – one of six produced. This one had appropriate decals – for tacos!

The walls and roof were cut out from the foam board, and hot-glued from the interior – as it was not going to be seen. The roof was recessed into the walls, leaving a shallow, raised section. An additional small room was added to the corner of the roof using more foam-board. Holes were drilled into the upper wall sections, using just a drill bit turned by hand, as it was only drilling through thin card and foam. These holes took short lengths of wooden dowel to represent the tree-trunks that would be used in the real structure to support the roof. Windows were arbitrarily positioned, and cut out and fitted with balsa frames, with the grain of the balsa adding to the overall effect. Doors were cut from thin balsa sheet. The wood sections were painted with thinned-down paint to give that washed-out look caused by constant exposure to the harsh Sun.

The exterior was painted with a stiff mix of plaster, with the red adobe colour already added. This was applied somewhat haphazardly, but not too haphazard, as the real plaster would not be that thick. The accessories mostly came from doll's-house pieces, including small pots and vases of various sizes. The snake is one of the many wild animals made by Schleich

LEFT If it's the future you are looking into, the buildings here were mostly built from EMA parts – dishes and hemispheres. The date in the 'future' is uncertain, though the old British Rail rolling stock may now be a bit out of place!

Buildings do not have to be built from bricks, stone, wood, or even from this world. Science-fiction and fantasy modellers can have an out-of-this-world time with their dioramas in that, well, they can literally do whatever they want. Here, a building can be anything, and an excellent opportunity for recycling pots, boxes, containers, and anything else you want – all can become buildings and structures in some setting far, far away!

RIGHT Sometimes the kit you are building can suggest alternatives. Here is the Walther's Cornerstone kit of a Hobby Shop…

BELOW … but the Hobby Shop is now on the Moon, with parking for Lunar Rovers and other transport found in the Airfix Astronauts Set. The Dragon Lunar Rover is also seen, and the out-of-this-world modellers are the Airfix astronauts taken from the set and also the Lunar Module kit.

Chapter 9

Example Builds

The main focus of this book is an overall look at the materials and techniques used to build dioramas, and the aim has not been to go into precise details of individual models. However, this chapter does take a more detailed look at some individual builds, and the reasoning behind why they were built.

BACK TO THE PAST

Many diorama ideas come from scenes in a movie or television show which is of interest to the builder, such as this first example.

Arguably one of the most iconic scenes from the past few decades comes from the movie *Back to the Future Part III*, and the scene where the wood-burning locomotive has to push the DeLorean up the magic 88mph to enable the car to travel through time. The aim of the diorama was not to precisely recreate the scene on the screen, just to give the impression and 'feel' of the scene.

First, the two main elements of the scene were built. The kit for the DeLorean, in 1:24scale, was produced by the Japanese company Aoshima, although it was also released for the US market by AMT, and the UK by Halcyon. Aoshima has made all four versions of the film DeLorean, one each from the film Parts I and II and two from Part III, where the car was seen with two sets of wheels – from the fifties with white-wall tyres, and with the railroad wheels it needed for the rail track, which were the ones used in the diorama. Aoshima has re-issued these kits a number of times with various modifications, such as including figures and supplying the body in an authentic 'stainless-steel' finish. (At the time of writing, it is also producing a brand-new kit incorporating even more detail.)

For the locomotive, things were slightly trickier… Railway modelling involves many scales and gauges, (there are well over 100), and trying to sort and classify them can be a minefield, with even dedicated rail experts disagreeing on some aspects. However, even within the vast range of scales available, 1:24/5-scale is not one of them. The nearest is G-scale, which is really a gauge (distance between the two rails), not a scale, but for all practical purposes usually equates to 1:22.5-scale. (This scale/gauge is otherwise known as LGB

The items used for the *Back To The Future Part III* scene. The MPC *General* (this is its most recent box, and the kit has also been issued under AMT and Airfix logos); the Aoshima kit of the appropriate version of the DeLorean; and a box of LGB track.

ABOVE Laying the track sections to fit the base.

ABOVE Cutting the LGB track down the centre on a hobby band saw.

or 'garden scale', and although the 'G' in 'LGB' is generally taken to mean 'Garden', it actually stands for Grosse – ie, German for 'large'!)

However, there are some static model kits of railway locos, and conveniently, a wood-burning loco of the correct era is one of them – *General* made by MPC. As MPC primarily makes model cars, in 1:25-scale, *General* conveniently comes in the scale of 1:25. However, it has a 4-4-0 wheel layout, (four leading wheels, four driving wheels, no trailing wheels), whereas the loco in the movie is a 4-6-0 (six driving wheels), so from the very beginning, using this loco kit was always going to be a compromise. Sometimes that has to be the case – and it is the 'overall feel' of the scene that was being attempted, rather than 100 per cent authenticity.

With the two models mostly built, the next task was to lay them out in position to see what size of base board was going to be required. Of course, there was also the track. The

BELOW Fitting the two halves of the cut tracks onto the baseboard, and starting the basic painting. Here, an old tin of matt light-blue was used, as it uses up paint and will be covered in vegetation in any case.

Adding the vegetation. Lichen is used a great deal, and real wooden twigs that can be turned into fallen trees. The PVA glue – centre – holds most of this in place.

RIGHT The modified MPC *General* wood-burning loco in its pre-painted state. A new cab and smokestack have been made.

BELOW Finishing the interior of the DeLorean. Marty McFly comes with this version of the kit (the poncho and hat have been added), as does the speed indictor on the passenger seat.

General kit is actually supplied with a section of track as its own display base (as is this version of the DeLorean), and although it may have been possible to utilise this, it would be necessary to use two kits to get sufficient length of track to accommodate both the loco and tender, plus the DeLorean. Instead, some LGB-gauge track was utilised. This is narrow-gauge track which, ironically, at 1:22.5-scale, is actually narrower than the required 1:24/5-scale, and the overall width (gauge) of the track in 1:24/5 scale is about half as much again as the LGB-gauge track. Consequently, twice the required length of track was sourced, each sleeper was marked at approximately half the required width, and then the track was cut down on a small band-saw. The cut track sections were then laid out on the baseboard, butting the cut sections of sleeper against each other to provide the increased width. The sections were then tacked into place, using very small wire nails, and any mismatches or gaps were hidden with superglue, filler and ballast. The overall track length needed to be adequate to accommodate the models, and to provide a bit of space either end, so the base ended up a little over 36in (91mm) long, as the track was angled from the front end of the base, in order to offset it from a straight line. This is invariably better than having everything exactly square – life rarely happens in straight lines!

The ends of the track were cut off to make them flush with the edges of the baseboard, and attention then turned to the scenery.

Most of time, the speeding duo are travelling in a shallow cutting, so banks were needed each side. These are not particularly high – around 2in (50 mm) – so it was decided to make them from expanded polystyrene (EPS). Because it will be further shaped, and covered with texture, it didn't really matter whether the EPS was one sheet, or made up from lots of bits! It can be held in place with a non-volatile glue, such as PVA, just paint, or most likely a combination of the two. Once dry, the EPS could be shaped – a wire brush and coarse abrasive paper was easiest in this case. The surface was them covered - railway-layout style - with plaster bandage. The usual trade name for this plaster bandage is Mod-Roc, though ordinary plaster bandage is equally effective – and cheaper! This is actually infused with dental plaster/Plaster of Paris, so it cures quickly, although there is usually enough time to allow for a small amount of 'prodding into shape' to be done.

A base coat of paint followed. Here, an old can of light blue was used, as the surface would be covered again anyway. Some top layers were actually added while the paint/plaster mix was still wet – various modelling flocks and grasses of all shades were used, as no surface is ever going to be one single colour, so a mix of shades is vital. Standard model-railway ballast was glued in place with PVA glue. Some small model bushes were used, though most 'shrubbery' came from aquarium-type lichens, which make very good bases for model bushes. Even real wood can be used, and small, dead twigs, snapped into various lengths, are perfectly acceptable as fallen tree trunks.

The loco and DeLorean – the latter with Marty McFly in poncho and hat, driving – were then be placed in position. Both were suitably weathered, and 'smoke' from the stack was added using teased-out cotton-wool, tinted with suitable aerosol paints.

The completed *Back to The Future Part III* diorama. The smoke is made from teased-out cotton-wool.

A CAT AT SEA

A diorama set 'at sea' may not exclusively include ships, but other vehicles or figures, and in this case an amphibious aircraft in the form of a Consolidated PBY Catalina landing on the water.

Kevin Khoo, an airline pilot himself, built an Academy Catalina having landed on the sea, finished in markings depicting an aircraft from RAF Seletar (Singapore) during World War II.

He took a sheet of expanded polystyrene, and began by carving out a general 'choppy wave' shape. He then covered this with Sculptamold (a water-based filler) and marked out the shape of the Catalina's fuselage with a felt-tip pen. This area was then carved out to give a round shape, so that the fuselage would sit at the correct stance 'in the water'. Waves were then added. Kevin worked out that the Cat produces three distinct wave patterns – bow and stern, plus a third from the 'step' in the fuselage halfway along. The surface of the waves was then covered with wet tissue, which interestingly can produce a very similar surface to the moving wave pattern, though the filler itself could be adequate. The final finish for the water was Vallejo Atlantic Blue water texture, with the white airbrushed on. The whole surface was finished with several coats of Pledge Floor Polish (what was originally Future Floor Polish) – a modellers' favourite for reproducing clear surfaces.

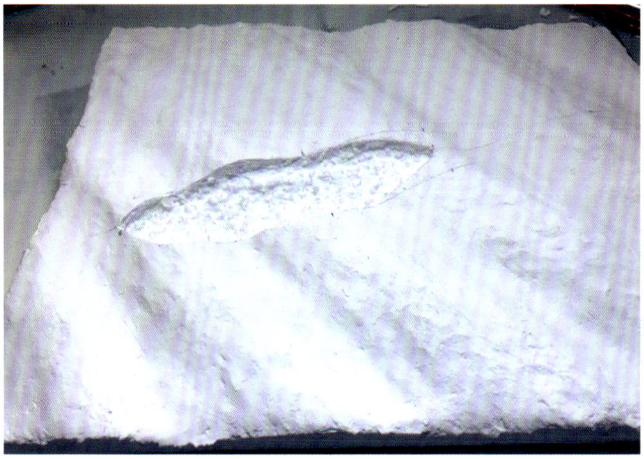

The initial base for the Catalina diorama. The base is expanded polystyrene, and has been covered in Sculptamold. Once dry a 'slot' has been cut for the fuselage of the Catalina. *Model and photo by Kevin Khoo*

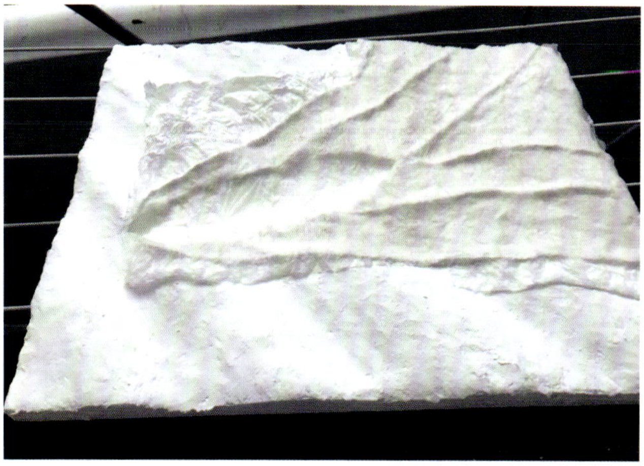

The base has been covered with ordinary facial-tissue paper, wetted and opened out, placed over the base and stuck down with Future floor polish. The wrinkles in the tissue help to simulate the general disturbance of the water. *Model and photo by Kevin Khoo*

Test fitting the Academy Catalina in its 'slot' The water colour has been added with 'Atlantic Blue' from Vallejo, and the tint around the fuselage is airbrushed Tamiya Transparent Blue. *Model and photo by Kevin Khoo*

Close-up detail of the area behind the Catalina fuselage. The crests of the waves have been added using a broad (10mm) brush, blended in 'backwards', in the direction of the wind. *Model and photo by Kevin Khoo*

The finished RAF Catalina on the waves. The expanded polystyrene base has been dropped into a specially-made wood frame. Note the model is not square onto the frame and in fact the wings hang over the edge, which makes it appear less regimented. *Model and photo by Kevin Khoo*

SNAKES ARE A PLANE

The World War II German experimental Bachem Natter, designed to intercept allied aircraft, was intended to be a cheap and quick aircraft to build, and one which could be moved and readied for launch very quickly. To this end, a number of prototypes were built, primarily from wood, and launched courtesy of a modified telegraph pole! The Natter (it actually translates into English as 'grass snake', and not the more usually quoted 'viper' or 'adder'), has been a popular subject for kit manufacturers over the years, and has appeared in a variety of scales. One of the most comprehensive kits is actually not the largest available, but is from Dragon in 1:48, later reissued in modified form by Revell. The Dragon kit features the Natter with its proposed launch tower of a converted telegraph pole.

Dragon later produced a kit of the prototype launch system which, somewhat ironically, was far more comprehensive than what would have been the production version. Given that the Natter is usually classified as one of Germany's 'Luftwaffe 46'

TOP RIGHT Models used in the recreation of the Bachem Natter launch-site diorama. All kits originate from Dragon, and Revell reissued the plane itself.

RIGHT A contemporary photograph showing the only pilot of a Natter – Lothar Sieber, with Erich Bachem (back to camera).

BELOW The completed combined Natter launch-pads diorama. The prototype pad is on the left and the production version on the right.

ABOVE LEFT Making and texturing the base, primarily using Tamiya acrylic paints.

ABOVE RIGHT The base for the prototype pad, which ironically is far more complex than the production pads.

LEFT The yellow prototype Natter, with the closed-in cockpit. This can be built from the Dragon kit – but the black stripes on the wings are incorrect, as they match – five on each. In reality, they were painted incorrectly, and the port wing had six stripes! The VW Beetle is the Tamiya 1:48-scale kit.

– craft that were designed, but usually never built, the Natter is one of the very few exceptions. Some literature has been produced on this bizarre craft, but not a great deal. The most comprehensive history came when aviation historian Brett Gooden wrote *Projekt Natter: Last of the Wonder Weapons*. The book contains many black-and-white photographs, augmented by colour drawings, to help explain exactly how the project came about, how it was built, and how the launching operation for the Natter was intended to proceed.

Consequently, this diorama is a classic case of being built using photographs of scenes found in a book. The two towers are reasonably well documented, as are a number of proposed designs and finishes on the Natters.

As a result, this diorama ended up as an 'artistic' mix, depicting both types of towers displayed side by side, with appropriate Natters in launching positions. A third Natter was then added 'being prepared', and a fourth one that shows the bright yellow scheme of the very first (un-manned) craft.

A base was cut from MDF. The photos of the Natters' launch sites – both prototype and proposed operational – show a bleak landscape, so the base was bolstered up with some thin layers of EPS polystyrene sheet, cut from electronic-equipment packaging. This was then covered with a coating of plaster. The prototype launch tower was built in a desolate flat area called the Ochsenkopf on the Heuberg plateau, close to the River Danube. There is not much detail to be seen at this site, but a roughly circular area was cleared and flattened, and a track was built, around which the tower could rotate. Although built, this 'rotating ability' was apparently never used. For the diorama, a semblance of this circular track was marked out with a pair of compasses on the base, and its sides were built up slightly with the plaster (in reality this track was never actually employed, and so much of the depth of the track was allowed to naturally fill in again with the surrounding soil).

Although the planned operational sites would be situated in a completely different location, a test version was built close to the prototype tower on the Heuberg plateau, on a circular concrete base – though not quite as close as depicted in the diorama.

As with the prototype pad, the operational pad was reproduced on the model base by drawing out a circle, then

RIGHT A production Natter (not that they really went into production), which has the wider tail-plane. This is on the production launch pad. The vehicles come from Tamiya's 1:48-scale range.

BELOW Figures of Sieber and Bachem, converted from those in the Tamiya Kübelwagen kit. The Citroën 11CV is also a Tamiya kit.

drilling a hole at the centre. This took the place of the 'socket' provided in the kit into which the 'peg' on the end of the launch pole fits. The surface was then roughed with course abrasive paper, and the circle was painted a concrete colour. The base was finished in greens and browns, blending in the two sites, with a sprinkling of 'grass' and 'earth' from various bags of materials sold for railway layouts. Most colouring came from Tamiya acrylic paints. In this instance, the base spread to the very edge of the set-up, so the edges of the MDF were sanded and filled, and the 'ground' finish and colour taken over the edges.

The actual numbers are somewhat vague, but there appear to have been around 34 prototype Natters built. These ranged from glider versions with fixed undercarriage, flown horizontally-slung under Heinkel He-111 aircraft, through test versions that were not intended to fly, to the versions that were indeed launched vertically. Between them, kit manufacturers Dragon and Revell issued several versions of the Natter, and a number of decals sets, so most proposed Natters could be built.

For this diorama, two more Natters were added. One is the garish bright yellow of the (unmanned) second successful launch, numbered M17 (a reproduction of which is on display in the Deutsche Museum in Munich). This had a blanked-off cockpit, bright red boosters and non-matching black stripes on the wings (one wing has five stripes, the other six, and even with German efficiency, this is reckoned to be down to pure error!).

The remaining Natter has crew working on the rocket engine, the craft sitting on cradles. Two crew are provided in the kit, but it was reckoned than more 'action' was needed. There is no shortage of World War II-era vehicles in 1:35 scale, but this model is in the aircraft scale of 1:48. Fortunately, Tamiya decided to add 1:48 as a military scale, almost certainly as it meant the kits could be used alongside 1:48 aircraft.

Amongst many vehicles Tamiya have produced in 1:48 scale was the early VW Beetle (split rear-window type), and the Citroën 11CV Traction Avant (captured examples being very popular in Germany). Also added was a Kübelwagen (the German Army version of the Beetle), and the Krupp 6x4 Protze open-top truck. Finally came the tracked motorcycle – the Kettenkraftrad – first produced as a tow vehicle in several of Tamiya's aircraft kits. It was then issued separately, now with a power-supply trailer and several pieces of equipment

The Kübelwagen kit also usefully supplied two figures – a German pilot and Luftwaffe officer. One photograph in the Natter book shows the only Natter pilot of a powered flight, Lothar Sieber, talking with the Natter's designer, Erich Bachem, before his first (and unfortunately his last) flight. The Kübelwagen figures were therefore modelled to represent these two. The pilot was built more or less as per the kit. Colours of the flight suit are unknown, as the photos are black and white, but it appears not to be a Luftwaffe dark blue colour, but a more non-descript tan or light brown. Bachem was usually pictured wearing a long trench coat (often with camera and binoculars slung round his neck), so the 'officer' figure was modified with thin plastic sheet to represent the coat, and a hat added from model filler.

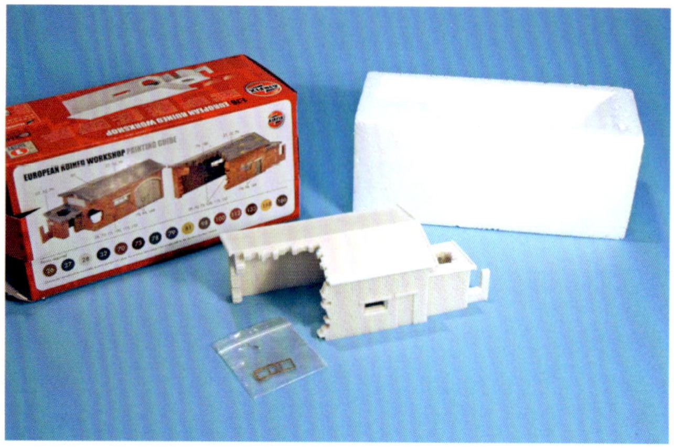

ABOVE LEFT The basic kits and accessories used for the 'Moonstrike' diorama: the later Airfix Lysander kit, with the 'spy' option; the Airfix European Ruined Workshop; the Airfix Farm Stock animal set; the Caesar Miniatures underground-resistance figures; and the ExtraTech Citroën 11CV.

ABOVE RIGHT The basic Ruined Workshop is a simple moulding, with photo-etched window frames, so the end result is dependent on painting and weathering.

LEFT Here, the Airfix Lysander has been built and the spy added, climbing down the supplied ladder.

MOONSTRIKE

Mentioned in previous chapters was the fact that some of the mainstream model companies have issued kits in resin, primarily for builders of war-time dioramas. One such Airfix kit was a ruined workshop, and this is ideal as the basis for a classic wartime scenario – the dropping of an agent behind enemy lines. Consequently, this diorama revolves around that mainstay of wartime RAF undercover work, the Westland Lysander, a plane able to fly in what would likely be called these days 'stealth mode', and land on unprepared runways in the dead of night.

The base was built from MDF which – to mix imperial and metric, as is often done when model-making – was 18in x 18in (460mm x 460mm), by 12mm (0.5in) thick. The scene needed to be reasonably flat (even a Lysander needs a reasonably flat surface on which to land), but has a raised area at the back. This was built from scraps of EPS covered in plaster to give a round 'hilly' look. Colouring came from railway landscape finishes of greens, browns and greys.

The Lysander was one of Airfix's first aircraft kits, and the very first edition was as early as 1956. This early kit was very basic, and did not include the 'spy' options, although it is very likely many modellers did their own conversions. However, in 1974 a new kit was produced, and this time the undercover options were included, for 161 Squadron 'Special Duties', with the ability to add the built-in ladder, to which could be attached the 'passenger' alighting '*quelque part en France*' (somewhere in France).

This later kit was a vast improvement on the original, in that it now featured wings in top and bottom halves (the original kit featured one-piece mouldings), separate wheels in their distinctive spats with clear landing lights, and this time around, a multi-piece cockpit canopy. All in all, almost 50 parts (the original had fewer than 20). Of course, even this 'new' kit is now 50 years old, and that too is beginning to show its age, but with a bit of work can be made to look very presentable.

The only modification made to this kit was that the stationary propeller was replaced with a clear acetate disc, as the engine would not have been stopped on such a mission – drop or pick up the passenger and get back into the air as quickly as possible to avoid those pesky Messerschmitt 109s! The scene also uses a 1:72-scale Citroën Traction Avant from Extra-Tech – a resin and photo-etch kit, and the figures are from the appropriate set of French Underground Partisans from Caesar Miniatures. They are joined by a few animals, from the Airfix Farm Stock set. The final photograph also show what the scene would really have been like – ie, at night, which does of course hide many details.

The diorama items added to a base, made from small amount of expanded polystyrene glued to a block-board base. The plane has taxied near to the ruined workshop, and the French partisans have come to help the debarking spy. Note the propeller has been replaced with a clear disc, as the engine would not have been stopped.

Perhaps this whole scene would look better at night… though by now the cows would likely have retired to their stalls!

ROBERT IN ROSWELL

This idea for this diorama originates from the designer and builder of the world's first liquid-fuelled rocket, Dr Robert H. Goddard. He began his experiments in Worcester, Massachusetts, but these did not last long, as the neighbours started to complain! So, Dr Goddard and his new wife, Esther, took the long drive south in his new Packard, to New Mexico and the town of Roswell (yes 'that' Roswell). There, he built a much larger launch site and much larger rockets. This could have formed the basis for the diorama, but it was something more compact that caught the eye. To transport the rockets from his new workshop to the launch site, he bought a Ford Model T van and trailer. Because it was black (Henry Ford's motto, 'Any color as long as it's black…'), and basically a long van, it got nick-named 'The Hearse'. However, a van and trailer by itself, a diorama does not make, so one other item that could be added was the firing hut. Built a safe distance from the launch pad in case the rocket blew up – they occasionally did – it was basically a wooden shed,

TOP LEFT The starting point for the 'Robert in Roswell' diorama idea. The model of the hearse is based on a contemporary photograph. *Black and white image courtesy of NASA/Goddard Spaceflight Center*

LEFT Contemporary image of Goddard's firing hut in Roswell, New Mexico. *Courtesy NASA/Goddard Spaceflight Center*

BELOW Close-up of the Goddard firing hut, made from sheet styrene, thin strips of wood and acetate for the windows. The sandbags are from one of the military accessory kits, and the figure is the mechanic from ICM's Henry Ford set of figures. The car is AMT's Ford Model T Depot Hack.

LEFT The Goddard diorama with the figure sets used to provide the figures in the scene. Goddard himself (bottom left) is the engineer from the Henry Ford & Co set; the mechanic (centre, by the door), is the mechanic from same set; Esther Goddard (bottom, with camera), is from the American Mechanics set; while the guy carrying the red fuel can and the man in the background carrying the plank are from the American Gasoline Loaders set.

BELOW A close-up of the rear of the firing hut, with ladder, the corrugated walls and more spare parts scattered around.

with The Hearse often parked alongside. So now we have the beginnings of a diorama.

On a base of MDF around 18in (46cm) square, the firing hut was built from thick plastic sheet, then covered with 'corrugated' embossed plastic; the few photographs of the shed seem to indicate this. The roof sloped to the back, and was covered in sandbags to keep the whole structure on the ground (it can get very windy in New Mexico). A ladder to the roof appears in some images. There are no images of the

BELOW Some of the military accessory packs used, particularly for supplying the sand bags. Note the Italeri set (top) is 1:35-scale, while the Tamiya, is 1:48, demonstrating that scales can be often mixed to good effect.

Another view of the compete diorama of the Dr Robert H. Goddard firing hut in Roswell, New Mexico during the 1930s.

Contemporary photo of Goddard at the doorway of the firing hut, with the actual launch pad in the distance. *Courtesy NASA/Goddard Spaceflight Center*

interior, though in a few images it can be seen through the doors that some items were present – tables, chairs and some sort of stove, as there is a chimney sticking out through the roof. The chimney was constructed from plastic tube. The door itself is also shown reasonably clearly in photographs, and this was built up from balsa-wood strips.

In the few images available, outside there is little to see, but one can assume that this would vary day-to-day, so spare girders, planks and fuel cans were scattered around. The Hearse was built mainly from various early AMT Ford Model T kits and the 1934 Ford Pick-Up from the same company. Two more vehicles were added, based on AMT's Depot Hack Ford – one intended for transporting the crew, the other for materials – planks, girders and fuel. Goddard himself was modified from the ICM kit of 'Henry Ford and Co' – three figures, including Ford himself, plus a designer and engineer. Goddard ending up being modified from the engineer figure. Mrs Goddard was also present for most of the time, and she had developed into the record keeper, photographing the action, both with still and film cameras. ICM also offer a set of female car mechanics, one of whom was modified into Esther Goddard, wearing overalls, which would seem appropriate.

Chapter 10

Variations on the Theme

Two professional areas where model dioramas play a part arc thosc uscd for architecture and those made for museums, or temporary displays. Both of which have their own styles, though both could provide inspiration for models of your own.

ARCHITECTURAL MODELS

An architectural model tends to be focused purely on a specific building in isolation, and so itself is not exactly a diorama. However, when it comes to models of new developments, or a new town-plan showing the buildings in-situ, these models start to take on the traits of dioramas. To this end, many model companies grew up to supply the types of materials required to build these models. One of the main companies that grew from these beginnings was EMA – Engineering Model Associates. Admittedly, the company was set up primarily to aid professional modellers to build structures such as power stations, chemical plants and the like, but many parts were adapted to use for pure architectural models (and for that matter, special-effects models). Architectural models also introduced small scales that the home hobbyist would not normally be using. Architectural scales tend to start around 1:100, which admittedly is already an 'amateur' scale, but then there is 1:200, 1:250, 1:500, 1:1000 and even 1:2000. Some of these models fit into ship scales (and spaceship scales), but not much else. If you do use such scales, you can obtain figures and vehicles, though the smaller the scale, the less defined the details will be. For example figures in 1:500-scale and below are, in effect, 2D 'cut-outs', usually produced as shapes on a photo-etched brass sheet, or these days more likely 3D printing. Vehicles tend to be generic shapes, but you can get lookalike cars, trucks, buses and coaches. Some of the larger vehicles are moulded in clear plastic, so you can, with care, paint the bodywork and retain the clear windows of the vehicles.

Even though architectural models tend to be built in the smaller scales previously mentioned, some are much larger. One specific example also has connections to another aspect of model building (which is dealt with in detail in the next chapter), that of special-effects model making, as it is a recreation of the

An architectural model prepared to show the proposed design and layout of the Samuel Oschin Air + Space Center – part of the California Science Center in Los Angeles.

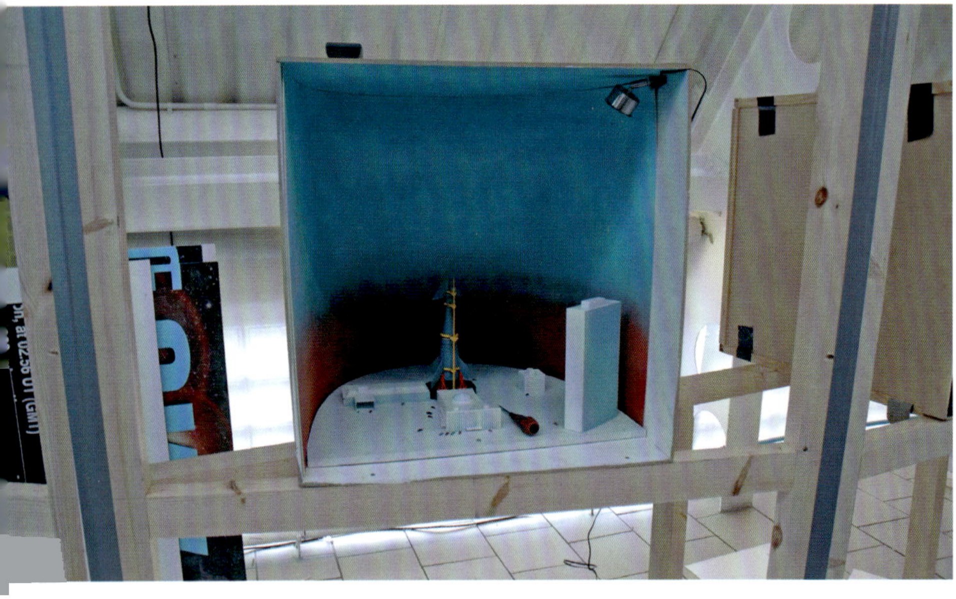

LEFT Using a very small-scale vehicle for an architectural model depicting a display of a 1950s rocket being readied for launch, for the One Small Step travelling exhibition. The screwdriver on the baseboard gives an idea of the overall size.

BELOW The 1950s rocket launcher in completed form, showing the scales. The vehicles are nominally scaled at 1:200.

BOTTOM Another set-up from the One Small Step exhibition, showing the Apollo 11 Lunar Module on the Moon. The diorama has to be basic, as the lunar landscape is fairly homogenous, here created with several bags of plaster. The Lunar Module is the 1:48-scale Monogram kit.

original AP Studios in Slough, west of London, where Gerry Anderson first made his mark on both TV productions and, for that matter, modelling in general.

The idea came from writer Sam Denham, who required the model for a future project. He contacted Simon Atkinson, himself a renowned model-maker. He had worked on the large *Liberator* spacecraft model for the *Blake's 7* TV series, and built the model of the prison ship, *London* for the same series, during his time at Space Models in Feltham, West London. At the time Sam Denham approached him though, he was running a design and model course at the City of Glasgow College, and so the idea became a reality, as Simon could use the project to teach his students, and Sam would end up with the required model.

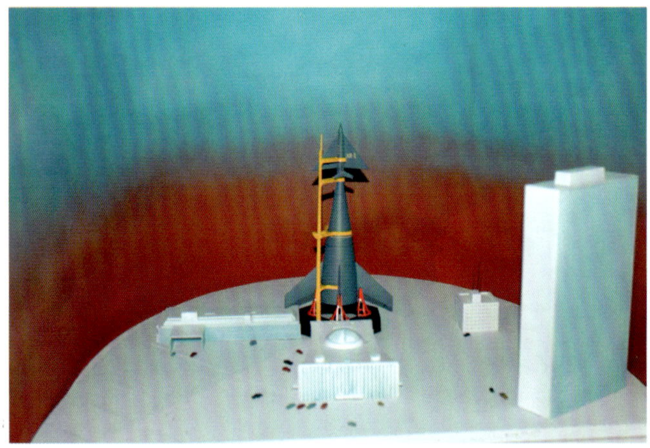

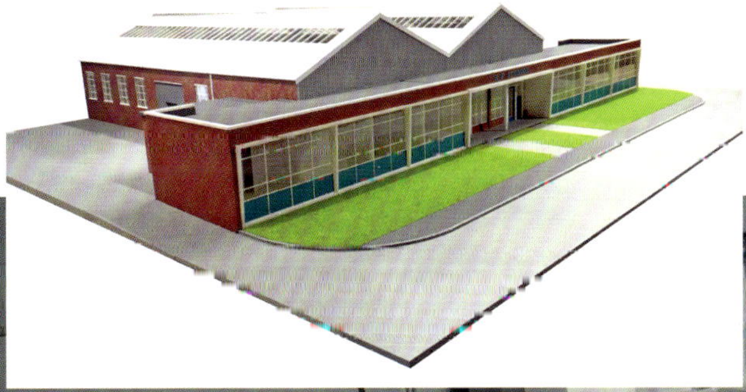

LEFT A computer-generated image of what the original AP Film Studios in Slough looked like. This was used as a starting point to build the model. *Photo by Sam Denham/Simon Atkinson*

BELOW Starting work on the AP Film Studios building – with some main walls and windows laser cut. *Photo by Sam Denham/ Simon Atkinson*

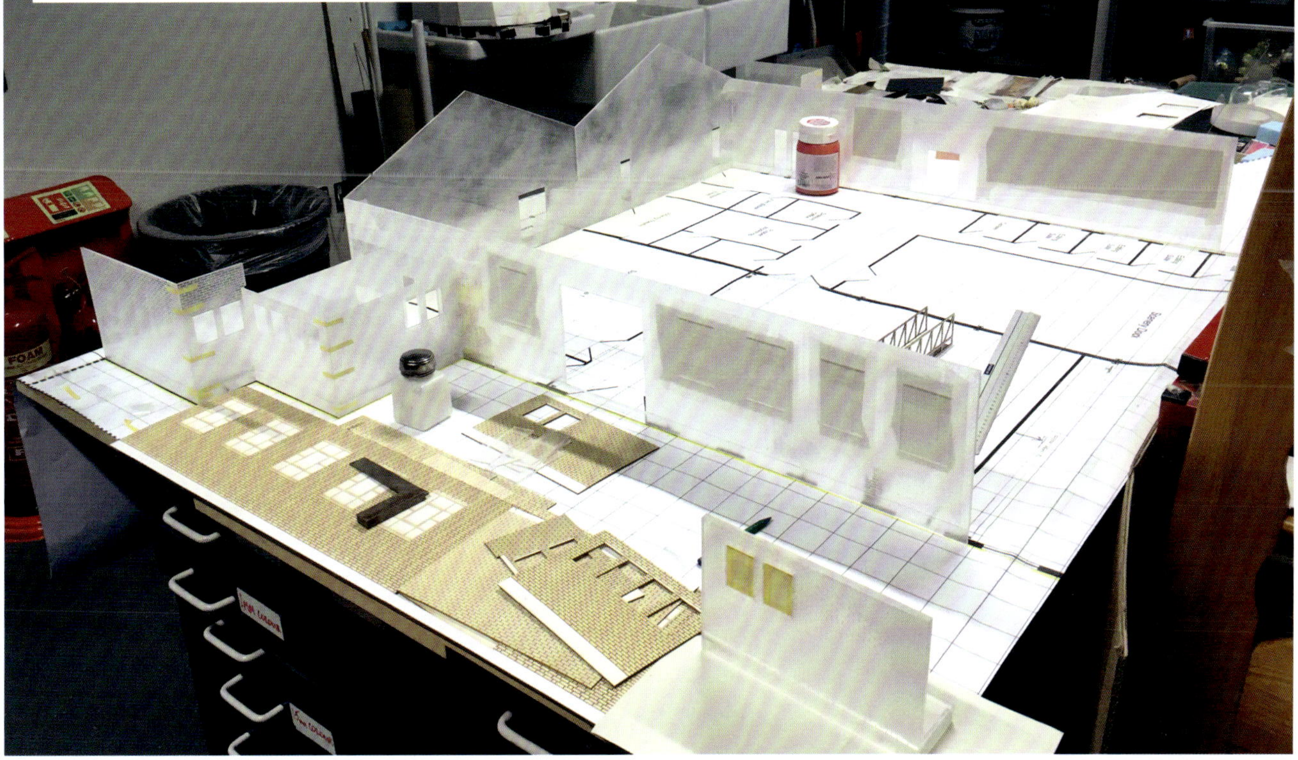

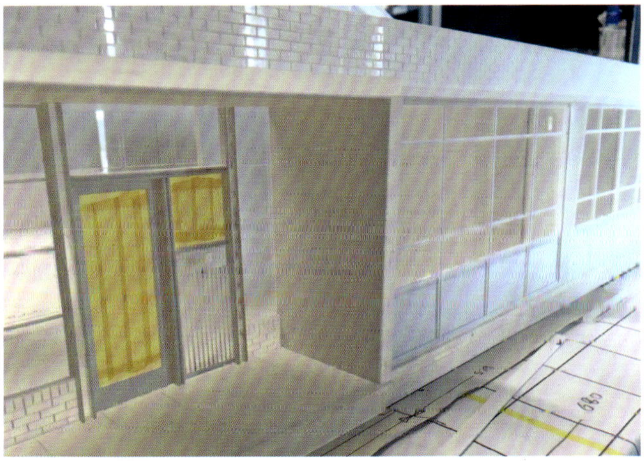

The model was built using standard architectural-style techniques, which tend to be dedicated solely to this type of model-making, but elements of which could certainly be adapted for the home hobbyist.

ABOVE LEFT A close-up of the doors and windows for the AP Film Studios buildings. The door and adjacent window have had masking tape applied, ready for painting. *Photo by Sam Denham/ Simon Atkinson*

ABOVE RIGHT The exterior walls and doors in finished form. The 'brick' pattern has been added by laser etching. *Photo by Sam Denham/Simon Atkinson*

A model within a model. One of the rooms in the model building of the AP Film Studios includes the classic set of Thunderbird 2 taking off – complete with folding palm trees! *Photo by Sam Denham/Simon Atkinson*

THE THUNDERBIRDS STUDIO

Architectural models certainly also need detailed plans, but this was not straightforward in the case of AP Studios. The original plans could not be located, and the situation was not exactly helped by the fact that the building itself has been demolished. However, original photographs of the building certainly did exist, and some of the original plans were eventually found. Using this information, new plans were drawn up, aided by memories from people who had actually worked at the building back in the 1960s, such as production designer Mike Trim and model-maker Alan Shubrook. This is precisely what many model-makers will do when creating a diorama – building up information from a variety of sources.

Architectural model-making invariably relies on the use of a lot of acrylic sheet, the main trade names in the UK and US respectively being Perspex and Plexiglass. The acrylic sheet was mainly used in its clear form, enabling the 'window glass' to be built in. Sheets of acrylic were cut to size for a whole wall, using three layers – outer and inner walls, with the 'window glass' being the central core. For professional – or semi-professional work – acrylic can be cut and etched using lasers, though this is unlikely to be available for home use. In this case, etching was used for the exterior finish – brickwork and the roof – while the interior layers could incorporate doors and other detailing.

Acrylic sheet can be cut by scoring with a special knife blade (it has a hooked edge for the task), and then carefully snapping the sheet along the score-line.

Project leader Simon Atkinson (left) and Charlie Morrison putting finishing touches to the completed AP Film Studios model. *Photo by Sam Denham/Simon Atkinson*

Sam Denham, who commissioned the AP Film Studios model, standing behind it. 1:24-scale model cars parked on the street help turn a basic architectural model into a diorama. *Photo by Sam Denham/Simon Atkinson*

Somewhat obviously, thinner sheets snap more easily than thicker sheets, and it is advisable not to try the scoring method on sheets over 4mm thick. Also, the newer the acrylic sheet, the more reliable is the scoring method (acrylic tends to 'dry out' as it ages, and the 'snapping' method my not be as reliable, as the sheet will likely shatter or not snap cleanly). However, thicker acrylic sheets can also be cut using band-saws, or even circular-saws, though extreme care has to be taken that this is done very slowly, as heat builds up and the sheet is very prone to burning and melting!

As Simon Atkinson relates: 'I used cast acrylic sheet, harder than the extruded stuff – it's ideal for laser-cutting and etching, and that's the way all of the walls were created from CAD drawings my students and I produced.

'The laser has different options, so you can etch, emboss or cut through. The walls were laminated from three layers, with the glazing forming the core – all masked off during construction to prevent scratching. The window frames were laser-cut from HIP [High Impact Polystyrene] styrene sheet.'

The whole building, including all the interior rooms, was eventually completed. Of course, the original building had been fitted out as a filming studio, for the filming the Anderson puppet series, so had film stages built in. Consequently, these areas we added to the model. The main area was set up with a stage, with a miniature set – and even the overhead gantry on which the puppeteers would operate the puppets. There was also a room where Thunderbird 2 was being set-up, so in effect it was creating 'a model of a model'. Once the building was completed, the road outside had scale cars added, so it became a diorama.

FALSE PERSPECTIVE

The *Thunderbirds* studio model was built to the same 1:24 scale throughout, so you can walk round and everything you see is in scale. However, that is not always the case with 'false perspective' models often seen in museums. Here, a fixed view point is used – at the front of the model – so the background fades off into… the background! This notion of false perspective was used a great deal when building the London Science Museum's period farm layout, designed to show how farming (in the UK at least) has developed over the years, decades and for that matter centuries. In the foreground are three-dimensional models (many using existing die-cast models of farm machinery), with accompanying details – trees, hedges, fences and gates. As the viewer glances towards

One of the traditional farming models in the London Science Museum, showing three-dimensional models in the foreground, while the background is a two-dimensional painted backdrop.

A slightly more-modern farm scene. The barn and figure on the left, along with the red tractor, are 3D, and the 2D background starts just behind the line of the barn, and includes the baler attached to the red tractor. The change here is barely discernable.

RIGHT Also on display in the London Science Museum, another example of forced perspective, but moving through time. Here though, both elements are three-dimensional. For 'Holidaying on Mars', the kid's bucket and spade are full-size, while the Viking Lander in the background is a 1:24-scale model, built from the RealSpace Models kit.

BELOW A shadow box that shows the interior of a seventies-style American house. This is in 1:12scale.

the back of the diorama, the 3D aspect fades, and becomes 2D, as it has been painted on a scenic backing. When done well, the join should not be apparent. However, this type of scenic diorama only work from the front; look from the side or from the back (if the viewing angle for the set-up allows this), and it will completely destroy the illusion.

The same applies to what are generally called 'shadow boxes'. These are the small diorama scenes that are viewed as 'three-dimensional pictures'. As with the previously described false-perspective examples, you view these only from the front. Many are set indoors, for example to show what a living room may have looked like a century ago. A perspective is provided, as the items within are three dimensional, and shadow boxes are a classic method of adding atmosphere with lighting. A table lamp could be lit, or the fire in a grate, or lighting could provide an impression of the time of day outside a window. In fact, this duplicates much of what Daguerre and Bouton (see Chapter 1) were doing with their 'theatrical dioramas' back in the 1820s – though here on a much smaller scale.

ABOVE A shadow box showing a twenties American café.

RIGHT A shadow box on display at the Chicago Art Institute. It is 1:12-scale and shows the entrance hall of a California house in the 1950s.

BELOW A shadow box that shows the interior of a Spanish or Mexican 'Pueblo-style' house.

RECRUITING AMATEUR MODEL-MAKERS

There is an interesting trend with some museums, especially aerospace museums that are dealing with subjects close to the heart of model-makers, in that they will use commercial models as the basis for many dioramas. Museums invariably have their own workshops, not only for restoring the full-size objects themselves, but that can also turn out models of the same aircraft to show different varieties, or maybe to be included in a diorama of a wartime airfield. At some point, someone somewhere must have wondered 'why are we spending time scratch-building all these models of a Spitfire when there are many commercial model kits out there of this particular plane?' Consequently, it was far easier to go down to

the local hobby shop and buy half a dozen scale Spitfire kits, rather than spending considerably longer building each one from scratch individually. So, model displays and dioramas began to change in museums, as the older, scratch-built model planes, usually constructed from wood, were replaced by more up-to-date, and usually more detailed, plastic versions of the same. To this end, many such museums sought out local model clubs or chapters of the IPMS (International Plastic Modellers' Society) and commissioned them to supply and build appropriate models of the aircraft. The use of the commercial kits, especially modern kits, enabled more far more intricate details to be built in, so an aircraft production line say, using commercial kits as the basis, could perhaps show engines and propellers removed, as they were separate parts in the kit. More time could therefore be spent on building the surrounding hangar section of the diorama from scratch.

ABOVE A diorama showing Waco GC-4 Hadrian gliders landing 'somewhere in France' and unloading personnel and vehicles. This is a display at the Cradle of Aviation Museum in Long Island, New York. The glider models were built from Italeri/Testor 1:72-scale kits. The buildings almost certainly come from Cornerstone kits. These will be HO, 1:87-scale kits, but close enough to 1:72-scale, to be used in this scenario.

RIGHT A diorama showing the assembly line for Boeing B-29 bombers during World War II. This diorama is on display the at SAC (Strategic Air Command) Museum in Nebraska, USA, and built by members of the Fort Crook Chapter of the IMPS and the Lincoln Area Modeler's Society. The models are Monogram 1:48-scale B-29s.

A diorama in 1:48 scale at the SAC Museum, depicted General Eisenhower's visit to troops about to embark on a parachute drop over Normandy. The DC-3 is the Monogram kit and the vehicles and figures are from Tamiya.

A simple diorama showing a P-40 being readied for take-off during the North African campaign. All items are based around commercial model kits.

ABOVE One of several UFO-based dioramas at the UFO Museum in Roswell, New Mexico. Here, a supposed German 'UFO' has been discovered by troops. The craft is a highly-modified Lindberg Flying Saucer (the first 'space' kit ever to be made in injection-moulded styrene), with a Monogram half-track.

LEFT Even if a diorama has to be simple as it is a craft on water – in the case a Short S25 Sandringham (the Sunderland military flying boat converted to civilian use), the diorama element can be enhanced, as in this case, by the addition of its mooring buoy. This model, almost certainly based on a modified Airfix kit, is on display at the Flying Boat Museum in Foynes, Ireland.

Some such dioramas show scenes 'closer to the action', such as preparing for take-off, or delivering urgent supplies. Given that the scale chosen for the diorama, if using commercial aircraft kits, is going to be one of the traditional ones, likely 1:72 or 1:48, there is usually a great deal of other equipment, including vehicles, that can also be incorporated. This also applies to figures. Landscaping the terrain and adding vegetation is also going to follow the home-hobbyist route, rather than the old professional model-maker style. The distinction between professional and amateur model-making is gradually fading – and the styles are coming closer together – and if anything veer more towards the 'amateur' side of things.

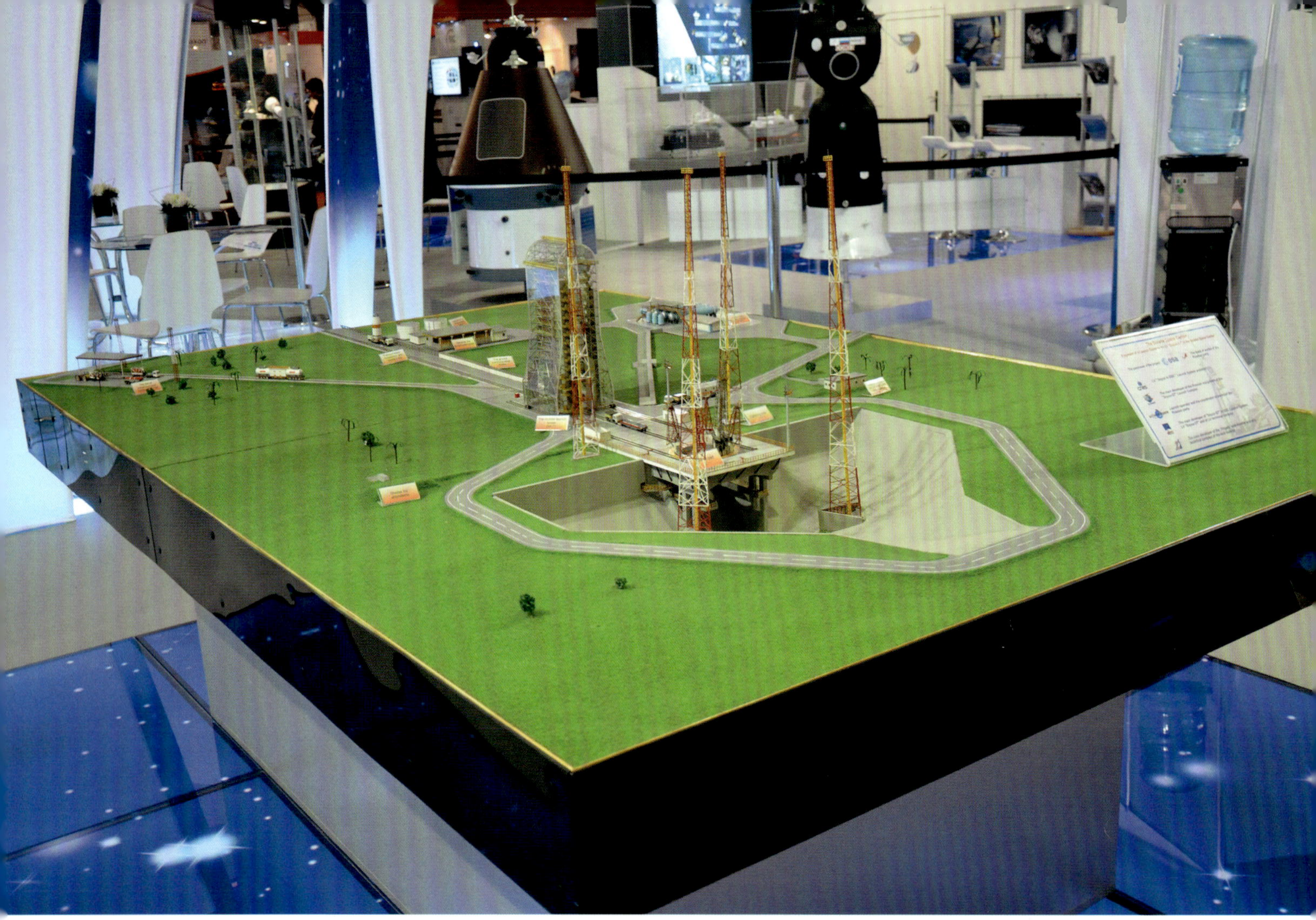

ABOVE A simple, almost architectural, model depicting part of the European Space Agency's launch-site at Kourou, in French Guiana. Seen here at the 2012 Farnborough International Air Show.

RIGHT The V2 launch site display at the London Science Museum. Here, all the contents of the diorama were scratch-built, including the trees.

OUT IN THE WILD

Some outdoor visitor attractions, such as castles, and other historical sites, will have dioramas of the whole site in the form of a model in the visitor centre. Although photographs and video from drones are becoming increasingly common to give an impression of a site, there is nothing like a scale model for visitors to ponder over.

Sometimes, companies, or sites can also use a miniature display to celebrate an important event. In 2013, Fermilab in Batavia, west of Chicago, moved a very large and heavy piece of equipment from Brookhaven in New York. This Muon g-2 detector is now in place, but the way it was transported was built as a model, using commercial H0-scale trucks and cars, and displayed in visitor centre.

ABOVE Commercial railway items have been used here for a specially constructed model of Hotel Escalante that was located in Ash Fork, Arizona, on Route 66, from 1907 to 1968. This diorama is on display in the town museum.

ABOVE Dioramas can also be useful to depict a particular event. This shows how the giant Muon g-2 detector – 50ft (15.5m) in diameter – was moved from Brookhaven, (Long Island, New York) to Fermilab (Batavia, Illinois) in 2013. The diorama was based around existing H0-scale vehicles, and was on display in the foyer of Fermilab's Wilson Hall building.

LEFT The actual Muon g-2 detector being installed at Fermilab.

DISPLAYS FOR SHOPS

Directly linked to the home hobbyist, model shops sometimes use dioramas to show off the latest fare from the model companies. Touched on briefly in previous chapters, these 'store displays' are made by the model companies themselves especially for this purpose. The models are sometimes simplified compared to the retail versions. A model of a car may, for example, not have an engine fitted, if it is not going to be visible in the diorama. In addition, the store display may just be a simple support to hold the model and provide some details. In the past however, some store displays took on a definite diorama look, though this was usually built up from card. Although much simplified, many looked very effective, and because of their comparative rarity – none were ever produced in great numbers – they have become collectible, and hence gained a value of their own.

ABOVE An example of shop displays made by the manufacturers for hobby stores, especially in the 1960s. These are both Monogram aircraft and the card diorama element bring something 'extra' to the actual model. The Ford Tri-Motor (left), besides the diorama figures included, has the addition of a suitably snowy Antarctic scene; while the Wright Brothers plane diorama (right) includes the monument, in card, now built on the original launch site at Kill Devil Hills, North Carolina. *Models from the Dean Milano Collection*

RIGHT A shop display that makes a diorama, of sorts. Regularly featured in Katrickets, a craft shop in Addison, Illinois (west of Chicago) is a large Halloween display using the many buildings and figures made by Department 56.

Chapter 11

On The Screen

Although this book is primarily dealing with amateur modellers working from home, it is relevant to look at the way the special-effects profession deals with similar subjects for the movies and television. This is invariably on a larger scale, sometime a much larger scale, though many of the techniques and details used are very similar, and often identical to the home hobbyist. Many special effects (SFX) supervisors, designers and technicians were also 'amateurs' in the sense that they started building models and dioramas at home in their earlier years, maybe even photographing or filming them, before they made it their profession (as happened for this author). Consequently, many techniques have been transferred from a 'home' environment to professional use.

MINIATURE SETS

The idea of building films sets in a small scale is as old as the film industry, and still plays a large part in making movies and TV series. Yes, many special effects are now produced using digital technology with CGI (Computer Generated Imaging), but professional model makers breathed a sigh of relief when it was realised that a lot of directors still like to shoot footage 'for real', and many still shoot the original footage on photographic film, even if it is then immediately digitised for post-production.

So, is a miniature set built for filming a 'diorama'? Although not really referred to as such – it's usually termed a 'miniature set' – yes, it is a diorama, as it is building a scene that tells a story, though there are some additional factors that may come into play.

Miniature sets will invariably have moving or working features – though this really only mimics what Daguerre and Bouton were doing with their 'theatrical dioramas' way back in the 1820s (see Chapter 1). They are also specially lit, and effects such as smoke or mist may be added, which is unlikely to be the case with an amateur build. What is certainly different to an hobby build in most cases is that special-effects miniature sets are never permanent.

GOING FILMING

The term 'filming' is still generically used whether the image is going onto traditional film stock, as many directors still use, onto video tape, or more likely these days, totally digital onto a hard-drive or smart-cards.

Professionally build Moon Bases need a lot of moondust – here a bag of plaster was probably used, as although it is in a thin layer, the area covered is quite large.

ABOVE Dyed sawdust, a bag of which is on the left, being used to build up a miniature desert scene. The mountains are carved expanded polystyrene, and the cloudy sky was hired from a specialist supplier (though it has yet to be tensioned, hence the creases!).

LEFT Using a rostrum to get the whole miniature filming set 'off the ground'. This firstly allows a camera on a dolly to slowly track past the whole scene, and also makes general working on the miniature set a lot easier!

BUILDING AN SFX SET

A miniature set is built to purely to fulfil a specific task – and a temporary one at that. Once consigned to film, it all moves on – the set is broken up, and maybe part of it re-dressed into the next set, or the various bits and pieces go back on the shelves and into boxes for re-use next time around.

Although the materials used for professional miniature sets are generally much the same as the amateur modeller would use, invariably they are used in much larger quantities! Whereas a lunar landscape built at home would maybe use the equivalent of a couple of handfuls of plaster, a special-effects miniature set would easily get through a couple of bag-fulls.

The size of the base is also going to be a lot larger than the model maker at home would – or could – deal with. To this end, a miniature set is invariably built on rostra. This gets the whole layout off the floor, where working is not that easy, and to a height which it makes it much easier to film.

One aspect of filming miniatures scenes that is different to producing a model diorama at home, is that you are trying to make it real from the viewpoint of the human eye. To this end, most 'scenes' are viewed at human-eye height, so around 70in (180cm) from the 'ground'. On a miniature set, even a fairly large miniature set, this is only going to be a matter of millimetres off the surface, with the axis of the camera lens having to be at a corresponding level. Trying to get the camera low enough to the miniature 'ground' has always been a problem – another reason for building the set on a raised platform. This challenge also led to the addition of a sloping front edge in the foreground of any miniature set, so the body of the camera and lens could be positioned lower than the supposed 'ground level'. Although modern filming equipment is generally much smaller than older versions, the professional lenses still remain on the large size, as they have to allow sufficient light through – and the larger the diameter of the lens, the better. Special periscope lenses are available, that can get into places traditional lenses cannot, so achieving this 'eye level' on miniature sets can be less of a problem today.

Building filming miniature sets on raised platforms also

ABOVE A top view of a large miniature set, showing expanded polystyrene carved into mountains (top), and general landscape (centre). Peat substitute is used to dress the forward landscape. Note also the sections are separated – with gaps in between, which are hidden when viewed from the front.

RIGHT This is a periscope lenses, fitted to a Mitchell R35 film camera. It is used to get in extremely close to the model house.

Overhead shots of miniature dioramas can be filmed. Being set 'on the Moon' also helps, as it is already somewhat 'unreal'.

Sometimes a miniature set is actually built on the floor and not on rostrum, as it is then easier to get studio TV cameras to 'look down' at it.

ABOVE An aircraft model shot at night, in a mist, and raining. The set is extremely simple, with painted runways, loose peat for the non-concrete area, and miniature lamps. The glare and reflections from the light greatly assist making the scene appear more real.

RIGHT A model sailing ship on the ocean at night. Here the 'ocean' is actually black polythene sheet, being gently shaken to give the illusion of waves. The background, painted as for a storm greatly helps.

'REAL' vs 'REEL'

The two words 'real' and 'reel' are used here as a play on words, as in English they are coincidentally homonyms, for describing aspects in film and TV, where the actual reality of making the film is 'real', but the story behind what appears in that film, can be termed 'reel' – itself a play on 'reel of film'.

As an example of an object, occasionally associated with this author, *Doctor Who*'s robotic dog. K-9, was invented for the story 'The Invisible Enemy', written by Bob Baker and Dave Martin, designed by Visual Effects Designer Tony Harding and built in the BBC Visual Effects workshop. This is the 'real' story.

However in the 'Whovian Universe', K-9 was built by Professor Marius on-board the space-station orbiting Saturn's largest satellite, Titan, and then passed on to The Doctor. This is the 'reel story'.

(However K-9 maintains he is the 'cleverest dog in the Universe' anyway – whatever definitions are being used …)

helps the camera, as this can then be mounted on a dolly (a movable camera support on wheels), for tracking shots. Dollies are not exactly small or light, as besides the camera itself, they will usually be carrying the camera operator, so they have to be heavy to maintain stability and reduce shake – and with the model set already at eye level, this greatly helps the whole mechanics of the shooting process. (And if you've ever wondered in film credits what a 'dolly grip' is – it is the person that skilfully moves and controls the dolly!)

All this is not to say, of course, that 'top shots', where the camera is above the scene, are not possible. They are used a great deal, but care has to be taken to maintain the belief in the viewer that the scene is 'real', and it is this 'suspending disbelief' that is at the core of any professional miniature-set filming

Not surprisingly, this business of suspending disbelief and making the scene real is greatly assisted if they are set at

A futuristic cityscape, again at night, with mist and fog – and (real) lasers.

night. There are far less problems with details, a lot can be hidden in the shadows and if the set is, say a cityscape with a lot of lights, these create glare and reflections, all of which adds to the illusion. Throw some rain in as well, and you are well on the way to completely suspending disbelief! *Blade Runner* – especially the original movie – does this for the vast majority of its scenes (miniature and full-size), as do many scenes in various Batman movies.

This 'night' aspect applies especially with ships, as the larger the object is in real life, the greater the difficulty in making the model look realistic. Set that scene at night, and add wind and rain, and you have a far greater chance of that suspension of disbelief.

KIT BASHING

The models themselves built for special-effects work do not differ all that much from what the amateur model-maker will build at home – in fact there's a great deal of travel the other way, with hobbyists recreating what they have seen on the screen. There is also exploitation of model kits themselves. The idea of 'kit bashing' – taking parts from model kits and applying them to special-effects models now has a history as old as the construction kit. This can probably be traced back to when the early Gerry Anderson productions were being made – *Supercar*, *Fireball XL5*, *Stingray* and, of course, *Thunderbirds*. Kit bashing was used not only for the models themselves, but to create the miniature sets – or dioramas. The vast majority of miniature sets were specially constructed, using similar materials to the home modeller – metal, wood, card, plaster and paint. However, for the finishing and general scenery parts, the hobby model kit came into its own. Two almost complete Revell Jupiter C rocket gantries formed the basis for the Marineville HQ in *Stingray*, tipping back just like the full-size rocket versions.

Standard model car kits could be converted into vehicles suitable for a particular story. For example, scenes in *Thunderbirds* used a stock Monogram 1958 Ford Thunderbird, and the custom car, the Silhouette from AMT, both bedecked in police-car markings. In another scene, the box-top of an AMT Dream Rod kit was cut out and used complete as a car showroom window.

These miniature sets took great advantage of the Airfix trackside accessories. There was no point in painstakingly constructing girders from plastic strip, when Airfix made a girder bridge, signal gantry and turntable, all with suitable parts that could be used. Many were just used 'as is', and maybe formed into simple shapes as 'background' material then, after filming, consigned back to the 'bits and pieces' box. A lot were stored in tea-chests and when Gerry Anderson's production company ceased operation, the BBC Visual Effect Department (VFX) bought a large selection of this background material – all still packed in the tea-chests. In fact the author, while working at the VFX Department, often reckoned the tea-chests seemed to contain more girder bridge parts than Airfix ever made! A number of the original employees of the Anderson production company, including Ian Scoones, Tony Harding, Richard Conway and Peter Wragg, moved to the

A recreation of a generic Gerry Anderson puppet set-up, involving both *Thunderbirds* (in the form of Thunderbird 1), and *UFO* (in the form of a SHADOmobile). Thunderbird 1 is actually hung on very fine tungsten wires, and the SHADOmobile is radio controlled, using modern RC systems.

Recreations of early *Thunderbirds* police cars that here – and for the originals – used the Monogram 1958 (appropriately) Ford Thunderbird (left), and the AMT Silhouette custom show car.

BBC VFX Department, and brought many skills with them. Consequently, similar techniques began to be employed in such BBC science-fiction series as *Doctor Who*, *Blake's 7*, *The Hitchhikers Guide to the Galaxy* and the short-lived *Moonbase 3*, and later were still being used in such as *Captain Zep*, *Star Cops*, *Space Vets* and *Red Dwarf*.

A landscape made for a TV classical drama, which shows a distant train making its way across a bleak landscape.

A side shot of the same set-up, showing various real twigs being used for the trees without their leaves, stuck into sheet of expanded polystyrene. The train (not visible here) was a 00-gauge model steam loco and carriages, painted black.

CONSTRUCTING THE SCENE

Buildings, vehicles and 'general bits and pieces' were one thing, but they then needed some sort of base material to sit on. Although hobbyists would build a solid base, with the structures firmly fixed, film work takes the opposite approach, and miniature sets would always be left 'soft'.

The basic structure would be built up using blocks of expanded polystyrene (invariable EPS, as it was cheaper and usually there was a plentiful supply, as it was also used for carving full-size scenery). This would be used as the basis for hilly or mountainous structures, roughly cut to shape, or even covered with cloth, which could then be roughly pushed into

LEFT Making large-scale miniature scenery, here SFX Designer Colin Mapson is working on plaster bandage-covered expanded polystyrene. *Design and photo by Mike Tucker*

BELOW Creating an 'alien landscape', using some purpose-made buildings (foreground), and borrowing existing structures from previous shoots for the background.

ABOVE The alien landscape from the side, showing how the set appears as rather a mess when not viewed from the intended angle, ie the front. Note also how low the camera is – almost touching the base, the edge of which slopes down.

LEFT A close-up of the building showing lights inside the window, and other external lamps giving an odd 'unearthly' lighting texture to the exterior.

'valleys' and 'gullies'. Bags of various materials were then literally poured onto this base. Favourites included peat (today it would have to be 'peat substitute'), along with such materials as vermiculite (used for loft insulation), both materials very useful for bulk. Plaster or real sand would then be sprinkled over the top. Colours and textures could be added with flock, available in bulk and purely sprinkled over the top. The buildings, vehicles and other structure were then placed in position, and everything was then teased and shaped into place, with dry paint brushes being handy for the smaller tasks, or even the soft brush from a brush and dustpan set if larger amounted needed to be moved.

Lights may have been added in the windows of buildings, with self-contained batteries, or wires hidden by the landscape. Movement could also be incorporated, and for a moving vehicle, a favourite method used by the Anderson crews was simply pulling it along on very thin fishing line, kept as low as possible. This was helped if the relevant stretch of road had a banked edge or hedges to 'hide the string'. Suspension was built in by the simple, and ingenious, process of supporting and suspending the axles and wheels using elastic bands and foam rubber.

Interestingly, at that time radio-control was rarely used, as it was bulky, heavy, expensive, and not necessarily all that reliable. However, today, all four 'problems' have mainly been solved - radio-control equipment is a lot smaller, a lot lighter, a lot cheaper (relatively), and a lot more reliable, so it can be fitted to the smallest of models.

In order to move flying craft, very thin tungsten wires could be used – so thin that they became virtually invisible when lit correctly. These had the advantage that as they were metal, a current could be passed down them, perhaps for activating landing gear, or even firing small explosives. (Care had to be taken as to exactly how much current was passed down these wires – too much and the wire acted as a fuse-wire and melted, so causing the model to crash down on the set, whether or not this was the intention.)

As movies in particular got more grandiose, the miniature sets used grew larger, more detailed and more expensive to both build and film. If a scene was water-based, models of ships and submarines had to be built large, primarily so the water itself was not visible, as water does not 'scale' at all, so with early 'water-based' series such as Gerry Anderson's *Stingray*, you had to accept that the scale of the water never looked correct.

This problem of scaling water became apparent with many James Bond movies that involved craft at sea. Miniatures had to be built large enough so the water itself was 'small' enough in-frame to ensure that it was not obvious that the scale was incorrect.

Alternatively, where possible, the use of water was avoided altogether. A ship at sea could be represented by the model mounted on a pivot so it could be 'tossed and turned', and it could be 'sailing' on a sea of black polythene sheet. Salt spray could be added by throwing salt through a large fan, though this technique was really only effective if the scene was set at night.

Expanded polystyrene creating hills, and red-tinted plaster creating a Martian surface for this 'future' Viking Rover. This model used simple radio control.

Underwater scenes, however, were slightly easier, as here it was a matter of not using water at all for the miniature sets. All that was required was a small amount of smoke, left undisturbed so that it evened out, purely to 'dull' the scene, and then maybe a few reflecting ripples from a flexible mirror above. The scene could also be shot through a thin foreground tank of water, maybe with a few bubbles rising, and real seaweed and water plants, plus perhaps the odd live fish swimming around could be added to the illusion!

Using a thin aquarium in front of an underwater model set. The pipe on the left will supply occasional streams of bubbles to prove it is water. Fake underwater plants can be seen on the model set in the background. Real ones will be added to the tank.

A QUESTION OF SCALE

Scale is also one specific aspect where the worlds of the amateur and professional model-maker can differ. Hobby models are almost always built to a scale, though perspective differences may be built in. Elements of false perspective will invariably involve smaller scales in the background rather than the foreground, but the vast majority of hobby model dioramas will be built to a single scale.

However, professional model sets certainly don't have to be built to a single scale. The size is usually dictated by the scene, what any objects in the scene have to do, and how long the shot is on the screen. When cutting from one shot, or scene, to another, the scale is irrelevant, and scales could vary considerably throughout a sequence. Many different sizes of models were built for the *Star Wars* Millennium Falcon, from one the 'size of a dime', through many intermediate sizes, right up to one that was full-size.

ABOVE Scales are not usually that important with miniature sets built for filming. The models are built to whatever size the scene dictates. In this case, showing cooling ponds for a drama, in effect it ended up at 1:76-scale, as an 00-gauge locomotive was used in the background. As it need to be watertight, the whole model set was built in a pre-formed plastic garden pond.

LEFT The special-effects technicians show the size when it comes to positioning the working rig for the cooling ponds.

The Aurora Model Company built the 1:10-scale Black Beauty for the TV series *The Green Hornet*, including part of the living room. *Photo by Andy Yanchus*

Individual miniatures are built in various sizes (as opposed to actual scales), depending on the task they need to perform and how much detail will be visible. So, larger models will be used for the foreground, smaller models for background, even though the miniature set is identical for both shots. In addition, some of the larger models may be just a section of a craft – a close-up of a moving arm for example, to fulfil a specific task.

Professional model-makers rarely get involved with scales – they will build the design to whatever specification the SFX supervisor or production designer hands them, where a scale is rarely noted. This especially applies to objects that would be very large in real life – a factor that especially comes into play when building spaceship miniatures. The 'real' size of the *USS Enterprise* from the original *Star Trek* series was never established, given that the miniature on screen was almost never seen in relation to its crew. The full size of the star ship was only really established when the first model kit came onto the market (that from AMT), when model-kit historian, the late Andy Yanchus, who at that time one of the Project Managers at Aurora (that was also involved with the issuing of the kit for the non-US market), actually calculated the scale of the kit – and by default what would be the size of the 'reel' craft. He used calculations and measurements based on the size of doors and windows, and the fact that the majority of the crew were human (or at least human-sized), to come up with a reasonable scale, which happens to have worked out at 1:635. That was then 'officially' adopted, and all scales since then can be traced back to Andy's initial work.

AURORA AND THE TV COMPANY

It is well-known that commercial model kits, or rather parts from them, find their way into special-effects models and miniatures, but it is not often that the actual company does. However, that did happen in the case of Aurora and the TV series The Green Hornet. Aurora wanted to make the kit of the car – the Black Beauty, a highly modified Chrysler Imperial – and part of the agreement was that the company, including Andy Yanchus (see main text), made the 1:10 scale models used in the series.

BUILDINGS FOR SFX

In many cases, the SFX model makers will use the same techniques as the hobbyist – especially as, professionally 'time is money', and if you spend time building something you could get off the shelf, it is costing money!

This applies especially to buildings, and one ready-made source of materials is the doll's-house-miniatures market. Here, the two main scales are 1:24 and 1:12. 1:24-scale is especially useful, as it matches the car scale of 1:24/5, and although this is really too small for the SFX industry, 1:12-scale is ideal. So, this means – conversely to what was previously stated – that professional modellers may consequently find, by default, that they are working to a specific scale, in this case 1:12-scale.

ABOVE An American house and street scene, set in the 1930s, which is indicated by the car – a 1937 Cord – parked on the street. *Photo by Nick Kool*

LEFT A closer shot of the American house and street scene. *Photo by Nick Kool*

As an example of this scenario, a classic twenties/thirties American house was required for a television comedy series, filmed in the UK. Yes, you could go on location and find a suitable house – America, not surprisingly, is full of them, and there are also suitable examples in the UK. However, that does mean a location shoot, with a number of crew required to travel, and be housed and fed, all of which costs (even the author, with all his years in the business, is still amazed at the number of people required to shoot one minute of film!). So, an alternative is to build a miniature set instead. This means that you don't have to worry about the environment if it rains, and can set the mood, night or day, with a few flicks of switches. So, in this particular case, the model was built using traditional model-making techniques and materials, including doll's-house parts. Fake snow was added, and even a car of suitable scale (in this case a 1:12-scale 1937 Cord from AMT, built and supplied by the author). Yes it cost money to build and film, for what is purely an 'establishing shot', but it was still a lot cheaper than taking all those folks on location and relying on the weather!

RIGHT The actual size of the miniature set – or diorama – compared to camera and crew. This is actually built to 1:12-scale, as many doll's-house fittings were used throughout the build, and 1:12 is one of the major scales. *Photo by Nick Kool*

BELOW A miniature set for a program on tornados. Note the metal barrels on the right and far left. *Design and photo by Mike Tucker*

1:12-scale also came into the miniature set for a lead mine, designed to be blown apart when hit by a tornado for a documentary. 1:12-scale was used for the rear of the set, but – using false perspective – the front was built in 1:6-scale. Here, a number of items from the model company Dragon were used. Dragon makes a number of items in 1:6-scale, to go with the vehicles and other items made to match the scale of GI Joe (or Action Man for that matter). In this case, the foreground oil drums were Dragon originals, suitably weathered.

RIGHT The barrels – Dragon items – in 1:6-scale, being weathered by effects technician Alan Brannan. *Design and photo by Mike Tucker*

BELOW To give an impression of the overall size of the tornado diorama, Pete Tyler, director of photography, stands in front of the complete set. Note that the set is raised off the floor. *Design and photo by Mike Tucker*

FOREGROUND VS BACKGROUND

Models – and model sets – can also be used as 'foreground miniatures', where they are close to the camera, whereas real people are in the background. Careful camera angles and lenses can fool the viewer into thinking the model is far larger than it is – and so must be in the background.

In many cases the foreground miniature is actually that – a model. In other cases the 'foreground' is painted on glass – called a 'glass shot' – or maybe a two-dimensional photo is incorporated into the main scene, itself built in three dimensions. In the case of a film looking at just what would happen if the Leaning Tower of Pisa actually lent too far and fell over, the Tower was built as a 3D model, and the buildings in the foreground were actually a cut-out photograph.

RIGHT If the Leaning Tower of Pisa should ever collapse – the pressure would make it explode – as in this miniature diorama scene. However, although the Tower is a 3D model, the foreground building as a 2D photo cut out!

ABOVE A typical scene in an aircraft hangar – the plane itself and people milling around… *Design and photo by Steve Begg*

LEFT … except that the airliner is a model – admittedly a very large model – but the hangar is real. The shot uses the model as a foreground miniature, with the people standing under the plane actually positioned much further away in the hangar. Only the people in the foreground are in their 'correct' positions. *Design and photo by Steve Begg*

FILMING WITH DINOSAURS

Although many historical aspects of special effects in both films and TV remain today, more or less as they were when first invented, some have admittedly changed. The main reason for this is, of course, down to computers and CGI. These days you won't find any dinosaur story being made without what are now more or less 'off-the-shelf' computer programs to general the basis of the beasts. However, that wasn't always the case. The first instance of CGI being used to create dinosaurs in a film was *Jurassic Park* in 1993, and the technology was used in the TV series *Walking With Dinosaurs* in 1999. What came before the CGI? Animated puppets could be used (as they were for some scenes in *Walking With Dinosaurs*), but that has its limitations. Another option was to try not to move the dinosaurs, but purely move the camera.

ABOVE Two brontosaurus wallowing in water in a prehistoric scene. The dinosaurs are modified commercial kits, and the foreground plants are real.

LEFT A dimetrodon on a rock stares out over a prehistoric landscape. The dinosaur is from Airfix, the rocks are expanded polystyrene and the landscape is a bag of peat substitute.

Two corythosaurus dine off the upper branches of a pre-historic plant. Again, the dinosaurs are from commercial kits and the plants are real.

The prehistoric landscape being set-up, by SFX technician Morag McLean. Note the real plants being used, still in their pots so they can be kept watered. The pots are then sunk into holes cut into the baseboard, so they can be 'dressed in'.

This was done in a science programme on pre-history, where standard model-kit dinosaurs were bought – different manufacturers' products so they would look different to each other, and many were re-modelled anyway. The models were then placed on a large diorama base, in suitable scenarios, such as a brontosaurus (or whatever they were termed at that time) in a lake. The scenery was then surround by plants, but here real ferns and similar were used – again, far cheaper than trying to model each plant separately, and they looked real, as they were real. As it is reckoned many modern ferns are small version of what existed in prehistoric times, the scales worked to the advantage of the filming. 'Movement' was then created by slow camera tracking along the large baseboard, revealing dinosaurs in the distance – the viewer's eye assuming that they were wallowing about the water! This is obviously one technique that would not now be used in movie – or TV – making these methods somewhat obsolete. However, it could be used by the amateur hobbyist, who could combine model-making and gardening! Just make sure the plants are kept well-watered.

ABOVE Another view of the prehistoric landscape being set, with the holes for the plant pots cut in the baseboard. Many modern plants match their prehistoric counterparts – except they are a lot smaller – hence they are ideal for re-creating their far larger cousins from a much earlier time.

RIGHT A mix of real and fake greenery being used to create an alien forest scene. The real branches in the foreground are attached to a lighting stand (top right) so they dangle in front of the camera lens.

WHETHER TO WEATHER

Something that almost certainly did originate with special-effects model-making is weathering, also described as 'distressing' or just 'dirtying down'. This is another difference between the amateur diorama and the professional miniature set. For the hobbyist environment, you don't actually have to weather the model, whether in a diorama setting or not. Maybe the subject is a car just off the production line, or an aircraft for that matter. Military vehicles do actually start clean, and the same goes for ships, so the choice is down to the builder.

With the SFX industry though, miniatures were regularly 'dirtied down', to make them look real, as nothing in this life is perfectly clean. If a brand-new clean car is driven out of the showroom, the tyres will immediately start to wear and pick up road dirt. This dirt will be transferred to the bodywork, and the pristine showroom car starts to look less than pristine. Aircraft take on similar dirt from runways, and they pick it up from the air they travel through. Similarly, locomotives and rolling-stock pick up debris and dirt from the track, and if they are steam engines, from all the smut and smoke from the chimney. Ships sailing in water are also going to accumulate weathering, from flotsam and general sea conditions. It is certainly the case with military vehicles, where dirt comes into play naturally as tanks churn up fields, and mud gets everywhere.

So, it is this overall idea that everything in everyday use will pick up a patina, which prompted the SFX industry to weather its miniatures. Many of the techniques used would be the same, or at least similar, to hobby model-making, although the final purpose was not for the model to take pride of place on the mantelpiece, but to take its place in the overall story arc, with the intention of becoming integrated seamlessly with the live action.

RIGHT The vast majority of miniatures for filming are 'weathered' – even those set in space. Here, long-time special effects supervisor Ian Scoones weathers a spaceship before filming. Note that this set also features a model base with a sloping front edge.

LEFT Although on a far smaller scale, the SFX weathering techniques can be equally applied to the home hobbyist. And to this end many manufacturers make suitable products to allow you to give your Rat Rod that appropriate finish!

Appendix

Useful Contacts and Resources

INTERNET SEARCHES

These days, when considering research, it is very easy to say that it'll all be found 'on the 'net'. To a great extent this is true, though with the proviso that sometimes there is too much information on the Internet, and sorting what you want from want you don't is not always straightforward, and in many cases can lead to extreme frustration! However, do not forget that good old-fashioned paper references, in the form of books and magazines, still have an important role to play.

Assuming that you have internet access, one very important point to remember when searching is that the results are only as good as the information or question you are putting in – and even then it doesn't always work. For example, make sure you type in 'Supermarine Spitfire', or 'Spitfire aircraft' if you are looking for the aircraft, as otherwise, you will probably also receive results including Triumph Spitfire sports cars, etc!

Also be aware when searching, that the term 'models' has more than one meaning – you have been warned!

THE COMPANIES

The listings here cover most of the world's model companies, though the list is not exhaustive.

Very broadly, model companies can be split into two types. Firstly, the mainstream companies that produce kits in injection-moulded polystyrene, the type of kits produced by such as Airfix, Revell and Tamiya, to use three of the best known names. Secondly, there are the specialist companies, which are often one-person operations that produce kits using a range of materials – except injection-moulded styrene – and which are normally only available from specialist hobby shops and/or by mail direct from the companies' websites. These are the companies that are also generally known as the cottage or garage industries.

However, even this division is not always clear, as some specialist companies may use limited-run injection-moulded styrene techniques, and many mainstream companies produce kits which include parts made from 'specialist' materials, such as white metal and photo-etching.

MAINSTREAM COMPANIES

This list included the majority of the major companies that currently appear to be producing kits, though it isn't guaranteed to be fully comprehensive. To be listed as 'Mainstream', the primary moulding material is polystyrene (though some other materials - resin, photo-etch, white metal - may be included). If the primary moulding material is resin or white metal, these companies are listed under 'Specialist companies'.

ACADEMY
Academy Plastic Model Co Ltd., 521-1, Yonghyeon-dong, Uijeangbu-si, Gyeonggi-du, South Korea
www.academyhobby.com
The major Korean model producer that used to work with Minicraft in the US, though that connection was severed in 1997.

ACE MODEL
Ace Model, Ukraine
www.acemodel.co.ua
Makes military subjects in 1:72 and 1:35-scale.

AFV-CLUB
Hobby Fan Trading Co, No 7, Alley 7, Lane 225, Mintsu West Road, Taipei, Taiwan
www.hobbyfan.com.tw
Created in the late 1980s to produce kits of subjects not covered by other companies. These were primarily military, but now including aircraft.

AIRFIX
Hornby Hobbies Ltd, Margate, Kent CT9 4JX, UK
www.airfix.com
One of the first model-kit companies, and still one of the best-known names world-wide. Over the years, produced a wide range of subjects, particularly aircraft. Now owned by Hornby, along with Humbrol, Corgi, Scalextric and Hornby Railways.

AMODEL
Distribution: IBG, Benedykta Hertza 2 04 – 603, Warsaw, Poland
www.ibg.com.pl
Ukraine company, created in 1995 with a wide range of aircraft models in most conventional scales, from 1:32 to 1:144. Uses preformed parts for some of the large-fuselage models such as the Myasishchev and Buran space orbiter.

AMP
Dnepr, Ukraine
www.mikro-mir.com
Specialises in slightly obscure aerospace items, including helicopters, 'Luftwaffe 46' projects and the Sanger Silver Bird spaceplane. The company was created alongside Mikro-Mir, but the names were then split.

AMT
Round 2 Models, 4073 Meghan Beeler Drive, South Bend, IN 46628, USA
www.round2models.com/models/amt
One of the original American model companies, best-known for its car models. It then introduced the first *Star Trek* kits, and its famous five-piece 'Man in Space' set. Having been taken over by Lesney, it was then acquired by Ertl, which itself was taken over by RC2 (Racing Champions). Consequently, it joined its original rival, MPC, as that had also been bought by Ertl. Both companies were then acquired by the new Round 2 company in 2009.

AOSHIMA
Aoshima Bunka Kyozai Co Ltd, 12-3 Ryutsu Centre, Shizuoka City, Japan 420
www.aoshima-bk.co.jp
One of the oldest model companies in the world, with beginnings in the 1920s making wooden kits. Moved to plastic in the early 1960s and is still producing a wide range of models.

ATLANTIS MODELS
Atlantis Toy and Hobby Inc, 435 Brook Avenue Unit-16, Deer Park, NY 11729, USA
www.atlantis-models.com
Founded in 2009 by the former owners of Megahobby.com, Peter Vetri and Rick DelFavero. Initially reissued kits from other tooling, though making its own series of 'flying saucers'. In early 2018, acquired much of the Revell-Monogram, Aurora and Renwal tooling, when the Revell Group stopped trading after the Hobbico collapse.

AZ MODEL
AZ Model, Above Calcium 364, Křenice u Říčan 250 84, Prague East, Czech Republic.
www.azmodel.cz
Created in 1997. Produces aircraft kits in 1:144, 1:72 and 1:48 scales, plus decals.

BACHMANN
Bachmann Industries Inc,1400 East Erie Avenue, Philadelphia, PA 19124, USA
www.bachmanntrains.com
One of the main American model-railway suppliers. Makes a number of American-style buildings as kits, working in H0 scale/gauge. Has a UK-based operation that deals with 00 scale/gauge items.

BANDAI
Bandai Co, Ltd, 5-4 2-chome, Komagata, Taito-ku, Tokyo, Japan
www.bandai-hobby.net
Well-known Japanese toy manufacturer, that had also made kits over the years. Many are classic Japanese anime characters, though the company has also produced kits for more traditional modelling subjects. Recently has produced new and highly detailed *Star Wars* craft, some reissued for Europe by Revell-Germany.

BIGMODEL
'Bielwood', 43-332, Pisarzowice Ul. Szkolna 59, Poland.
www.bigmodel.eu
Primarily produces airliners in 1:144-scale. Other aircraft and military subjects are planned in standard scales.

BRENGUN
Jan Sobotka, Moravská 38, 620 00 Brno, Czech Republic
www.brengun.cz
Company making a wide range of models, including complete kits, plus add-on and diorama parts. Scales include 1:35, 1:48 and 1:72 – and also rail gauges such as H0 and N. Includes HAULER name.

BRONCO
Ningbo Weijun (Bronco) Mould & Plastic Co Ltd, D Building No.688, Ling Feng Shan Road, Beilun, Ningbo, China
www.cn.bronco.com
One of the newer Chinese companies, established in November 2004. Makes a wide range of aircraft, military and ships, in various standard model scales.

CAESAR MINIATURES
Miniknight Miniatures, PO Box 48-23, Taipei, Taiwan 105
www.minitoysoldier.com
Producer of wide range of 1:72-scale figures, including modern, ancient, science-fiction and fantasy. Intended for wargaming, as well as general model-making.

DAPOL
Dapol Ltd, Chirk, Wrexham, UK
www.dapol.co.uk
Founded by David Boyle in 1983, Dapol primarily deals with UK 00 and N-gauge rail items. It acquired the Airfix range of trackside accessories and rolling stock (that included the Kitmaster range), in 1985.

DORA WINGS
Dnipro, Kvitneva 19/1, 49066, Ukraine
www.dorawings.com
Unusual aircraft kits in 1:72, 1:48 and 1:32-scale.

DOYUSHA
Doyusha Model Co Ltd, 4-27-21, Arakawa, Arakawa-ku, Tokyo, Japan
www.doyusha-model.com
One of the older Japanese names, still producing a wide range of kits.

DRAGON
Dragon Models Ltd, B1, 10/F, Kong Nam Industrial Building, 603-609 Castle Peak Road, Tsuen Wan New Territories, Hong Kong
www.dragon-models.com
Producer of aircraft, military and space kits.

EBBRO
Ebbro, 7-7 Chiyoda 7-chome, Aoi-ku, Shizuoka City, Japan
www.ebbro.co.jp
Created in 1998. Specialises in 1:20-scale F1 and 1:24 French vehicles. Also a 1:48-scale Honda Jet.

EASTERN EXPRESS
Nizhnyaya Syromyatnicheskaya, 11, Moscow, Russia
www.ee-models.ru
Founded in 1992 in Moscow. Primarily makes aircraft and military models, but with some figures and – oddly – the ex-Frog South Goodwin lightship!

EDUARD
Eduard Model Accessories, Mirova 170, 435 21 Obrnice, Czech Republic
www.eduard.com
Created in 1989, initially to make accessories, mainly photo-etched, for other manufacturers' kits. Later moved into highly detailed injection styrene kits of their own, mainly aircraft in the standard scales.

EMHAR
Bachmann-Europe PLC, 13 Moat Way, Barwell, Leicester LE9 8EY, UK
www.pocketbond.co.uk
A brand initially set up by Toyway, which was taken over by Pocketbond, itself then acquired by Bachmann-Europe. Makes 1:72-scale aircraft and military models, and a unique range of 1:24-scale Bedford lorries.

ENCORE MODELS
Squadron, 1115 Crowley Drive, Carrollton, TX 75006-1312, USA
www.squadron.com
Name used by the model distribution company, Squadron, for kits that it has adapted from other manufacturers. See also SQUADRON under 'Distributors'.

FALLER
Gebr. Faller GmbH, Kreuzstraße 9, 78148 Gütenbach, Germany
www.faller.de
Germany's best-known model-railway manufacturer. Much is pre-assembled and 'ready-to-roll', but many of the buildings are available in kit form, and adaptable to other scenarios. In the past, Faller also made aircraft kits.

FINEMOLDS
53-2 Matoba, Oitsu, Toyohashi, Aichi 441-3301, Japan
www.finemolds.co.jp
Specialist model-kit producer, including Star Wars subjects.

FLY
Jiří Válek, Ďáblova kolonie 814, 735 53 Dolní Lutyně, Czech Republic
www.fly814.cz
Makes a range of aircraft kits, from airliners in 1:144-scale to trainers, gliders and other unusual aircraft in 1:48-scale.

FROG
Hobby Bounties & Morgan Hobbycraft Centre, 865 Mountbatten Road #0291/92 , Katong Shopping Centre, Singapore 437844, Republic of Singapore
www.hobbybounties.com
The original British model name, now owned by Hobby Bounties as an Anglo-Singapore company. Issuing some new kits and some Frog originals.

FUJIMI
Fujimi Mokei Co. Ltd, 4-21-1 Toro, Shizuoka City, Japan
www.fujimimokie.com
Founded in 1948, making wooden ship models. Started its plastic range around 1970, with kits across the range; aircraft, cars, ships and military. It is one of the larger of the Japanese model companies.

GLENCOE MODELS
Glencoe Models LLC, PO Box 337, Rochdale, MA 01542, USA
www.glencoemodels.com
Created by Nick Argento in 1987, the company has reissued many classic kits, including those from Strombecker, ITC, Adams and Hawk.

GREAT WALL HOBBY/G.W.H.
Shanghai Lion Roar Art Model Co., Ltd., Room 210, No 87 Lane 410, Long Wu Road, Shanghai P.R., China
www.lionroar.net/www.lionroarmodel.cn
Model-kit division of Lion Roar, making large-scale aircraft and Chinese spacecraft. The Lion Roar name is used for conversion kits.

HASEGAWA
Hasegawa Seisakuso Co Ltd, 3-1-2 Yagusu Yaizu Shizuoka 425-8711, Japan
www.hasegawa-model.co.jp
One of the major Japanese kit companies, with a wide range of subjects, including military, aircraft, cars, ships and airliners.

HÄT INDUSTRIES
Hat Industries Inc, PO Box 50284, Bellevue, WA 98015, USA
www.hat.com
Manufactures of a wide range of model figures, mainly in 1:72-scale, but some in 1:32. Includes some sets that originated with Airfix.

HAWK
Round 2 Models, 4073 Meghan Beeler Drive, South Bend, IN 46628, USA
www.round2models.com/models/hawk
One of the earliest model names in the USA, making a wide range of models. The name and tooling was acquired by Round 2 in 2013. Some Hawk kits have been reissued.

HELJAN
Heljan A/S, Rebslagervej 6, 5471 Søndersø, Denmark
www.heljan.dk/www.heljan.co.uk
Model rail manufacturer. Primarily H0 items, though now does have a UK division dealing in 00.

HELLER
Heller Joustra S.A, Chemin de la Porte, 61160 Trun, France
www.heller.fr
Founded in 1957 by Léo Jahiel. Since then the company has been through several owners, including being joined to Airfix when both were owned by Humbrol. However, Heller was not acquired along with Airfix and Humbrol when they were bought by Hornby, and Heller now runs as an independent company. It issues many of its own classic kits, and some new, across the range of aircraft, ships and galleons, and cars. Uses its own (unique) 1:125-scale, for some aerospace subjects.

HK MODELS
Hong Kong Models, Flat 12, 12/F, Tak Lee Industries Center, Tsing Yeung Street, Tuen Mun, New Territories, Hong Kong
www.hk-models.com
Created in 2010 to produce large, highly-detailed aircraft models in 1:32-scale.

HOBBY BOSS
Yatai Electric Appliances Co, Ltd., Nan Long Industrial Park, San Xiang, Zhong Shan, Guang Dong 528463, China
www.hobbyboss.com
One of the newer Chinese companies, making high quality aircraft, ship and military kits.

HORIZON MODELS
Horizon Models Pty Ltd, PO Box 305, Drummoyne NSW 2047, Australia
www.horizon-models.com
A new company started by Tony Radosevic in 2015, with its first kits dealing with early American space subjects. Uses injection-moulded styrene and photo-etch.

IBG MODELS
IBG, Benedykta Hertza 2 04 – 603, Warsaw, Poland.
www.ibgmodels.com
Manufacturer of a wide range of military, ship and aircraft models in traditional scales. Makes accessories using 3D printing.

ICM
ICM Holding, 9 Borispolskyya str., Building 64, Kiev 02660, Ukraine.
www.icm.com.ua
One of the new companies to emerge from Ukraine. ICM makes aircraft and military items, many from the inter-war era, plus figures and civilian vehicles in the 1:35 military scale. Some have been up-scaled to 1:24, including Ford Model T kits.

ITALERI
Italeri SpA, via Pradazzo, 6/b, 1-40012 Calderara di Reno, Bologna, Italy.
www.italeri.com
Founded in 1960s, and has gone through two name changes. It was originally Artiplast, but this was changed to Italereri, then to the simplified Italeri. In recent years it taken over former Italian rivals ESCI (acquired from Ertl) and Protar, and works in conjunction with Testors in the US, and Revell-Germany. Makes a wide range of kit subjects.

KAIYODO
Kaiyodo 19-3, Yanagi-machi Kadoma-shi, Osaka, 571-0041 Japan.
www.kaiyodo.co.jp
Produces mostly Japanese-based items, primarily figures. It also makes an even larger 2001: A Space Odyssey Discovery than the Moebius kit.

KARAYA
Karaya Ii Ltd, Legionow Polskich 16/54, 32-700 Bochnia, Poland
www.karaya.pl
Aircraft kit, decal and accessory manufacturer, using injection-moulded styrene and resin.

KINETIC MODELS
Kinetic Model (HK) Ltd, Room 11, 3/F, Mansfield Industrial Center, 19 Hong Yip Street, Yuen Long, N.T. Hong Kong.
www.kineticmodel.com
Aircraft kits in conventional scales including 1:24, and AFVs in 1:35-scale.

KORA
Robert Koraba, J.Wolkera 874, 756 61 Rožnov p.R, Czech Republic
www.lfmodels.cz/kora
Manufacturer of aircraft kits, using multi-material techniques, plus detailing parts, accessories and decals.

KP MODELS/KOVOZAVODY PROSTEJOV
Kovozávody Prostějov, Nad vápenkou 364, 250 84, Praha východ, Czech Republic
www.kovozavody.cz
Producer of 1:144, 1:72 and 1:48-scale aircraft models.

LF MODELS
711788 03, Novy Malin, Czech Republic
www.lfmodels.com
Manufacturer of aircraft and helicopter kits.

LINDBERG
Round 2 Models, 4073 Meghan Beeler Drive, South Bend, IN 46628, USA
www.round2models.com/models/lindberg
One of the earliest American kit names that started as O-Lin in the 1930s. Producer of the first 'all plastic space kit', the Flying Saucer/UFO in 1954. The name and tooling was acquired by Round 2 in 2013, with some kits being reissued as 'New Lindberg'.

MAC DISTRIBUTION
Branická 9, 147 00 Praha 4, Czech Republic
www.mackits.cz
Manufacturer of World War I and World War II aircraft and military vehicles in 1:72-scale.

MACH-2
17 rue Emile Combs, 78800 Houilles, France
www.mach2.fr
Proprietor: Didier Palix. Mach-2 mostly deals with aircraft, and some vehicles. Includes the Lift-Off range of 1:48-scale models based around the Thor-Delta rocket launcher and a 1:72 range of Soviet/Russian A-Type launchers. Moulded in styrene, but using short-run injection techniques.

MARS
www.marsfigures.com
Wide range of figures in 1:72 and 1:32-scales. Includes factual and fantasy.

MARUI
Tokyo-Marui, A5-17-1 Ayase, Adachi-ku, Tokyo 120, Japan
www.tokyo-marui.co.jp
Founded in 1965, initially making construction kits, as well as motorised cars and ships, and tools. Started to produce 1:1-scale guns and arms, variously gas- and electric-powered, and this has become the company's speciality. Beside sporting use, many are also used in the movie industry. The radio-control car side is still strong, but the conventional kit side has declined. Marui is often incorrectly referred to as 'TILT', as the Japanese Katakana letters for 'Marui' look similar to the Roman letters for 'T, I, L, and T'!

MASTER BOX
Ukraine
www.mbltd.info
One of the new companies emerging from Ukraine. Master Box has a range of military vehicle and many figures sets in the same 1:35-scale. It has also introduced a range of highly detailed figures in 1:24-scale, which include modern truckers and hitch-hikers, US cops and robbers, the Old West, space operas and Greek mythology.

MENG
Rui Ye Century (Shenzhen) Hobby Co. Ltd., Rm. 3016, Blk. A, Galaxy Century Bldg., 3069 Caitian Road, Futian District, Shenzhen, Guangdong, China
www.meng-model.com
Founded in 2011 to produce high-quality models, mostly military, with some ships and cars. There are a number of modern, soft-skinned military vehicles in 1:35, and a 1:24-scale Hummer. Intriguingly, most catalogue divisions are named after dinosaurs – some more appropriate than others. For example ships come under the Plesiosaurus Series! Has taken over many of Wingnut Wings models.

MIKRO-MIR
Dnepr, Ukraine
www.mikro-mir.com
Manufacturer of injection-moulded kits of unusual subjects. Aircraft and submarines in 1:144-scale, aircraft in 1:72 and 1:48, and ships in 1:35 and 1:350. Was created with AMP, but the company names then split.

MINIART
MiniArt Models Ltd, 144 B Kharkivske Highway, 02091 Kiev, Ukraine.
www.miniart-models.com
Established in 2001, MiniArt was one of the new companies to emerge from the Ukraine. It makes a number of 1:35 military vehicles, but also a wide range of diorama buildings, parts and accessories, arguably more than any other company. These are in 1:35, though could be adapted to other scales. Some buildings are made in 1:72. There is also a range of 1:16-scale figures.

MINICRAFT
Minicraft Models (US) Inc, 1501 Commerce Drive, Elgin IL 60123, USA
www.minicraftmodels.com
Started by Al Trendle in 1970 as a US importer of Japanese kits, Minicraft now designs and issues many of its own kits.

MODELCOLLECT
ModelCollect Ltd., Guangzhou, China
www.modelcollect.com
Created in 2012, a Chinese model company specialising in military subjects in 1:72 and 1:35, and large aircraft models in 1:72. The catalogue includes a slightly surreal mix of both real and 'what if?' subjects.

MODELSVIT
www.modelsvit-eshop.modelsvit-shop.com
Aircraft models, some 1:48-scale, mostly 1:72-scale, including some very large models such as a 1:72 Tupolev Tu-144 and Antonov An-225.

MOEBIUS MODELS
Pegasus Hobbies, 1458 W 7th St, Upland, CA 91786, USA
www.moebiusmodels.com/www.pegasushobbies.com
Created by Frank Winspur in 2006. One of the first companies to recreate some of Aurora's old science-fiction and fantasy figures. Later produced new tooling for similar subjects and branched out into 1:25-scale American cars and trucks. Acquired by Pegasus Hobbies in 2018, but continues to run as an independent name.

MONOGRAM
See Revell–Monogram

MPC
Round 2 Models, 4073 Meghan Beeler Drive, South Bend, IN 46628, USA
www.round2models.com/models/mpc
Similar to AMT, MPC was created in the 1960s to make model-car kits. It became famous for producing the first Star Wars kits. Acquired by Round 2 in 2009.

MRC
Model Rectifier Corp, 80 Newfield Avenue, Eldon, NJ 08837, USA
www.modelrectifier.com
An importer of kits for the US market, including many from Academy and Italeri.

NOY's MINIATURES
Israel
www.facebook.com/noysminiatures
Produces a very wide range of printed bases and background hangars for aircraft dioramas.

PECO
Peco, Underleys, Beer, Devon, EX12 3NA, UK
www.peco-uk.com
One of the oldest and best-known manufacturers of model-railway items in the UK.

PEGASUS HOBBIES
Pegasus Hobbies, 1458 W 7th St, Upland, CA 91786, USA
www.pegasushobbies.com
Created by Larry Thompson and Tom Macomber in 1987. The company runs a large model store in Montclair, and initially produced aftermarket parts for model cars. It then moved into wargaming buildings, then science-fiction and fantasy models and some aircraft. These are moulded, unusually, not in standard styrene, but in ABS. In 2018 it took over Moebius Models, though that continues to run as an independent name.

PLATZ
Platz Hobby Ltd., 3-1-1 Kusanagi Shimizuku, Shizuokashi, Shizuoka 424-0882, Japan
www.platz-hobby.com
Founded in 2000, Platz makes a range of aircraft kits and some military. Some of these are also tied into the very Japanese anime series 'Girls und Panzer'. Platz also produces modelling tools and is a distributor and retailer.

POLAR LIGHTS
Round 2 Models, 4073 Meghan Beeler Drive, South Bend, IN 46628, USA
www.round2models.com/models/polar-lights
Originally set up as the kit name for the Playing Mantis section of RC2, and an obvious play on the 'Aurora' name, the first kits from Polar Lights were recreations of old Aurora kits. New kits then started to be produced, including a series from Star Trek. Polar Lights was acquired by Round 2 in 2009.

PST
PST (PromSnabTorg), JSC, Minsk, Belarus
www.pstmodel.com
Producer of mainly AFVs and missile subjects in 1:72.

RED BOX, THE
Ukraine
www.theredbox.com.ua
Producer of a wide range of 1:72-scale figure sets.

RENWAL
See Revell–Monogram

REVELL–MONOGRAM
Revell USA LLC, 728, Northwest Highway, Ste 302, Fox River Grove, IL 60021, USA
www.revell.com
Two of the best-known names in modelling, combined since 1986. Both companies have issued many model kits, across the subject ranges, and in the past Revell had acquired the Renwal name and tooling, and Monogram much of the Aurora tooling. Revell-Monogram was acquired by the large model and hobby distribution company Hobbico in 2007. Hobbico, however, went into liquidation in early 2018. When Revell-Germany was taken over by Blitz in mid-2018, this holding company also acquired the Revell-Monogram US name and much – though not all – of the tooling. The remainder went to Atlantis Hobbies, though the NASCAR tooling was sold to the new company, Salvinos JR Models. The 'Monogram' name now tends to only appear on classic kits.

REVELL–Germany
Revell GmbH & Co KG, Henschelstrasse 20-30, D-32257, Bünde, Germany
www.revell.de
Although part of the overall Revell Group, it ran very much as an independent company, and although was eventually acquired by Hobbico, this wasn't until 2011, four years later than Revell/Monogram. It was consequently in a better position than Revell-Monogram when Hobbico went into liquidation in early 2018. Revell-Germany was taken over by the German company Quantum Capital Partners, under the name Blitz, in mid-2018.

RIICH MODELS
China
www.riichmodel.com
Producer of mainly military-orientated models, including civilian sets, plus aircraft and submarine models.

RODEN
Roden Ltd, 7a Nevska Str., OF.35, Kiev, Ukraine
www.roden.eu
Manufacturer of military-vehicle and aircraft kits in various scales. Part of a larger company that does more general injection-moulding, engineering and CAD-CAM work.

ROUND-2
Round 2 Models, 4073 Meghan Beeler Drive, South Bend, IN 46628, USA
www.round2models.com
Parent company that owns, AMT, MPC, Polar Lights, Lindberg and Hawk model-kit names.

RS MODELS
U Lomu 513/7, 795 01 Rýmařov; Czech Republic
www.rsmodels.cz
Producer of aircraft mostly in 1:72, some in 1:48.

SMER
Směr Production Team, Bellova 124, 109 00 Praha 10 - Petrovice, Czech Republic
www.smer.cz
Czech company founded 1952. Carries out a wide range of product manufacturing. Toys and kits are only a part of the business, the majority being from existing tooling.

SPECIAL HOBBY
Special Hobby, sro, Mezilesí 718/78, 193 00 Prague, Czech Republic
www.specialhobby.eu
Now the overall name for what started as the MPM range of companies, and still has a number of other associated names – including Azur, Special Armour and Planet Models. Produces a wide range of aircraft and military items.

SALVINOS JR MODELS
Salvino JR Models, 1240 E Ontario Ave #102 PMB 327, Corona, CA 92881, USA
salvinosjrmodels.com
A new company, purely dealing with American race cars, using new tooling. It also acquired the NASCAR tooling from Revell-Monogram in 2018.

TAKOM
Takom (HK) International Co. Ltd, Dong Guan, China
www.takom-world.com
Founded in 2013 in Hong Kong, Takom mainly specialises in military kits in 1:72, 1:35, 1:16-scales, including many unusual subjects.

TAMIYA
Tamiya Inc, 307 Ondawara, Suruga-Ku, Shizuoka 422-8610, Japan
www.tamiya.com
One of the major Japanese model companies and arguably the best-known name. Created in 1948 by Shunska Tamiya, initially making wooden ship kits, later moving to plastic. Tamiya's ranges encompass most modelling subjects, and it has large radio-control, robotic and educational-model divisions.

THUNDER MODELS
Discovery Technology Ltd, HaoSan ShangXing, Industry Zone, No.71 NanHuan Road,ShaJin Street, Bao'an, Shenzhen, China
www.thundermodels.com
Specialist military kits in 1:35-scale, including ancillary items, such as tractors, railway wagons and motorbikes.

TRUMPETER
Wasan Plastic Model Co, Nang Long Industrial Area, San Xiang, Zhong Shan, Guang Dong, China
www.trumpeter-china.com
The largest, and best-known of all the relatively new Chinese model companies, Trumpeter makes a wide range of aircraft, military and ship kits, and some American cars.

UM-MT (MILITARY TECHNICS)
Russia
www.ukrmodels.wixsite.com/ummt
Producer of military kits in 1:72 and 1:35-scale, including a number of armoured rail items.

UNIMODEL/UM
www.um-models.com
Ukrainian company, specialising in World War II range of AFVs in 1:72 and 1:48, and aircraft in 1:72.

VALOM
Zlešická 1808/10, Praha 4 – Chodov, 148 00, Czech Republic
www.valom.net
Founded in 2002. Produces aircraft, including many unusual subjects, in 1:48, 1:72 and 1:144-scales.

WALTHERS
Wm. K. Walthers, Inc., 5601 West Florist Avenue, Milwaukee, WI 53218, USA
www.walthers.com
America's major model-railway manufacturer. Much is pre-assembled, but many of the layout buildings and accessories are available as kits, and adaptable to other subject-matter.

WAVE
Wave Corporation, 1-10-1 Kiboshida Higashi-machi, Musashino-shi, Tokyo, 180-0002, Japan
www.hobby-wave.com
Founded in 1987, Wave produces model kits, accessories and tools. The vast majority of kits are classic Japanese anime subjects.

WINGNUT WINGS
Wingnut Wings Ltd, PO Box 15-319, Miramar, Wellington 6022, New Zealand
www.wingwings.com
Specialist in 1:32-scale World War I aircraft kits and decal sets. Now ceased trading, with much of the stock going to Meng Models

ZEBRANO
Zebrano, Minsk, Belarus
www.zebrano-model.com
Created in 2009 by Vladimir Kiselev. Initially working with such as PST. Makes unusual subjects of mainly Soviet armour and figures in 1:72, 1:43 and 1:35-scale. Kits in injection-moulded styrene, accessories in resin.

ZOUKEI MURA
Zoukei-mura Inc., Kyoto, Japan
www.zoukeimura.co.jp/en
One of the newer Japanese companies, created by Akihiro Nakatani and specialising in highly detailed aircraft models, primarily in 1:32-scale.

ZVEZDA
Zvezda LLC, Promyshlenna str.2, Moscow Region, Russia
www.zvezda.com
A new-style Russian kit company, created in the early 1990s, on the break-up of the Soviet Union. Uses modern techniques and primarily produces military and aircraft models. Also makes a wide range of figure sets in 1:72-scale, and some modern and historical ships. Some production is in conjunction with Revell – Germany.

SPECIALIST COMPANIES

AIM (Aircraft in Miniature)
19 Watling Street, Nuneaton, Warwickshire, CV11 6JJ, UK
www.aim72.co.uk
Manufacturer of specialist aircraft kits and accessories.

ANIGRAND CRAFTSWORK
Flat F, 23 Floor, Block 4, Waterside Plaza, Wing Shun Street, Tune Wan, NT, Hong Kong
www.anigrand.com
Specialist producer of resin kits, featuring a number of aircraft, space and X-plane subjects.

ATOMIC CITY
Atomic City Engineering, Hanford, CA 93230, USA
www.atomiccitymodels.com
Proprietor: Scott Alexander. Atomic City makes short runs of science-fiction subjects, plus a 1:12-scale injection-moulded styrene kit of the Mercury Capsule. Distributed though MRC. [See also MRC in the Mainstream listing.]

COZMIC SCALE MODELS
Unit 2, Denholme Business Centre, Halifax Road, Denholme Gate, Bradford BD13 4EN, UK
www.cozmicscalemodels.com
Proprietors: Keith and Adele Tomlinson. Manufacturer of a wide range of science-fiction-based kits and accessories. Most are 3D printed.

FANTASTIC PLASTIC
Fantastic Plastic Models, LLC, 25501 Willow Wood Street, Lake Forest, CA 92630, USA
www.fantastic-plastic.com
Proprietor: Allen B. Ury. Manufacturer of a wide variety of multi-material, mainly resin-based aerospace models.

GIBLETS CREATIONS
Giblets Creations, Oxford, UK
www.gibletscreations.co.uk
Started by James Gilbert in 2016 primarily to make parts for modellers using 3D printing. Most subjects are science-fiction in nature, though anything can be printed.

GREAT NORTH ROADS
19a Waverley Road, Southsea, Portsmouth, PO5 2PH, UK
www.greatnorthroads.co.uk
Proprietor: Simon Farrugia. Makes a wide range of primarily 1:35-scale wrecked buildings in plaster for military dioramas.

KORA MODELS
J. Wolkera 74, 756 61 Roznov pod Radhostem, Czech Republic
www.lfmodels.cz
Proprietor: Robert Koraba. Kora produces many resin armoured-vehicle kits, and, with NewWare, a series of V-2 rocket conversions, based on the Condor kit.

LUKGRAPH
Lukgraph, Zamłynie 28A, 30-898 Kraków, Poland
www.lukgraph.pl
Special company making large, highly-detailed multi-material kits, primarily of early British and American aircraft. Listed under 'specialist', as the main moulding material is resin, not injection-moulded styrene.

LVM STUDIOS
Goudplevier 106, 5348 ZG Oss, The Netherlands
www.LVM-Studios.com
Proprietor: Leon van Munster. Was a producer of complete multi-material kits of space subjects such as Soyuz, plus photo-etch sets for detailing existing kits, including the Hasegawa Voyager space probe. Also produced complex launch gantries for the Soyuz and Mercury Atlas launch pads. Here for reference only as the company ceased trading in 2018

NEW WARE
Zelazneho 6, 71200 Ostava 2, Czech Republic
mek.kosmo.cz/newware
Proprietors: Tomas Kladiva, Peter Cigan and Andi Wuestner. Producer of many specialist accessory sets for space modellers to update kits such as Revell's International Space Station and Mir kits, plus complete kits of Soviet/Russian craft such as Soyuz and Vostok.

REALSPACE MODELS
813 Watt Drive, Tallahassee, FL 32303, USA
www.realspacemodels.com
Proprietor: Glenn Johnson. RealSpace Models has the largest range of specialist-material spacecraft kits in the USA, making everything from a 1:200 Skylab adaptor for the AMT Saturn 5 kit, to Voyager, Viking and Magellan space-probes in 1:24-scale. Also made are detailing sets and decal sheets. The company distributes the detailed plans of David Weeks.

SHARKITS
9 rue de la Picardiere, 78200 Perdreauville, France
www.sharkit.com
Proprietor: Renaud Mangallon. Founded by Franck 'Sharky' Wagner to make specialist aerospace subjects, mostly in resin. The range includes several missiles and some science-fiction subjects.

TREEMENDUS
Treemendus Scenics, Atlantic Business Centre, Atlantic St, Broadheath, Altrincham, WA14 5NQ
www.treemendus-scenics.co.uk
Manufacturer of all types of model scenic materials – including trees. The company started in 2003.

STRATOSPHERE MODELS
www.picturetrail.com/stratospheremodels
Proprietor: Stéphane Cochin. Specialist manufacturers of limited-edition kits of science-fiction subjects, plus some real craft, including the DC-X. Now also does 3D design.

UNICRAFT
Ukraine
www.unicraft.biz
Proprietor: Igor Shestakov. Specialist producer of resin kits, featuring a number of aircraft, space and X-plane subjects.

3D PRINTING

This subject has a separate heading, as 3D printing companies tend to work in a completely different way to conventional model companies. Most of the many 3D/adaptive-manufacturing companies that now exist around the world deal directly with commercial applications designing and producing industrial items, but using 3D printing as against more traditional methods. Although in theory they could produce a part for a model kit, they may not be set up to deal with individual requests. Consequently, this listing has to be limited to those companies that either cater specifically for the modeller, or can accept small printing runs. Even then, this may only be part of an overall business.

This can only be a representative list, as more companies are regularly appearing offering these services.

BUILDPARTS
C.Ideas, 125 Erick Street, Suite# A115, Crystal Lake, IL 60014, USA
www.buildparts.com
Founded in 1998, C.Ideas can produce a wide range of subjects from a wide range of materials.

BOYCE AEROSPACE HOBBIES
Boyce Aerospace Hobbies, San Diego, California, USA
www.boyceaerospacehobbies.com
Started originally by Alex and Sheree Boyce in 1995, making traditional flying rocket parts. Re-vamped in 2015, now exclusively using 3D printing to make similar parts.

MODELU
3 Tyny Sarn, Llanwnog, Powys, SY17 5JF, UK
www.modelu3d.co.uk
Created in 2016, mainly to make life-captures of people to reproduce as figures for railway layouts, but includes many other subjects.

MODDLER
Moddler, 2325 Third St. Suite 224 San Francisco, CA 94107, USA
www.moddler.com
Started by special-effects veteran John Vegher, to produce 3D-printed parts, mainly for the SFX industry, but can deal with any type of part.

PART2PRINT
Part2Print, U Krcske vodarny 1134/63, 140 00 Prague 4, Czech Republic
www.part2print.cz
Created in 2003, dealing with all types of 3D printing, including that for model-making.

SCULPTEO
Sculpteo, 10 Rue Auguste Perret, 94800 Villejuif, France
Sculpteo, 169, 11th Street, San Francisco, CA 94103, USA
www.sculpteo.com
Created by Eric Carreel and Clément Moreau in 2009. Can deal with large commercial orders, or smaller personal work. Able to print using a wide variety of materials.

SHAPEWAYS
Shapeways, Long Island City, NY, USA
Shapeways, Eindhoven, The Netherlands
www.shapeways.com/marketplace
Currently the best-known name in 3D-printer parts for the modeller. The service works via 'communities' that supply designs and printing facilities. Using the on-line service, you can order pre-listed items to your required scale and quality, or upload your own designs to be printed.

GENERAL SUPPLIES

AK INTERACTIVE
AK Interactive, SL, Logroño, La Rioja, Spain
www.ak-interactive.com
Started by Fernando Vallejo in 2009, to manufacture a very wide range of paints and weathering materials for modellers. Initially used the 'Vallejo' name.

BARE-METAL FOIL
Bare Metal Foil Co, PO Box 82, Farmington, MI 48332, USA
www.bare-metal.com
Producer of Bare-Metal Foil, and other modelling accessories.

EMA and PLASTRUCT
Engineering Model Associates, 1020 S. Wallace Place, City of Industry, CA 91748, USA
EMA Model Supplies Ltd., 14 Beadman Street, London SE27 0DN, UK
www.plastruct.com/www.ema-models.co.uk
EMA is the major producer of specialist model parts made initially for professional modellers of chemical-plant models and the like. These can be adapted to a wide range of modelling projects, from the special-effects industry to the hobbyist. For the hobbyist, the 'Plastruct' division was introduced to supply the smaller ranges of EMA parts.

HUMBROL
Hornby Hobbies Ltd., Margate, Kent CT9 4JX, UK
www.humbrol.com
The UK's major model-paint manufacturer. Founded in 1919 in Kingston-upon-Hull as the Humber Oil Company. It moved into modelling paints, then other accessories, from the 1950s and became Humbrol. Acquired by Borden in 1976. Acquired by Hornby in 2006.

MR HOBBY
GSI Creos Corporation, 2-3-1, Kudan Minami, Chiyoda-ku, Tokyo,102-0074, Japan
www.mr-hobby.com
Major Japanese producer of hobby paints and accessories. The overall company was initially created in 1931, and became Gunze Sangyo in 1971. Changed to GSI Creos in 2001. Has used the Gunze Sangyo name in the past, for both paints and model kits. Now uses the 'Mr Hobby' name for all hobby-related items.

TESTORS
The Testor Corporation, 440 Blackhawk Park Avenue, Rockford, IL 61104, USA
www.testors.com
America's main model-paint and accessory supplier, Testors also issued kits from companies it has acquired over the years, including Hawk and IMC. It also produced a series of UFO kits of its own. Most kit names and tooling have now been acquired by Round 2.

DISTRIBUTORS

Even with the demise of many model shops and hobby stores around the world, some do fortunately remain, and many have moved over to online-ordering and mail-order. It is impossible to list all distributors here – check local listings or carry out a general internet search, but below are companies of which the author has personal experience and would recommend.

CULT TV MAN SHOP
CultTVMan, 248 E. Crogan St., Suite 202, Lawrenceville, GA 30046, USA
www.culttvmanshop.com
Proprietor: Steve Iverson. Very wide section of all types of science-fiction, fantasy and factual space kits, plus accessories.

FEDERATION MODELS
P.O. Box 110796, Palm Bay, FL 32911-0796, USA
www.federationmodels.com
Supplier of many muti-material science-fiction kits.

HANNANTS
H.G. Hannant Ltd, Harbour Road, Oulton Broad, Lowestoft, Suffolk NR32 3LR, UK
www.hannants.co.uk
Proprietor: Nigel Hannant. UK's largest model-kit distributor, specialising primarily in aircraft and military. Many decals and accessory sets, and its own paint and decal ranges.

HOBBY BOUNTIES
Hobby Bounties & Morgan Hobbycraft Centre, 865 Mountbatten Road #0291/92 , Katong Shopping Centre, Singapore 437844, Republic of Singapore
www.hobbybounties.com
Proprietor: Peter Chiang. Large general hobby-supply shop. Also owner of the FROG name.

HOBBY LINK JAPAN
Hobby Link Japan Ltd., Tatebayashi-shi, Nishitakane-cho 43-6, Gunma 374-0075, Japan
www.hlj.com
Proprietor: Scott T. Hards. Excellent source for Japanese kits, tools and accessories. Mail–order world-wide

MEGAHOBBY
MegaHobby.com,110 Hurlock Avenue, Magnolia, NJ 08049, USA
www.megahobby.com
Proprietor: Alan Bass. Created in 1999 as a distributor of all types of model items.

MODELSFORSALE.COM
Unit 3, Dean Close, Raunds, Northants, NN9 6BD, UK
www.modelsforsale.com
Proprietor: Vince Brown. Specialist kit supplier, including paints. Mail order and some UK model shows.

SQUADRON
Squadron, 1115 Crowley Drive, Carrollton, TX 75006-1313, USA
www.squadron.com
Originally created in 1968 in Detroit, Squadron is one of America's major model-distribution companies, dealing with hobby products from around the world, including kits, accessories and tools. It uses the ENCORE MODELS name for its own kits.

STARSHIP MODELER
PO Box 549, Lake Villa, IL 60046, USA
www.starshipmodeler.com
Proprietor: John Lester. Mainly science-fiction, plus paint, tools, books and magazines.

TIMELESS HOBBIES
Timeless Hobbies Ltd., Unit 6, Leys Farm, Chelmsford Road, High Ongar, Essex, CM5 9NW, UK
www.timeless-hobbies.com
Proprietor: Tony James. The UK's largest specialist science-fiction model, toy and 'collectible' supplier.

And finally, if you still cannot locate something you need, you may just have to resort to eBay.

OTHER USEFUL WEBSITES

The various International Plastic Modellers' Society (IPMS) websites from around the world:

UK: www.ipmsuk.org
US: www.ipmsusa.org
Canada: www.ipmscanada.org
Australia: www.ipmsaustralia.com.au
New Zealand: ipmsnz.hobbyvista.com

Most other countries follow similar syntax, or use a search engine.

Scale Model News: www.scalemodelnews.com

The author's site is: www.matirvine.com

Acknowledgements

As with any book, there are many people to thank – from maybe a small, but vital, question, to going over a number of points.

I would like to thank the following in particular:

Jean-Christophe 'J.C.' Carbonel
Paul Fitzmaurice
Tony James
David Jefferis
Dean Milano
Brian Sampson
Mike Tucker
Jim Webb
Andy Yanchus

For use of his article on the Consolidated PBY Catalina: Kevin Khoo

For details of the design and build of the AP Film Studios building:

Simon Atkinson and Sam Denham

For use of – and advice on – some photographs, including the models therein:

Nick Allen
Matt Bacon
Alan Bean
Steve Begg
Peter Chiang
David Hart
Rod & Ian Knott
Nick Kool
Bill Lastovich
Mark Mattei
Tory Mucaro
Suresh Nathan
Keng Leong Ng
Ian Peacock
Roger Penny
Spencer Pollard
Andy Preston
Patrick Pycke
Ed Sexton
Cris Simmonds
Patricia Yanchus

NASA and the Goddard Spaceflight Center for use of photographs of Dr Robert H. Goddard

Peter Vetri and Rick DelFavero, of Atlantis Models. www.atlantis-models.com

And The Elmhurst Model Railroad Club, based in Elmhurst, Illinois, for allowing me free rein of their wonderful railroad layout to photograph anything I needed. www.emrrc.net

If I have missed anyone, my apologies.

Index

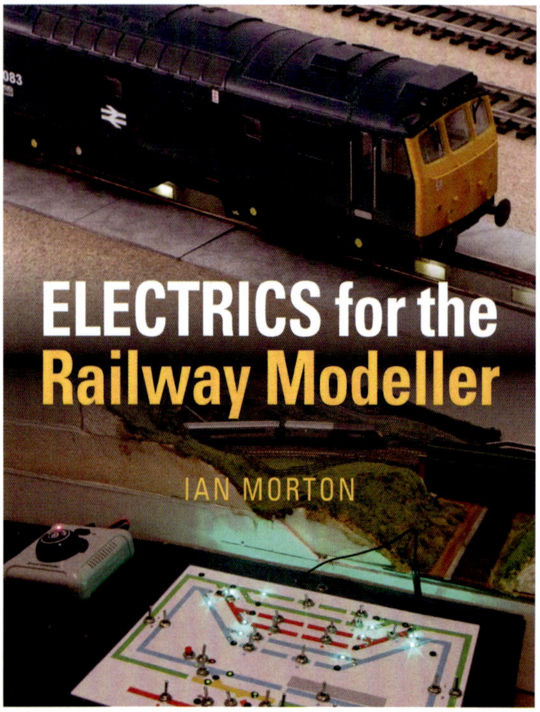

Electrics for the Railway Modeller

Ian Morton

In this fast changing modern world nothing stays the way it is for long and this particularly applies to model railways which rely so completely on basic low voltage electronics. This is often the aspect of the hobby that is most daunting and off-putting both for experienced modellers and those new to the pursuit.

One of the best guides to this subject was published about ten years ago by professional modeller and layout builder Ian Morton. This has been long overdue for revision given the way the electronics applicable to model railways has moved on in that time. This much revised edition introduces the concepts and practice of wiring model railway layouts in an easy and accessible manner. Starting from the assumption that the reader has no knowledge beyond connecting up a train set, the book guides us through the various techniques used until we have the knowledge to wire up a complex model railway.

Beginning with the basics, the book moves on to covers cab control, the operation of points and signals, train detection and lighting. Technology that was not widely available to modellers when the book was first published, such as the use of LEDs, is also reviewed in this new edition.

ISBN: 9781910809785
Price: £14.95
Order at **www.crecy.co.uk**